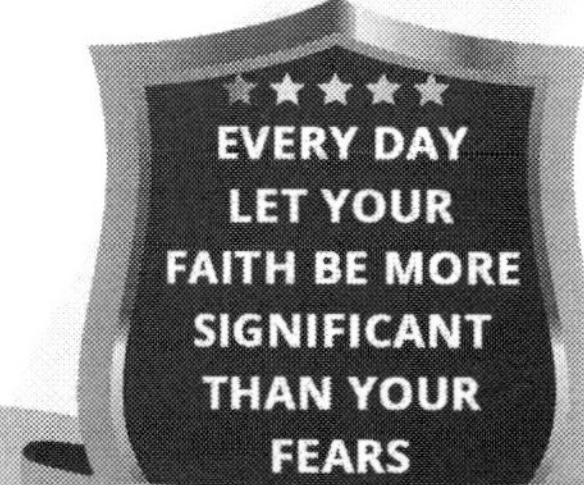

365 Live Fearlessly

A Fearless Faith Devotional & Journal for Life's Journey

QUARTER 3 OF 4

NICOLA MCFADDEN

365 Live Fearlessly:
A Fearless Faith Devotional & Journal for Life's Journey
(Quarter 3 of 4)

ISBN: 978-1-7780627-1-1
Nikimac Solutions Inc.

Credit, Permission, and Licensed for Use.

TABLE OF CONTENTS

Dedication vi
365 Live Fearlessly 1
Welcome 2
Faith Over Fear! 3
Get up & Let's go! 4
Feel Your Emotions Wheel 5
Keep a Gratitude Journal 6
365 Journal Prompts 7
365 Journal 8

DAY 182-188 - MEASURE YOUR HAPPINESS 9
Day 182 - The Fullness of Life! 10
Day 183 - His Protection is for You! 14
Day 184 - Season Changing... 18
Day 185 - God Fixed it! 22
Day 186 - Status Checked? About to Arrive! 26
Day 187 - God Reverses the Curse! 30
Day 188 - Own it! 34

DAY 189 189 - 195 - USE YOUR STRENGTHS 38
Day 189 - Survivor, Victor, Overcomer! 40
Day 190 - Believe, & be Ready! 44
Day 191 - I'm Doing More Than That! 48
Day 192 - Hold on! 52
Day 193 - Trust God's Re-Direction! 56
Day 194 - Never Forget to be Thankful! 60
Day 195 - Thankful I Didn't Give up! 64

DAY 196 - 202 - GRATITUDE 68
Day 196 - Hello... You Matter! 70
Day 197 - Freedom of Forgiveness! 74
Day 198 - I'm Awake, Blessed, Grateful! 78
Day 199 - I Will be With You! 82
Day 200 - The joy of Worship! 86
Day 201 - I am His! 90
Day 202 - This Day! 94

DAY 203 - 209 - GIVE TO OTHERS 98
Day 203 - What if? 100
Day 204 - God's Speed! 104
Day 205 - God's got This! 108

Day 206 - Bigger, Better & More Rewarding 112
Day 207 - God is Faithful! 116
Day 208 - Good Riddance; Rest With God! 120
Day 209 - Let's Pray 124

DAY 210 - 216 - CONNNECT WITH OTHERS 128
Day 210 - I Choose joy 130
Day 211 - It is Your Season & Time! 134
Day 212 - God Says, "I AM.." 138
Day 213 - Proper Correction, a Bridge to Growth! 142
Day 214 - God has Ordered Your Restoration! 146
Day 215 - I am Waiting, not Wailing! 150
Day 216 - I Sought Him & He Sustained me! 154

DAY 217 - 223 - BE ACTIVE 158
Day 217 - God's Favor Shall Honor You! 160
Day 218 - You Shall Finish Strong! 164
Day 219 - You Serve an Influential God 168
Day 220 - You're a Victorious Warrior! 172
Day 221 - Let's Pray for Each Other! 175
Day 222 - Are you Checking if God can? 180
Day 223 - Today is the day, U-Power-Up! 184

DAY 224 - 237 - BE PRESENT 188
Day 224 - Positioned: In the Right Please and at the Right Time! 190
Day 225 - Making Moves? Seek God! 194
Day 226 - The Blood Still Works! 198
Day 227 - Yes, a Breakthrough is About to HIT Your House! 202
Day 228 - Reward for Your Faithfulness. 206
Day 229 - I am Coming out; God is my Way-Maker! 210
Day 230 - God Will Provide & Satisfy Every Need! 214
Day 231 - You Must Trust God & Take Him at His Word! 218
Day 232 - God Shall Remember & you Shall Rebound! 222
Day 233 - Do not Fear, I am With you Always! 226
Day 234 - Rescued From Stress; Rested & Blessed! 230
Day 235 - What Does God say? 234
Day 236 - "You are Going to Make it, Trust me!" Says God. 238
Day 237 - God has a Plan! 242

DAY 238 - 244 - LEARN NEW SKILLS 246
Day 238 - Nothing can Stop God's Plan for Me! 248
Day 239 - Don't Look Back! 252
Day 240 - Lord, I Would Never Have Made it Without You! 256

Day 241 - Annoyingly Positive Vibes: With God, I got this! 260
Day 242 - The Shift Happens; Happiness is in His Presence. 264
Day 243 - He did it Before, and Will do it Again! 268
Day 244 - Keep Alert; God Will Heal! 272

DAY 245 - 251 - SLEEP 275
Day 245 - Confidence and Courage for the Conqueror! 277
Day 246 - I'm Wailing, Not Worried. I'm Worshiping. 281
Day 247 - Let God Finish the Work He Started in You! 285
Day 248 - You Will Laugh, Love, Learn, Live be a Light, & Leap for joy! 289
Day 249 - Be Encouraged. Nope! God Never Fails. 293
Day 250 - Do not be Afraid; Your Reward Will be Grand! 297
Day 251 - God Hears. He Sees. He Knows. He Will Deliver! 301

DAY 252 - 258 - NUTRITION 305
Day 252 - I'm With you. I'll Bless you & Your Children. 307
Day 253 - You Will Give Birth to a Legacy 311
Day 254 - Tresure In Your Sacks! 315
Day 255 - Go! I am Going to Make you Into a Great Nation. 319
Day 256 - You're not Broken but Positioned With Grace. 323
Day 257 - Fear Not! You Serve a God of Second Chances. 327
Day 258 - Stand Your Ground & Watch God! 331

DAY 259 - 265 - SPEND TIME IN NATURE 335
Day 259 - Don't Panic! It is Only a Test. God is With You! 337
Day 260 - God Promises you His Blessings to Live for Him. 341
Day 261 - Don't Rebel Against God; Don't be Afriad of Them! 345
Day 262 - God Decided you Will Defeat This Enemy! 349
Day 263 - God has the Final say and Judgement. 353
Day 264 - When God Says go! Don't be Afraid! Just do it! 357
Day 265 - Don't be Frightened; Don't be Terrified by Them. 361

DAY 266 - 273 - REVIEW AND REFLECT 365
Day 266 - The Lord, Your God, Will Fight for you. 367
Day 267 - Remember What God Did & Promised! 370
Day 268 - Be Battle-Ready. Don't Panic & Run Away! 374
Day 269 - God Never Forsakes not Forgets you. 378
Day 270 - Be Strong and Courageous. Do not be Afraid. 382
Day 271 - I Have Delivered Them Into Your Hands. 386
Day 272 - God Will do it for you Even if it Takes a Miracle! 390
Day 273 - God has a Plan! 394

References 399

DEDICATION

I thank God for the assignment and anointing for the 365 Live Fearlessly movement; it is an awakening to faithfully and fearlessly. I dedicate this book to the supportive relationships and inspiration of my sons, Nicholas Stanley and Matthew Chambers, my purpose-partner, John Marvin, and my fearless family in the Chayah Club community.

As a testimony, when I started the 365 Live Fearlessly Journey in 2020, it was inspired by a devastating heartbreak I experienced in 2019, which resulted in severe panic attacks; God challenged me to let my faith in Him be more significant than the toxic fears and lies of the enemy which caused me to focus on what happened versus who God created me to be and designed me to do. In 2020, I worked through the 365 devotionals and self-care strategies. I extended the 365 Live Fearlessly Journey to my community, Chayah Club, after the 2021 Daniel Fast: Closing the GAP.

At the beginning of the 365 Live Fearlessly (Quarter 2) journey in April 2022, I wrote out my prayer request and big audacious goals in my 365 Journal and asked God for a godly husband, my Adam, my rib, and king, to locate me. At the time of writing this dedication for 365 Live Fearlessly (Quarter 3), I am thrilled to share that I am engaged.

Beloved, you serve a faithful Father who prepares you for what you prayed for, and you must believe God. He wastes nothing!

Completing the third quarter book in the 365 Live Fearlessly series has been a labor of love. I had to dig deep and work hard to devote my full attention to this book. The book is anointed to restore your health, happiness, and spiritual growth inside-out; considering the spiritual warfare, I fought to bring it to publication in my prophetic insight and wisdom; it will strike the adversary and set captives free from captivity. Your personal growth from applying the strategies in this will assist you in developing relationships, creative expression, professional fulfillment, and stress management skills. The book gives you the tools to live your best life and connect with others in a secure place where you may learn, love, live fully, and leap forward.

This unique book brings you to an extraordinary encounter with God's Spirit, a lifetime commitment to spiritual empowerment, and fearless faith in God's purpose for your life. This book is a toolkit to help you work with God and go deep to do the self-care tasks you've been putting off, equipping you with resources to increase your happiness over the next three months. I'm thrilled to share this seed of my Heavenly Father, my closest friend, best Performance Coach, Personal Lord and Savior Jesus, and most excellent Teacher, the mighty Holy Spirit. I pray that it be planted in you as an individual, family, and in the legacy of our community, Chayah Club, to become the best version of yourself and to live your best life, and Chayah! (an old Hebrew word that means to live fully).

365

Live Fearlessly

BOOST YOUR HAPPINESS & FEARLESSNESS

QUARTER THREE

TO THE TO 365 LIVE FEARLESSLY JOURNEY

Some of the essential practices of the 365 Live Fearlessly journey are to become emotionally aware of *feeling your feelings* and *expressing your emotions* using a one-word check-in, to be spiritually empowered with the power of the Holy Spirt, to be strong and courageous with the revelation of God's character, to be confident with knowing your royal identity, to cancel the enemy's lies with the truth of God's word, and to overcome every toxic fear with your fearless faith and His limitless love. Put a '*But-God*' on your current circumstance to change the plot line and narrative; your story will turn around for His glory, and victory is the only possible outcome and conclusion on this matter. Your feelings of pleasure or displeasure contribute to your mood, positive or negative energy, and arousal of emotions: happy, calm, strong, sad, mad, or scared. You can shift the valence and arousal through intentional tactics such as positive self-talk and thoughts, affirmations, declarations of scriptures, praise, worship, prayer, gratitude, and journaling. The joy of the Lord is your inner strength and increases your happiness. I'm excited to support you on your 365 Live Fearlessly experience with tools and tactics to improve your life's contentment, significance, and peace. Over the next quarter, Jesus will be your Coach to help you apply your faith to work on toxic fears in your life that negatively influence your level of happiness. This book provides the resources needed to get you on a healthier, happier, and fearless life. I pray that as you go through the pages, you will begin to encounter God and experience miraculous results. Let's get this celebration started!

NICOLA MCFADDEN
TRANSFORMATION CONSULTANT

Faith Over Fear!

"Remember Elijah? He was a man, no different from us. He prayed with great intensity, asking God to withhold the rain; God answered his prayers and did not allow a single drop of rain to fall for three and a half years." (James 5:17, VOICE). Elijah was a prophet of God, an ordinary man swayed by his emotions, just like you. Yet a man of God, who prayed intensely, fervently, and earnestly for the impossible, moved God's heart to perform creative miracles and control nature.

Elijah had a divine encounter with God in 1 Kings 18:30-39. Elijah went on a mission that began with repairing the Lord's altar, which was in disrepair. Are you on an assignment to rebuild your temple, life, heart, and home, where you previously trusted and worshipped God, but now a counterfeit god's altar has usurped because of fears? Elijah faced a battle between the deity of Baal and the Almighty God of Israel. The rules of the battlefield set: "*You call on the name of your god, and I will call on the name of the LORD. The God who answers by fire—he is God.*" The prophets of Baal would invoke their deity, while the Prophet of God, Elijah, would invoke the Almighty God. The people agreed on the criteria for victory: The God who responded with fire would receive honor and glory. The prophets of Baal called, but nothing! Elijah made it difficult for the false prophets to fool God's people in the future, giving instructions to *fill four large jars with water and pour it on the offering and the wood.* Elijah eliminated any possibility of denying God's magnificence or doubting the truth by substituting a lie for it. He poured much water on the sacrifice to keep it from spontaneously igniting.
Elijah then prayed to God to reveal Himself and affirm Elijah's identity, saying, *"Answer me, Lord, answer me, so these people will know that You, Lord, are God and that You are turning their hearts back again."* God responded with fire, tangibly revealing that He is God. *"Then the fire of the Lord fell and burned up the sacrifice, the wood, the stones, and the soil, and also licked up the water in the trench."* God receives the glory of the Only True God. Elijah and the congregation witnessed the physical manifestation of the Holy Spirit's Fire, an irrefutable God act! *"The Lord—He is God!"* (NIV).

Yet, in 1 Kings 19:3-5, meet Elijah fleeing for his life, fearful, faithless, discouraged, disheartened, despairing, and suicidal because he accepted Jezebel's falsehoods and threats and rejected God's truth, character, and the reality that God is always with us. *"Terrified, Elijah quickly ran for his life. He traveled the length of Israel in one day and finally arrived at Beersheba, the southern point of God's territory, which is in Judah. When he arrived, he instructed his servant to remain there while he sought solitude. He journeyed into the desert for one day and then decided to rest beneath the limbs of a broom tree. There he prayed that his life would be over quickly and that he would die there beneath the tree.* ***Elijah:*** *'I'm finished, Eternal One. Please end my life here and now, even though I have failed and I am no better than my ancestors. Elijah then laid himself down under the broom tree and entered into a deep sleep. While he was sleeping, a heavenly messenger came and touched him and gave him instructions.'* ***Messenger: '****Get up, and eat.'"* (1 Kings 19:3-5, VOICE).
Beloved, isn't this your predicament today, as the devil and his demons work hard, telling you lies that drive you into toxic fear to question God, the character of God, doubt His truth, word, love, plan, power, purpose, and promise for abundant and eternal life?
How do you feel today? What is happening? What *weight or significance* have you given the things, happenings, people, or conditions that you think are causing this feeling of fear, frustration, or failure? Isn't this pessimistic energy that is fueling the dread, despair, doubt, or wrath as a consequence of you believing the enemy's lies, so you reject God and His word? Believe today that you are triumphant and have love, hope, peace, joy, abundance, liberty, wellness, wholeness, and newness of life in Christ Jesus! Why not doubt the enemy lies, block the fears, and believe God's truth to unlock the positive energy of His revelation, light, fire, and power of the Holy Spirit. Making you feel joyful, powerful, hopeful, and peaceful that He has already won the battle and nailed this situation on the cross? The devil's tactic is to bring lies, driving fears, and set up idols. The enemy establishes falsehoods, strongholds, and counterfeit altars in your life to kill, steal, and destroy you, the temple of God. The enemy confuses the royalty of your identity that you belong to God; you are God's child; as a result, the plans and thought He has for you are to bless you and not to harm you, to give you new life and a future of victory that you hope and desire.
The Father says, *"Don't be afraid, for I am with you. Don't be discouraged, for I am your God. I will strengthen you and help you. I will hold you up with my victorious right hand."* (Isa 41:10, NLT). Get up; get dressed; go and get something to eat; feed on My word! *"I am the Lord your God, Who brought you out of the land of Egypt; Open your mouth wide, and I will fill it."* (Psa 81:10, NKJV). Today commit to moving forward and do it even if you are afraid! *Faith over fear!*

Get Up & Let's Go!

Over this quarter of 92 days or 13 weeks plus one day, you will be working on yourself, overcoming the lies of the enemy, opposing the liar, Satan, and his falsehood that comes to kill, steal and destroy your joy, inner strength, peace, power, authority, love, self-disciple, self-control, discernment, well-being, and good judgment. This evil liar brings the spirit of fear as it is not of God. God has not given you a fearful spirit but the Holy Spirit that is living in you, His devoted lover. You must, therefore, deliberately partner with God to tear down the demonic strongholds that the devil has established as pacifiers to comfort you as you wallow in sadness, worry, anxiety, anger, and fear to overtake and overwhelm your life, contributing to your discouragement, self-condemnation, guilt, negative energy, emotional turmoil, mental struggles, stigmatization, helplessness, and hopelessness.

You can intentionally make every day a miraculous day by practicing the 3C daily routine: **C**ommand your day, **C**ommit everything to God through faith-filled requests and gratitude, and **C**onverse with God, self, and others. You are prioritizing God, starting the day joyous in His presence, each morning using your *Dope Faith Journal*, praying, affirming, and declaring scriptures, self-reflecting throughout the day, and in the evening applying your *Fearless Journal* and a self-coaching tool.

The following 12 factors have been proven to help boost feelings of joy and peace.

1. Baseline your happiness for what you measure gets managed
2. Hone your inner strengths by delighting in the LORD's joy
3. Practice gratitude
4. Give and be kind to others
5. Socially connect with others (being empowered and engaged in Chayah Club)
6. Be active and get moving
7. Be present, self-aware, and mindful
8. Learn new skills (e.g., enrolling in courses in Chayah Club)
9. Sleep and rest
10. Eat healthy and nutritious foods
11. Spend time in nature
12. Review and reflect

The 365 Live Fearlessly Devotional and Journal (Quarter 3) will guide you through these 12 factors to increase your fearlessness and happiness. With its carefully selected devotionals, assessments, and resources, you'll have an excellent toolkit to help you live a happier and healthier life. Your inside-out transformation to invest in your best life.

This self-help book is intended to assist you over the next quarter, beginning with an evaluation to determine your current level of happiness. You'll then work on the several categories each day and week within the quarter, all of which have been shown to influence faithfulness, fearlessness, and joy levels. There will be a daily devotional, journals, and self-coaching assignment for you to do to help you spiritually mature, emotionally aware, and personally develop. You'll examine your progress and retake the assessments at the end of the quarter to see how you have learned and grown and evaluate how much your happiness levels have improved.

FEEL YOUR EMOTIONS *wheel*

This wheel can be helpful when conveying your emotions to yourself and others. When you feel and name your feelings, you will devise solutions for coping, adapting, and becoming resilient.

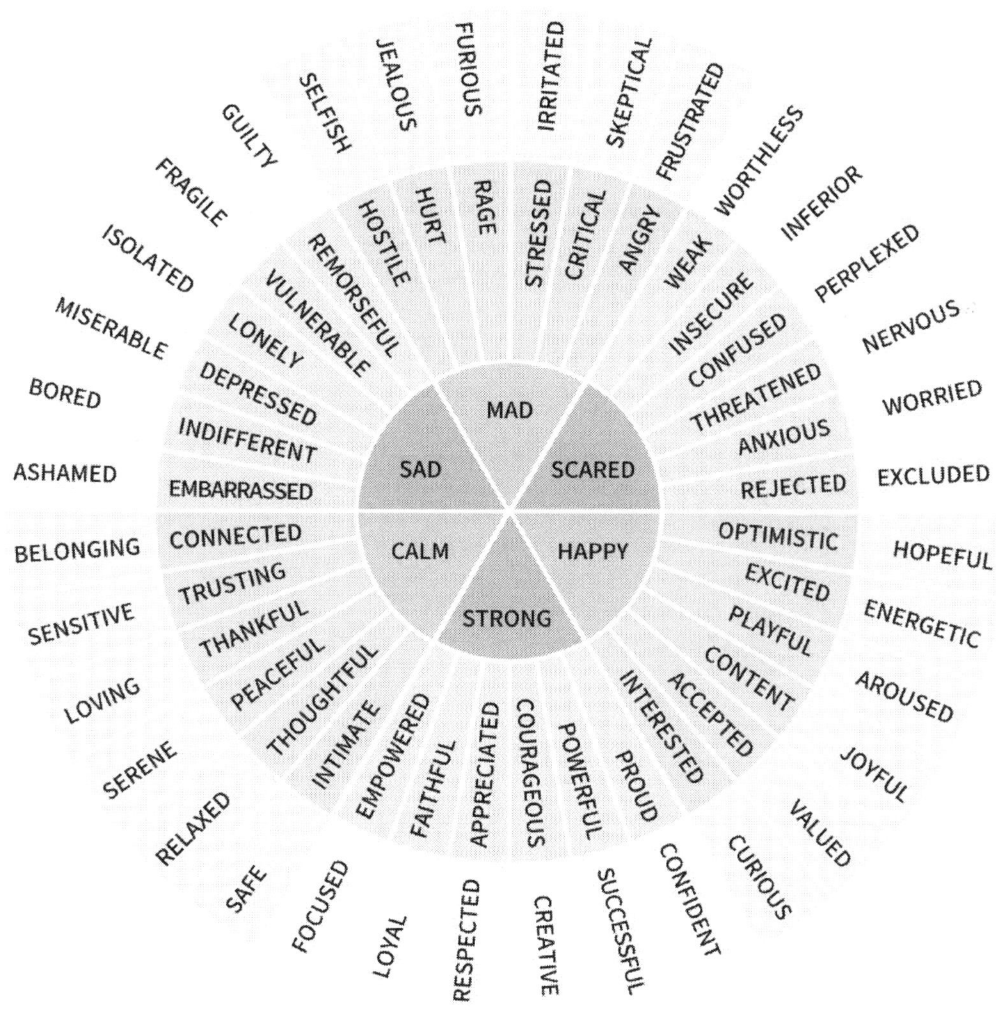

Source: Miri Campbell

Keep a Gratitude Journal

Keeping a Gratitude Journal may significantly impact your faithfulness, fearlessness, happiness, and relationships. You may build a stronger appreciation of God for the positive things and people in your life by penning gratitudes daily. As a result, you will become more sensitive to sources of God's presence, blessings, and joy in your surroundings. So be thankful no matter for this is God's will for you. (1 Thessalonians 5:16-18).

Here are five ideas to get you started with your Gratitude Journal.

1. Make a habit of listing three things for which you are thankful daily. This will help recall pleasant memories, be they of people, things, or occasions.

2. When writing, be as thorough and comprehensive as possible, and don't be afraid to go into the nitty-gritty.

3. Stop taking the beautiful things and people in your life for granted and start by embracing the idea that they are God-given gifts and blessings.

4. Make it a point to express gratitude frequently in your writing, thinking, speaking, and living.

5. You should imagine what your life would be like if you were to lose specific items or individuals. Be thankful for the things you were able to avoid, evade, or otherwise God prevent from happening because He is protecting you.

365 JOURNAL *prompts*

Journaling is a safe approach to overcoming the adversary's toxic fear and lies and self-reflecting on your thoughts and experiences. It helps alleviate anxiety, stress, and negative thoughts by letting you let go of them. Through your book, you will see the 365 Journal pages; write for 15 minutes on that day on whatever comes to mind using these prompts.

- Do I have any idea what my current situation is?
- What exactly do I have to be worried about?
- What caused this person to feel this way in the first place?
- Is there anything specific I hope to accomplish?
- What am I clutching to in my heart?
- In what way am I reacting?
- What is the sensation in each section of my body?
- How much more do I know about myself a month or a year ago than I do now?
- What are the things that impede me from getting things done?
- What would my best buddy say if I had to describe myself to someone?
- What is it that makes me smile?
- I have a long list of things I'd like to accomplish before I die:
- When I was a child, one of my favorite places was...
- What's the biggest worry I've got?
- Is there anything I'd like to alter about myself?
- This is a place that's on my travel bucket list:... What would I want if I could?
- What would I do with a superpower if I had one, and how can I put it to good use?
- In the next one to 10 years, where do I want to be?

365 Journal

DAY 182 - 188

Measure Your Happiness

Day 182 - The Fullness Of Life!

"The thief comes only in order to steal, kill, and destroy. I have come in order that you might have life—life in all its fullness."
— John 10:10, GNT

BELOVED,
It's easy to get discouraged by what other people say or think of you, how they treat you, or even how much they know about your previous failures, family background, personal secrets, or even their first impression of you. It would help if you asked them to update their database since you are a new creation, and their information is outdated because God created you to be evolving and becoming. But whose report will you accept? Believe in God's word about you. Jesus declared in John 10:10, "The thief comes to steal, kill, and destroy; I came to offer life in abundance."
Jesus' intent differs from the devil's. Jesus offers new life, the fullness of joy, and abundance, while the adversary attempts to murder, steal, and destroy. Therefore, as a believer, you live in Jesus' promise of fullness of joy, life, and wealth because He's already fulfilled it. You have God's already-established abundant and significant life. Life's challenges, disease, evil, sorrows, and adversaries may dispute God's promise of joy, strength, and peace. Jesus annulled Satan's plan to defeat, divide, destroy, and kill. Embrace Jesus' love, companionship, and closeness to experience the fullness of life. Life is rich, whole, and complete when you have Jesus. It's whom you have, not what you have or what others think. God's love isn't based on your worries, anxieties, frustrations, or failures. The abundance of life is a gift of God, not your works, but through Salvation, the cross, the empty tomb, His love, grace, and your faith from believing in Jesus and benefiting from your Kingdom's connection as a child of God.
Living the fullness of life is a *365 Live Fearlessly* pursuit, a daily purposeful living, faithfully and fully, seeking God, becoming emotionally aware, spiritually mature, cognitively renewed, spending time with God, growing, learning, developing, and transforming in a community of believers, Chayah Club. The fullness of life begins with the invitation to come (Salvation), coaching to conquer changes and challenges, and the commission to go and create disciples of all nations. The fullness of life realizes that it's not selfishness or self-centeredness but Kingdom-mindedness. You're invited on a mission to be a legend for Jesus and leave a legacy, store treasures in heaven, save lost souls, transform lives, empower others, give of yourself, be Jesus' hands and feet, and leave a mark that outlives and outlasts you. It is a new perspective, and the purpose in the promise to live abundantly; life in its fullness and fulfillment of Jesus' promise not to divide but multiply; not decrease but increase; not destroy but build; not cause depression but bring joy; not steal but bring recompense, restoration, and repayment and fully paid the wages of sin; not to die but to live and declare the glory of God.

AFFIRMATIONS & DECLARATION

- I am blessed. I am living life in its fullness, righteousness, abundance, joy, and peace.
- I come out of my barrenness, brokenness, loneliness, joblessness, and helplessness into blessedness.
- I am not hopeless because my hope comes from God; I am victorious, healed, happy, and healthy!
- I am positioned for my breakthrough and restoration. I am ready!

"You will not let them kill me, but I will live to tell the world what the Lord has done for me."
Psalm 118:17, TPT

PRAYER
Lord, Thank You for Psalm 118:17, which promises I shall live to tell of Your mighty works. In Jesus' name, I declare I will live and proclaim Your glory. Lord, in Jesus' name, Your peace will always guard my heart. (Phi 4:6-7). I won't be anxious, sad, or worried about anything, but I will continue praying and petitioning You with thanksgiving. I believe that Your peace, the peace that preserves my heart and mind in Christ Jesus, is mine. I stand on Deuteronomy 28:6 and acknowledge that as I obey You, I'll be blessed when I enter and go. My children, household, family, finances, the labor of our hands, ministry, career, business, vision, objectives, destiny, this day, this week, this month, this year, and the future are abundantly blessed. I will not labor in vain nor produce children for calamity, for my children are blessed. (Isa 65:23). In Jesus' name, my efforts, labor, abilities, and work will yield an abundant harvest, prosperity, exceptional performance, productivity, profits, the harvest of souls, and a lasting legacy. Use me as a financial pillar and grace steward to nations and a carrier of Your fullness of life, blessings, miracles, faith, love, and grace; globally and generationally. In Jesus' name, I pray, amen.

MY DOPE *faith journal*

Date S | M | T | W | T | F | S

Morning: I feel my emotion! My one-word check-in:

DECLARATION

Consider today's verse. I implore the Holy Spirit to reveal His wisdom and truth to me and I declare it over my life.

OBSERVATION

What does the message mean? Lord, help me see it.

PRAYER

What is my prayer request? Lord, I live fully in You.

EMPOWERMENT

How will Your word empower me? Lord, give me the insight to apply my faith to be more significant than my fears.

MY FEARLESS *journey*

Evening: Feel my emotion! My one-word check-up:

What is making me FEEL like this?

What lessons did I LEARNED?

What THOUGHTS did I had?

What prompted my GRATITUDE?

Who did I CONNECTED with?

What brought me JOY?

EVENING PRAYER

WATER:

FRUIT & VEG:

MY MOOD:

My treat for today is: ....

FEARLESS CONTRACT

I, (your name)

will (state your goal)

by (enter date)

because doing so will benefit me (explain why you set this goal)

When I'm finished, I will treat myself with (state your reward)

Signature:

Day 183 - His Protection Is For You!

Live under the protection of God Most High and stay in the shadow of God All-Powerful. Then you will say to the Lord, 'You are my fortress, my place of safety; you are my God, and I trust you.'
Psalm 91: 1-2, CEV

BELOVED,
You're sometimes afraid of what's in store for you in this life. Physical protection and shelter are fundamental requirements that must be satisfied to feel safe and secure in one's own life. In peril, it seems impossible to defend yourself sometimes, yet you must trust in God's protection. Spiritual, psychological, emotional, financial, physical, and social storms or confrontations make you feel afraid, vulnerable, and unsafe. God is your trustworthy, caring, and mighty Defender, according to the Bible. *Protection is the act of preventing someone or something from hurt, harm, or injury.* God is your Protector, a cloud pillar by day and a fire pillar at night; Put on God's whole armor and resist the devil; God will protect you and surround you with joyful salvation songs. God is your strength and refuge in times of trouble. Be strong and fearless. Do not be frightened, for the Lord your God is with you; He will never desert you. You may now say, "Lord, You are my Helper; I am not afraid. I'm under Your protective coverage: Blood covered and Blood washed. Who can hurt me? I am the Lord's servant, God's property, and the King's kid." The Father says no weapon made against you will prevail, and you will refute every accuser. This promise is your inheritance from Me. (Isaiah 54:17). Whatever your situation, seek Jesus, dwell in His shelter, rest in His shadow, hide in His presence, trust God, and say, "Lord, You're my refuge and protection." Activate His deliverance, redemption, and supernatural power. Unwaveringly believe! Confess Psalm 91 over your life, family, children, career, business, ministry, projects, aspirations, and destiny! God is ready and eager to fulfill His word for you. God is your refuge and strength, a constant and present aid in trouble. This God is your God forever and will guide you from abundant life to eternal life. God will bless you and command angels to carry you, fight for you, lead and help you. He keeps you at peace because you courageously trust Him.
Psalm 91 contains these three wisdom keys to God's protection.

1. **Seek Him as your shelter and rest in His shadow.** You seek the Lord, Most High's protection.
2. **Speak it aloud to God.** You must declare and claim it by saying, 'God, You are my Protector.'
3. **Surrender to Him.** You trust, believe, and are fearless in His love and power to protect you.

AFFIRMATIONS & DECLARATIONS
I await God's salvation. Only He sustains me. He's my defense and protection, and I won't lose. (Ps 62:1).

- I am covered and protected by the Blood of Jesus. I am confident and contented in God's protection.
- I am under His All-powerful divine protection, divine security, and divine nature.
- He is My Creator, Way-Maker, Redeemer, Promise-Keeper, Liberator, and Light-in-the-Darkness God.

Psalm 91:14-16, MSG: *"If you'll hold on to me for dear life," says God, "I'll get you out of any trouble. I'll give you the best of care if you'll only get to know and trust me. Call me and I'll answer, be at your side in bad times; I'll rescue you, then throw you a party. I'll give you a long life, give you a long drink of salvation!"*

PRAYER
Heavenly Father, will You please protect me from any adversity, persecution, and impediment with Your eternal all-powerful might? Surround me with Your power, grace, glory, and Blood. As I seek safety in You, let me rejoice, continually praise You, and delight in Your promise to keep me secure. For You, O LORD, are the One who acknowledges and honors the righteous; You surround me with 'favor like a shield.' O God, empower me in Your power and conceal me beneath Your wings - You are my Loving and Strong Protection, Refuge, Stronghold, Deliverer, and Safe-place. Dress me flawlessly and wonderfully in Your protective armor so I can endure, conquer, and beat the devil's schemes, diabolical plots, temptations, and falsehoods. My war is not against flesh and blood but rulers, powers, principalities, evil worldly forces of this darkness, and spiritual forces of wickedness in the high places. Lord, You are my Champion Defender, Commander, Controller, Guardian, Rock of Safety, Fortress, Shield, and Keeper. Protect me, my children, my household, my family, the work of our hands, heads, hearts, habits, and land from evil, and keep our souls safe and at peace. Watch our departures and entrances, going out and coming in, peaks and valleys, ups and downs, the ins and outs, nights and days forever. In the name of Jesus, I pray, Amen.

MY DOPE *faith journal*

Date S | M | T | W | T | F | S

Morning: I feel my emotion! My one-word check-in: ....

DECLARATION

Consider today's verse. I implore the Holy Spirit to reveal His wisdom and truth to me and I declare it over my life.

OBSERVATION

What does the message mean? Lord, help me see it.

PRAYER

What is my prayer request? Lord, I live fully in You.

EMPOWERMENT

How will Your word empower me? Lord, give me the insight to apply my faith to be more significant than my fears.

MY FEARLESS *journey*

Evening: Feel my emotion! My one-word check-up:

What is making me FEEL like this?

What lessons did I LEARNED?

What THOUGHTS did I had?

What prompted my GRATITUDE?

Who did I CONNECTED with?

What brought me JOY?

EVENING PRAYER

WATER:

FRUIT & VEG:

MY MOOD:

My treat for today is: ....

The Happiness Test

Give each assertion a score between 1 and 3, with 1 representing seldom true, 2 representing occasionally true, and 3 representing frequently true. When completed, add your points together to get your happiness score.	Seldom	Occasionally	Frequently
I am aware of my strengths.	1	2	3
My life has significance for me.	1	2	3
I have hope for the future.	1	2	3
I can concentrate on the current moment.	1	2	3
Every day, I take regular breaks from social media.	1	2	3
Every day, I engage in regular physical activity.	1	2	3
I frequently show others kindness.	1	2	3
By utilizing my abilities, I experience a strong sense of fulfillment in my life.	1	2	3
I express my emotions to family or friends.	1	2	3
People and circumstances have made me feel grateful.	1	2	3
I'm a part of a spiritual community or organization.	1	2	3
I participate in things that I find both complex and exciting.	1	2	3

Scores: 12 - 19

Not Happy

You are employing only a few abilities that add to your satisfaction. You may acquire pleasure by mastering these talents. Consider seeking professional help if you are going through a tough time.

Scores: 20 - 28

Moderately Happy

You have specific abilities that lead to happiness, but you might benefit from learning and implementing a few more happy habits to achieve satisfaction in all aspects of your life.

Scores: 29 - 36

Extremely Happy

You have many talents that contribute to your happiness, and as a result, you are happy in all aspects of your life. Continue to use these strategies and enjoy your pleasure.

YOUR HAPPINESS SCORE:	

Day 184 - Season Changing...

"Because of you, I know the path of life, as I taste the fullness of joy in your presence. At your right side, I experience divine pleasures forevermore!"
— Psalms 16:11 TPT

BELOVED,
Life seasons are described in Ecclesiastes 3:1-15 as *"A time for everything and a season for every activity under the heavens."* Spring, summer, fall, and winter are natural seasons each year. Like these seasons, changes and challenges in life need mental, emotional, and behavioral adjustments. Nightlong weeping ends with dawn's joy for the beloved who trusts the Lord and knows that darkness will pass. Mood, stamina, resilience, grit, and faith are honed with the changes in life seasons. How quickly you adapt to seasons and how you see the current season tell much about your spiritual maturity and personal growth. God's plan for you determines your identity and destiny, not you or your situation. God says everything has a time and a season, and you may be contented, peaceful, joyful, strong, courageous, developed, nurtured, fruitful, and thrive despite it all. Nature, people, the earth, times, tides, and seasons are in His hands. God is timeless and constant. Seasons change, but He remains the same, always faithful to keep His promises. He created you to *"be fulfilled, subdue it, multiply, conquer, and possess it."* His generosity, sovereignty, and magnificence aren't diminished by seasons. God speaks, and it creates, tables turn, storms quiet, and breakthroughs occur!
Bad breaks, setbacks, divorce, financial issues, heartbreak, failed relationships, career discontent, business stagnation, sickness, or death of a loved one can leave us in a dry, unproductive, fearful, and barren season. In times of difficulty, instability, and uncertainty, turn to God's word for truth, comfort, peace, wisdom, joy, and His promise. He'll revive you despite years the locusts have eaten. He'll recover lost time. Trust that He'll repair, refund, return, recoup, reimburse, and repay you. Those who trust God are blessed. Oh, happy new day! Greet this new season of fertility, wealth, possibility, nobility, royalty, vast fruitfulness, unique favor, and Zion's fortunes restoration that awaits you!

AFFIRMATIONS & DECLARATIONS
I declare: I am kingdom-minded! I have a kingdom purpose.
My Father says, *"And I will also give you what you did not ask for—riches and fame! No other king in all the world will be compared to you for the rest of your life!"* (1 Kings 3:13, NLT).

- I am sufficient by God.
- I am blessed and loved by God with wisdom, wealth, wholeness, and wellness.
- I am forgiven. I found new life in God.
- I believe that God has a great plan in my life.
- I believe God will keep me in perfect peace.
- I believe God is not punishing me; He is preparing me for what I am praying and expecting.
- God is at work for me; He is fighting on my behalf.
- I am made ready for my new season.

I am a seed. I am planted rather than buried. In Jesus' name, I bring forth peace, prosperity, wisdom, wealth, health, and wellness. I am fertile, fruitful, and flourishing. I own and possess my possessions. Even as the seasons change, my God's love remains constant. Throughout it all, He remains devoted.

"For I am planting seeds of peace and prosperity among you. The grapevines will be heavy with fruit.
The earth will produce its crops, and the heavens will release the dew.
Once more, I will cause the remnant in Judah and Israel to inherit these blessings."
Zechariah 8:12, NLT

PRAYER:
Heavenly Father, thank You for revealing Your eternal essence through the changing nature of creation, creative miracles, and Your divine nature by blessing me with everything for life, living, livelihood, and righteousness. God, You are the Eternal Controller and Sovereign God. Your love endures time, tides, and seasons. I am entering a magnificent, bountiful season filled with Your provision; it will happen suddenly; I'm ready. My character is altered, and I'm prepared for my calling and fresh beginnings. I'm excited, not anxious! I'm glad to live my mission, inspiring, and impactful life. Faith is my heritage; my life significance is Your purpose. Help me trust You courageously and confidently throughout this shift so I can walk fearlessly in Your plan, promise, and provision—May the season of change usher me in another beautiful season. Lord, I receive and activate every prophetic word, purpose, and path for my new life and seasons. I experience Your light, joy, delight, serenity, satisfaction, victory, wisdom, and wealth. My seasons are changing but God; You remain the same, pleasing God and faithful Father. In Jesus' name, I pray, Amen.

MY DOPE *faith journal*

Date	S | M | T | W | T | F | S

Morning: I feel my emotion! My one-word check-in: ....

DECLARATION

Consider today's verse. I implore the Holy Spirit to reveal His wisdom and truth to me and I declare it over my life.

OBSERVATION

What does the message mean? Lord, help me see it.

PRAYER

What is my prayer request? Lord, I live fully in You.

EMPOWERMENT

How will Your word empower me? Lord, give me the insight to apply my faith to be more significant than my fears.

MY FEARLESS *journey*

Evening: Feel my emotion! My one-word check-up:

What is making me FEEL like this?

What lessons did I LEARNED?

What THOUGHTS did I had?

What prompted my GRATITUDE?

Who did I CONNECTED with?

What brought me JOY?

EVENING PRAYER

My treat for today is: ....

Happiness Test

Use this scale, where 1 is very happy (extremely sad), and 10 is very happy (extremely pleased, to gauge your overall happiness during the past month in each of the categories provided. To calculate your total level of happiness, add your scores.

	Very unhappy									Very happy
General happiness	1	2	3	4	5	6	7	8	9	10
Health	1	2	3	4	5	6	7	8	9	10
Career	1	2	3	4	5	6	7	8	9	10
Sleep	1	2	3	4	5	6	7	8	9	10
Communication	1	2	3	4	5	6	7	8	9	10
Family	1	2	3	4	5	6	7	8	9	10
Relationships	1	2	3	4	5	6	7	8	9	10
Emotional life	1	2	3	4	5	6	7	8	9	10
Strengths & Talents	1	2	3	4	5	6	7	8	9	10
Fitness	1	2	3	4	5	6	7	8	9	10
Optimism	1	2	3	4	5	6	7	8	9	10
Spirituality	1	2	3	4	5	6	7	8	9	10
Sex life	1	2	3	4	5	6	7	8	9	10
Nutrition	1	2	3	4	5	6	7	8	9	10
Finances	1	2	3	4	5	6	7	8	9	10
Environment	1	2	3	4	5	6	7	8	9	10
Learning & education	1	2	3	4	5	6	7	8	9	10
Personal growth	1	2	3	4	5	6	7	8	9	10
Recreation	1	2	3	4	5	6	7	8	9	10
Friendships	1	2	3	4	5	6	7	8	9	10

YOUR HAPPINESS SCORE:	

Day 185 - God Fixed It!

"The Lord is close to all whose hearts are crushed by pain, and He is always ready to restore the repentant one. Even when bad things happen to the good and godly ones, the Lord will save them and not let them be defeated by what they face. God will be your bodyguard to protect you when trouble is near. Not one bone will be broken."

—Psalm 34:18-20, TPT

BELOVED,

Many times, you feel as if your life is in a state of disarray, your dreams have been dashed, your faith in others has been shaken, or you have abandoned God and set out on your own, only to be left bruised or broken by life's storms, whether caused by illness, financial ruin, or social collapse. You see yourself as an old, dilapidated house needing repair and restoration. God is still mending people's damaged lives and hopes; physical, spiritual, emotional, mental, social, and financial well-being, and relationships with their families and loved ones; He is the Ultimate Fixer. The Lord is the Supreme Fixer-Upper; He can fix anything and everything. Jesus, Son of God, trained as a carpenter, crucified as a Savior, and resurrected as a Liberator and Anointed One, can repair, renovate, restore, rebuild, recreate, redeem, repair, recover, reclaim, rescue, rebirth, refresh, renew, revive, reboot, and reset anything, regardless of the state or condition of your life's brokenness, barrenness, sickness, abandonment, damage, destruction, or devalue. It takes faith amidst fear, failure, and frustration to declare that my Father is fixing this!

The Father had a plan when the devil plotted and devised his diabolical and malevolent desire to kill, steal, and destroy God's perfect creation. The devil developed his tactic, duping Eve and Adam into disobeying God, causing them to sin, so sin invaded all people and the earth. Romans 5:12, AMP, says, *"Therefore, just as sin came into the world through one man, and death through sin, so death spread to all people [no one being able to stop it or escape its power] because they all sinned."* But God had a perfect plan for redemption and permanently resolving the sin problem. Jesus arrived and finished the work on the cross; He fixed it; He paid the wages in full! You experienced death through Adam but abundant and eternal life, new creation, joy, peace, hope, righteousness, and victory through Christ. 1 Corinthians 15:22, KJV says, *"For as in Adam all die, even so in Christ shall all be made alive."*

The Father says about your situation, "I just fixed it, it is finished, it's working, and it worked out! Jesus has broken every chain: loneliness, joblessness, sickness, wilderness, unfruitfulness, barrenness, sadness, hopelessness, homelessness, helplessness, poorness, and restlessness. He brought you newness of life, liberation, joy in fullness, limitless love, salvation, new trajectory, and a fresh start." *God fixed it!*

AFFIRMATIONS & DECLARATIONS

Christ has given me completeness, fullness, happiness, goodness, magnificence, and grace. I thank You, LORD, for Your holiness, righteousness, sweetness, and lovingkindness! My God provides a safe place for me, the lonely, and guides me, the captive, to liberty, wisdom, wealth, wholeness, and wellness. There will be no complaining or moaning, only acknowledging and claiming! As His child, I now request my Heavenly Father, Abba, to repair it, and I now believe! Thank You for mending it, Daddy! It may appear to be impossible, but it is not for You. It seems intimidating and intricate, yet it is neither too complex nor too chaotic for You. Look how you put everything together, used everything that is broken, useless, and abandoned, and made it all work, remarkable, purposeful, excellent, blessed, and valuable, a masterpiece indeed! It's all fixed now! Thanks, Extraordinary Strategist!

- My God is more significant than any problems. God loves me more than I could ever imagine.
- I am covered; I am redeemed; I am free, fearless, and fixed! I am loved. God's love set me right. Greater is God who dwells within me than the adversary who works against me. I am happy!

Hosea 6:1, TPT: *Come on, let's renew our loyalty to the Eternal One! He tore us like a lion, but He'll heal us; He wounded us, but He'll bandage us.*

PRAYER

Heavenly Father, You're needed today. Spiritual, psychological, emotional, physical, financial, and social healing are required. I need salvation from sin, shame, and suffering. Lord, remind me that You work incessantly, persistently, aggressively, miraculously, or meticulously and victoriously for me and others. Lord, forgive me for attempting to fix my problems and failing miserably. Lord, forgive me for seeking strategies, solutions, and support elsewhere when I can only find it in You. Please forgive me for forgetting how much I need to prioritize my faith over my feelings and fears. When I'm lost and feeling broken, unwell, damaged, humiliated, inadequate, insufficient, missing, or needed. In anguish, I come to my Master with the plan for His masterpiece, Infinite-Fixer, and The Finisher-God. Lord, You know all. You understand my pain, process, and purpose. Please change and fix it to fit your divine purpose, promises, and goals. You know where I need to heal, grow, and be released. Lord, cure, bless, and keep me. Fix it, Lord, even if it takes a miracle, every disease, wound, heartbreak, limitation, barrier, desire, lack, and mess. You can do more than I can ask, imagine, think, or believe. In Jesus' name, I pray, Amen.

MY DOPE *faith journal*

Date S | M | T | W | T | F | S

Morning: I feel my emotion! My one-word check-in: ....

DECLARATION

Consider today's verse. I implore the Holy Spirit to reveal His wisdom and truth to me and I declare it over my life.

OBSERVATION

What does the message mean? Lord, help me see it.

PRAYER

What is my prayer request? Lord, I live fully in You.

EMPOWERMENT

How will Your word empower me? Lord, give me the insight to apply my faith to be more significant than my fears.

MY FEARLESS *journey*

Evening: Feel my emotion! My one-word check-up:

What is making me FEEL like this?

What lessons did I LEARNED?

What THOUGHTS did I had?

What prompted my GRATITUDE?

Who did I CONNECTED with?

What brought me JOY?

EVENING PRAYER

WATER:

FRUIT & VEG:

MY MOOD:

My treat for today is: ....

The Life Cycle

Consider the ten cycle categories and evaluate how satisfied you are with your life in these areas. Draw a line through each section to symbolize your happiness rating out of 10. To see your Cycle of a Life map, connect the circles. Dedicate every area of your life to God, the Ultimate Fixer!

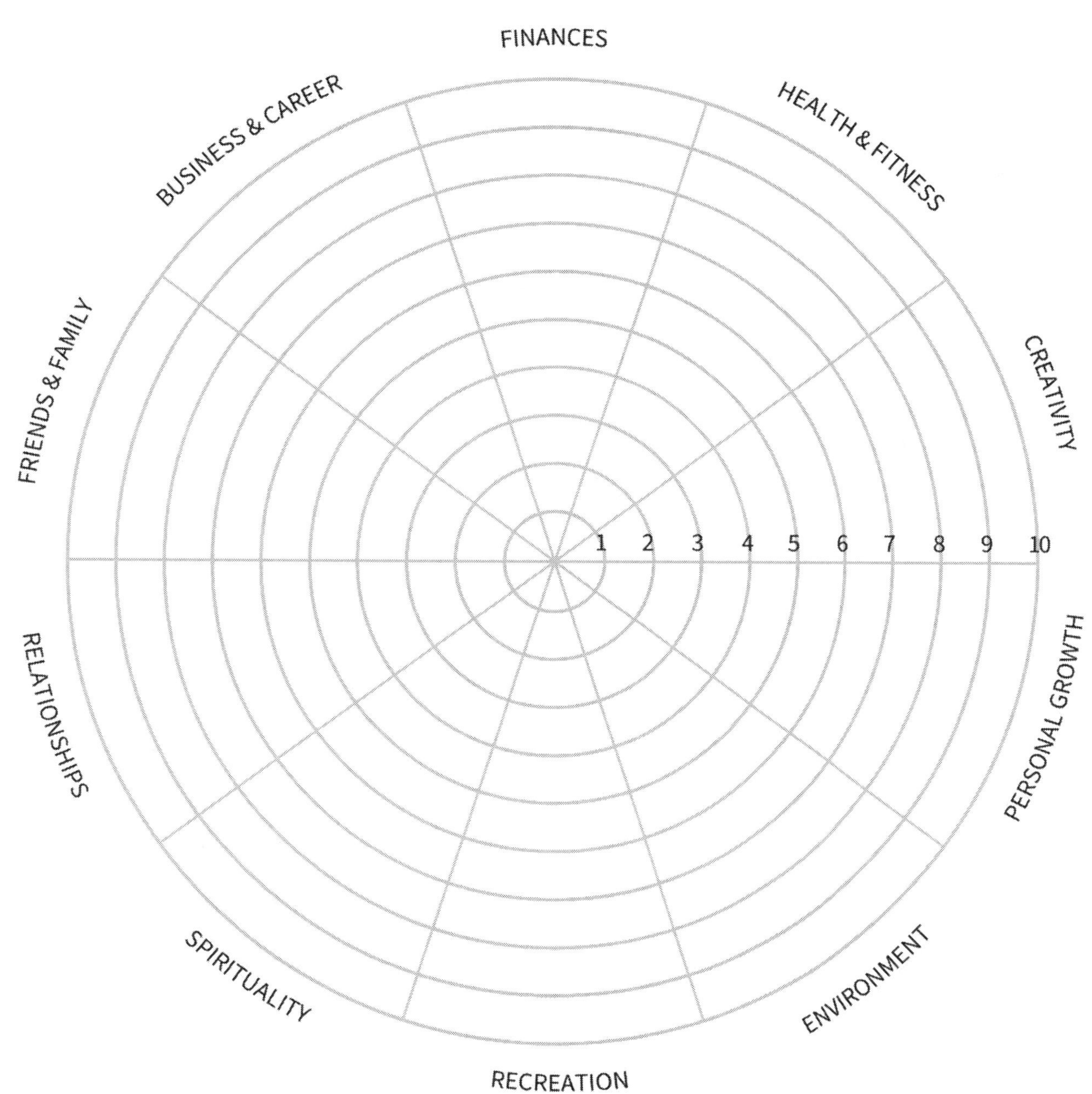

Day 186 - Status Checked? About To Arrive!

"A little one shall become a thousand, and a small one a strong nation: I the LORD will hasten it in his time".
Isaiah 60:22, KJV

BELOVED,
You are checking on your blessings, answered prayers, and delivered promises today, and the tracking information reads, "Your Blessings are Shipped and About to ARRIVE - Suddenly!" God said, I heard your plea the first time, Day 1, when you humbled yourself before Me and prayed, and I responded, but there's spiritual warfare for your breakthrough, and I'm sending help. I'm equipping My divine supply chain with Hosts of Angels. A priority status upgrade has been issued; it is arriving very soon. 'Your next is now!' I, God, gave a mandate when you pray. Chief Angels with fiery darts are dispatched, coming to intervene and inform you that I value you. Listen and be strengthened to comprehend the provision of your vision. (Dan 9:23, 10:12). Your blessings are in transit and on-route from heaven; neither Amazon nor FedEx are as trustworthy as your Faithful Father and His angels.
What will you do while waiting for your blessings? Worship, praise, and ponder God's word. In Genesis, God promised Sarah and Abraham a son. God did the impossible. At the proper time, the Lord gave a barren older lady the ability to give birth to a bouncing baby boy; she held Issac (laughter) in her hands. He blessed her barren womb to conceive by an impotent older man, and God gave them Issac. Sarah scoffed at the prophecy, yet, Sarah smiled when Isaac was born and embraced her son in her arms, exactly as God promised. God will make things happen at the perfect time, so delay isn't denial! Isaiah 60:22 say, *"At the right time, I, the LORD, will make it happen."* You are under an open heaven, a bridge between heaven and earth, and angels ascend and descend. (John1:51). Jesus Christ spans the divide between heaven and earth to fulfill His promise with His armies of angels blessing you. You can trust Him to keep His word because The Mediator, Intercessor, Redeemer, Promise-Keeper, Way-Maker, Miracle-working God, and Light of the World. Your deliverance, blessings, miracles, and breakthrough will happen at the given time.

AFFIRMATIONS & DECLARATIONS
God says I will do even better than you asked, immeasurably more!
"Now to Him who is able to [carry out His purpose and] do superabundantly more than all that we dare ask or think [infinitely beyond our greatest prayers, hopes, or dreams], according to His power that is at work within us." (Ephesians 3:20, AMP).

- God is currently showering me with His blessings! I am rejoicing and reveling in God's unexpected blessings, uncommon miracles, and unusual favor.
- God is blessing me with precisely what I require and everything I could desire by His will.
- I am blessed and prospered because God loves me! My mind is wide open to opportunities and all possibilities, my ability and character are prepared, and my faith is strong!
- I am in the proper position and at the right moment to get my unexpected, unforeseen, mind-blowing, and dream-like benefits; I am uniquely created for a memorable and magnificent purpose.
- I am unique, gifted, talented, purposeful, and created for a time such as this.
- I am creative, brilliant, valuable, and intentionally, fearfully, and wonderfully made for this time, place, and purpose. I am guided by God's Word and synchronized with His schedule.
- I am fearless. I am limitless. I am not lost, and it's not too late for me. My God is always on time and target. I did not miss my destiny; rather, it was ordained and predestined for me by my God.

PRAYER
Heavenly Father, thanks for the love, care, and all You've given me. Thank You for letting me bless others today. Lord, help me overcome my fear of failing and not seeking You. If I don't ask; therefore, You stated I don't have. You said Your children perish for lack of awareness of Your word's truth. You told me to write down my vision, and You'll make it happen at the perfect moment, even if it seems to delay. Satan wishes for me to be fearful and not live freely for You. Help me to live my life with brave confidence and daring faith in You. Jesus, the authority of Your Name, power of Your Spirit, and Your Body and Blood are my salvation, deliverance, redemption, healing, peace, joy, blessings, hope, prosperity, and a new beginning. In Jesus' name, I ask for breakthroughs, fulfilled promises, destiny alignment, miraculous healing, divine helpers, and answered prayers. Lord, I checked the status; You have verified and confirmed my deliverance with Your word; I am blessed. *Notification alert:* Arriving soon, suddenly, and immeasurably more blessings are on the way. In Jesus' name, I pray, Amen.

MY DOPE *faith journal*

Date S | M | T | W | T | F | S

Morning: I feel my emotion! My one-word check-in: ....

DECLARATION

Consider today's verse. I implore the Holy Spirit to reveal His wisdom and truth to me and I declare it over my life.

OBSERVATION

What does the message mean? Lord, help me see it.

PRAYER

What is my prayer request? Lord, I live fully in You.

EMPOWERMENT

How will Your word empower me? Lord, give me the insight to apply my faith to be more significant than my fears.

MY FEARLESS *journey*

Evening: Feel my emotion! My one-word check-up:

What is making me FEEL like this?

What lessons did I LEARNED?

What THOUGHTS did I had?

What prompted my GRATITUDE?

Who did I CONNECTED with?

What brought me JOY?

EVENING PRAYER

My treat for today is: ....

365 Journal

Day 187 - God Reverses The Curse!

No weapon that is formed against thee shall prosper; and every tongue that shall rise against thee in judgment thou shalt condemn. This is the heritage of the servants of the Lord, and their righteousness is of me, saith the Lord.
— Isaiah 54:17, KJV

BELOVED,
The repeated cycles of trauma, sickness, disease, mental disorders, poverty, teenage pregnancies, single-parent households, fatherlessness, toxic relationships, divorce, domestic abuse, incest, incarnation, addiction, almost making it out, untimely deaths, suicidal thoughts, identity crises, ungodly alliances, and demonic yokes are often seen and experienced by people of all generations, nationalities, and family backgrounds. You must intentionally break these vicious cycles, negative pronouncements, ancestral yokes, satanic bondage, and diabolical plots by the Blood of Christ, the power of the Holy Spirit, and in the authority of Jesus' name. It may run in your family, but you must stop it. As a believer, God utilizes even the enemy's ill intentions to help you; sets the table for you before your enemy; overflows with kindness, grace, and power. Weapons are formed but shall not prosper; They won't prevail. The pious receive light, peace, and joy. Open your mouth, reverse the curse, and reclaim joy, peace, liberation, and victory!

Proclaim it:
Lord, fear will not triumph since You have prevailed. Your affection soothes me and drowns away my anxiety. If I fall, I will rise; if I am in distress, the Lord is my everlasting light. I desire a supernatural experience to resurrect me, transform my circumstances, reroute my life, and deliver me from despair, sickness, poverty, and pain. The LORD God is a sun and shield, bringing grace, glory, favor, and honor.
The Lord will not withhold anything good from you, and He gives you, His beloved and favorite child, the ultimate best and promises generational blessings for my obedience. In the name of Jesus, every ancestral curse, demons of divorce or single-parent families, destiny pirate, identity thief, joblessness, career unhappiness, financial barrenness, poverty, depression, anxiety, and every form of mental disorder, toxic fear, sickness, and affliction are extinguished in Jesus' name, by the Blood of Jesus, and the Fire of the Holy Ghost.
God promises to care, cure, carry and bless you even into old age! The Father said, "I made you, and I'll carry you, rescue you, and save you. I am your Creator, Redeemer, Deliverer, Liberator, Curse-Reverser, Chain-Breaker, Corruption-Canceler, and Champion-Defender. I am reversing every curse!"

AFFIRMATIONS & DECLARATIONS
"Nevertheless, the Lord Your God was not willing to listen to Balaam, but the Lord, your God, turned the curse into a blessing for you because the Lord your God loves you." (Deuteronomy 23:5, VOICE).

- I am God's creation; no curse shall harm me, nor lies and accusations of my enemies.
- I reject the spirit of hindrance and delay in my life.
- I have been transferred from the kingdom of darkness to the Kingdom of Light, where I cannot be rejected, cursed, or abandoned. I reverse every curse in the name of Jesus.
- I am a chain-breaker. I am breaking the generational curse, it may run in my family, but it stops here.
- I am a legacy-builder. I am liberated. My God turned the curse into a blessing. I am loved.

"And I will make you a great nation, And I will bless you [abundantly], And make your name great (exalted, distinguished); And you shall be a blessing [a source of great good to others]; And I will bless (do good for, benefit) those who bless you,
And I will curse [that is, subject to My wrath and judgment] the one who curses (despises, dishonors, has contempt for) you. And in you, all the families (nations) of the earth will be blessed."
Genesis 12:2-3, AMP

PRAYER
Heavenly Father, glory to You, the One True, The Sovereign and Creator God, for I am, whom You say I am, to whom I belong, and everything You have created me to be and become. As my Creator, Redeemer, Architect, and Author, You are fully aware of the mountains, obstacles, opposition, oppression, temptation, trials, and the consequences of sin. When You died on the cross, You set me free from every sin, curse, hex, vex, wickedness, evil, captivity, and chain. I am grateful for the presence of the Holy Spirit, my Great Comforter, Advocate, and Helper in me, a Christ Follower. The power of sin and wages of death have been canceled over me because of Christ. Protect and deliver me from every generational curse, sinful tendencies, temptations, troubles, sickness, poverty, and strongholds I face. Lord, give me a boomerang anointing that every curse boom, reverse as a blessing, and return the evil intent to the pits of ell. Lord, please help me identify and bring them to You, confront them, and do the work necessary to ift my focus and magnify You, TO REVERSE EVERY CURSE TO A BLESSING. In Jesus' name, I pray, Amen.

MY DOPE *faith journal*

Date S | M | T | W | T | F | S

Morning: I feel my emotion! My one-word check-in:

DECLARATION

Consider today's verse. I implore the Holy Spirit to reveal His wisdom and truth to me and I declare it over my life.

OBSERVATION

What does the message mean? Lord, help me see it.

PRAYER

What is my prayer request? Lord, I live fully in You.

EMPOWERMENT

How will Your word empower me? Lord, give me the insight to apply my faith to be more significant than my fears.

MY FEARLESS *journey*

Evening: Feel my emotion! My one-word check-up:

What is making me FEEL like this?

What lessons did I LEARNED?

What THOUGHTS did I had?

What prompted my GRATITUDE?

Who did I CONNECTED with?

What brought me JOY?

EVENING PRAYER

My treat for today is: ....

The Life Cycle

Identify the areas you want to specialize in, then consider your objectives and the following measures you must take to achieve them. God is leading you into generational blessings.

FRIENDS & FAMILY	

BUSINESS & CAREER	

FINANCES	

HEALTH & FITNESS	

CREATIVITY	

PERSONAL GROWTH	

ENVIRONMENT	

RECREATION	

SPITITUALITY	

RELATIONSHIPS	

Day 188 - Own It!

"Take possession of the land and settle in it, because I have given it to you to occupy."
— Numbers 33:53, NLT

BELOVED,
You frequently hear that small, still voice from God that He has given you the go-ahead and anointing to move forward, start the business, return to school, publish the book, enter into ministry, leave that toxic relationship, cancel the enemy's lies, be the first person in your family to be different and break the mold; claim it, do it, and own it! However, fear paralyzes you; you're demotivated by the how, when, and why me? But why not you? Who are you not to arise, shine your light so that His brilliance in you might illuminate others? With Christ, you're a game-changer; You wield considerable power; You alter things!
You are leaving a legacy. You are shifting the narrative! It's yours; claim it! Leave the village thinking behind and adopt a Kingdom mindset. You're rewriting history and altering the story plot. You're working on revisions. You're making progress. You're taking chances, risking with Christ as there is no failure, and going somewhere wonderfully despite the challenging journey. Your choices change the outcome of your circumstance. You've revolutionized the game. Despite obstacles, you're considering new options, and God is making it happen for you. You're pumped! You are becoming more. You have choices, not constraints. You are recovering God's instructions on inhabiting and possessing the promised territory. The Father says, "You must drive out the people of the promised land, break their carved images and cast idols, and demolish their high places," The Father continues: "Enter the promised land righteously, confidently, and live in cleanliness and holiness. You're ready for a new era with a transformed character; you're brave, strong, and sure of God and yourself. Remove your old thinking, ungodly lifestyle, confining notions, sinful habits, idols, unhealthy lifestyle, terrible relationships, and carnal cravings. Take possession of the place I've given you and live there. Please do not claim you are outnumbered and cannot force them out because the Greater One is in you. Please stop trekking in the woods, affirming your fears, and move forward to acquire the Kingdom's wealth; Own it! I've promised you the promised land, a land flowing with milk and honey. I am the LORD, your God, who has set you apart; You are the King's kid; I have given you clarity and provision for the vision. How long will you postpone entering the land that the LORD, Your God, has given you? Suddenly, I will do it! Numbers 33:53, MSG, says, *'So that you take over the land and make yourself at home in it; I've given it to you. It's yours.'* Now go, and own it!"

AFFIRMATIONS & DECLARATIONS
"He gave them also the lands of the nations, That they might take possession of the fruit of the peoples' labor." (Ps 105:44, ESV). I am a game-changer because the Lord God Almighty is a Game-Changing, Creator, and Redeemer God. I know You didn't bring me this far to abandon me. I'm not going to trip. Jesus set me free from slavery. His Blood set me free from the bonds of sin and captivity. My shame, pain, and immorality were all on the cross. He accepted my sins, sickness, sadness, and sorrows and died in my place as a sacrificial lamb. He has ascended to Heaven. So not in the woods for me; I am victory-bound, so carrying these heavyweights felt insane when Jesus encouraged me to adopt His light yoke. I stand up and declare that I shall eat, drink, feast, and sit in front of my adversaries. In His promised land, I've tasted the milk and honey. In Jesus' name, I proclaim that all things are changing. I own it! There has been a significant alteration in my biography, story, and destiny in the name of Jesus. The ebb and flow of the tides in my storm. In my season, there has been a miraculous transformation—a case of conversion in my circumstances. No more moaning, wavering, roaming, questioning, squatting, asking, renting, venting, begging, and borrowing. I'm not going to wait any longer till I see it. I'm going into it with faith. God says, "I own it!" So, I own it! I am claiming it, possessing it, occupying it, and taking it over!

Nehemiah 9:25 NKJV: "And they took strong cities and a rich land, And possessed houses full of all goods, Cisterns already dug, vineyards, olive groves, And fruit trees in abundance. So they ate and were filled and grew fat, And delighted themselves in Your great goodness."

PRAYER
Heavenly Father, I'll quit complaining and claim it today. In Jesus' name, I believe. My destiny, story, purpose, biography, and legacy are changing. With Christ, I am liberated as I face my incarcerated existence and push myself to conquer its imprisonment, mental slavery, emotional bondage, sickness, and poverty! I manifest my aspirations, breakthroughs, fresh starts, and vision today. I boldly say that I will win, I can do it, *I own it*, and I will be whatever God has created me. I bind every adversary's hostile conduct to my life, every destiny thief, killer, and devourer. I proclaim that darkness will not succeed against my vision, work, children, household, relationships, career, finances, freedom, peace, joy, health, healing, wellness, wholeness, business, ministry, vocation, and destiny. In Jesus' name, I pray, Amen.

MY DOPE *faith journal*

Date S | M | T | W | T | F | S

Morning: I feel my emotion! My one-word check-in:

DECLARATION

Consider today's verse. I implore the Holy Spirit to reveal His wisdom and truth to me and I declare it over my life.

OBSERVATION

What does the message mean? Lord, help me see it.

PRAYER

What is my prayer request? Lord, I live fully in You.

EMPOWERMENT

How will Your word empower me? Lord, give me the insight to apply my faith to be more significant than my fears.

MY FEARLESS *journey*

Evening: Feel my emotion! My one-word check-up:

What is making me FEEL like this?

What lessons did I LEARNED?

What THOUGHTS did I had?

What prompted my GRATITUDE?

Who did I CONNECTED with?

What brought me JOY?

EVENING PRAYER

WATER:

FRUIT & VEG:

MY MOOD:

My treat for today is: ....

DAY 189 - 195

Use Your Strengths

“Then he said to them, “Go your way, eat the fat, drink the sweet, and send portions to those for whom nothing is prepared; for this day is holy to our Lord. Do not sorrow, for the joy of the Lord is your strength.”

— NEHEMIAH 8:10, NKJV

Day 189 - Survivor, Victor, Overcomer!

"But no matter what comes, we will always taste victory through Him who loved us."
— Romans 8:37, VOICE.

BELOVED,
They claim that God assigns the most brutal battles to His strongest warriors. He gives you spiritual strength, authority, wisdom, and power. He became the consuming fire for the three Hebrew boys in the blazing furnace. In the lion's lair, the Roaring Lion of Judah shuts the lion's mouth for Daniel. The Great I AM sided with Moses against Pharaoh. Gideon became the Mighty Warrior. David triumphed against Goliath. You may be battling a life-threatening illness or disease, facing a faith-shattering test, or witnessing the devastation of your family, home, life, and children resulting from a divorce, facing family troubles, financial difficulties, setbacks, the death of a loved one, business bankruptcy, being passed over for a promotion, job loss, or relationship heartbreak. Looking at these circumstances, you may not feel like a survivor, victor, or overcome. With all of the trials you've faced, you may not feel like you've triumphed, but you have because Christ has given you His victory and word. You are more than a conqueror, according to Romans 8:37, because He loves you so much that He died for you.

- A survivor lives through an event that killed others.
- The *victor* beats an opponent in a fight, battle, conflict, or championship.
- An overcomer has triumphed in a dispute or power struggle after overcoming a stumbling block or hindrance.

You are a survivor, a victor, not a victim of life's storms, an overcomer, a triumphant warrior, and more than a conqueror over the devil because of your faith in Christ Jesus.
There is no comparison of God's greatness to your opponents, vandals, bullies, and giants. You are a survivor, winner, and overcomer through Christ. Affirm His truth:

- *I am a survivor.* God is my source of power, help, and protection. Lord, You are always willing to help; I realize that my genuine support, strength, and security come from my Creator and Redeemer. You'll watch over me and never let me down. My God shall never forget me. You are my Guardian-God, and You never sleep, always keeping an eye on me and shielding me in Your presence. You are my night and day 365-24-27 Guardian-keeper. You protect me as You watch over me. You will keep me safe and defends me; I will go and return safely; You'll always stand up and fight for me. (Psalm 121). Who can stand in my way if God is on my side? With Christ, I am fearless. When cornered, I cry into You; despite the circumstance, I am relaxed, cool, calm, contented, and collected. (Ps 27:1-3).
- *I am a victor.* My God fights and wins my battles. You engage and conquer the opponents in every combat; I am confident the conquest is achieved, and victory is the only outcome. I am not afraid of this enormous army; the fight is for my God, the Champion Defender, and He wins! (2 Chro 20:15).
- *I am an overcomer.* My God divinely intervenes. You invade my mess, re-create me into a masterpiece. I am immovable and unshakeable. Dawn will expose Your divine assistance and light to me. (Psa 46:5).

AFFIRMATIONS & DECLARATION
In the name of Jesus, I decree and declare Your word. I stand on Your truth. Lord, You are active and ready to perform Your word. "*I trust You to save me, Lord God, and I won't be afraid. My power and my strength come from You, and You have saved me." (Isaiah 12:2 CEV).*
"Hello, new day; I am in control of my life, not circumstances. This day, I refuse to take on lies, fears, demons of chaos, and confusion. I remain undaunted - I am cool, calm, confident, courageous, and collected as a child of the King! I am a child of God. I am a joint heir with Christ. I am royalty and radiant. I am blessed. The Chain-Breaker breaks every chain. He is my Survivor, Victor, and an Overcomer God!"

- I am a survivor, a victor, an overcomer, and so much more than a conqueror!
- Worry is exchanged for adoration. With faith, I overcame my fear. I trade my anxiety for His anointing.
- I have survived because I have a powerful GOD.
- I am always ready, eager, and capable of succeeding.

Ezra 9:8, NLT: "But now we have been given a brief moment of grace, for the Lord our God has allowed a few of us to survive as a remnant. He has given us security in this holy place. Our God has brightened our eyes and granted us some relief from our slavery."

PRAYER
Heavenly Father, Oh God, Abba Father, I seek the fullness of your promises, purpose, and grace today. Fight and defend to protect Your soldiers and me on the front lines facing the battle of disease, poverty, financial crisis, personal struggle, and adverse life event. God of Resurrection comes in our midst and delivers a message of victory, consolation, peace, protection, security, and serenity. I am a survivor, victor, an overcomer with Christ, and more than a conqueror in Jesus' name; I pray, Amen.

MY DOPE *faith journal*

Date S | M | T | W | T | F | S

Morning: I feel my emotion! My one-word check-in: ....

DECLARATION

Consider today's verse. I implore the Holy Spirit to reveal His wisdom and truth to me and I declare it over my life.

OBSERVATION

What does the message mean? Lord, help me see it.

PRAYER

What is my prayer request? Lord, I live fully in You.

EMPOWERMENT

How will Your word empower me? Lord, give me the insight to apply my faith to be more significant than my fears.

MY FEARLESS *journey*

Evening: Feel my emotion! My one-word check-up:

What is making me FEEL like this?

What lessons did I LEARNED?

What THOUGHTS did I had?

What prompted my GRATITUDE?

Who did I CONNECTED with?

What brought me JOY?

EVENING PRAYER

My treat for today is: ....

Your Qualities & Strengths

According to the figure below from Peterson and Seligman's book Character Strengths and Virtues: A Handbook and Classification, there are 24 character strengths and 6 virtues. Look at the diagram, then list your main qualities and skills in the following table.

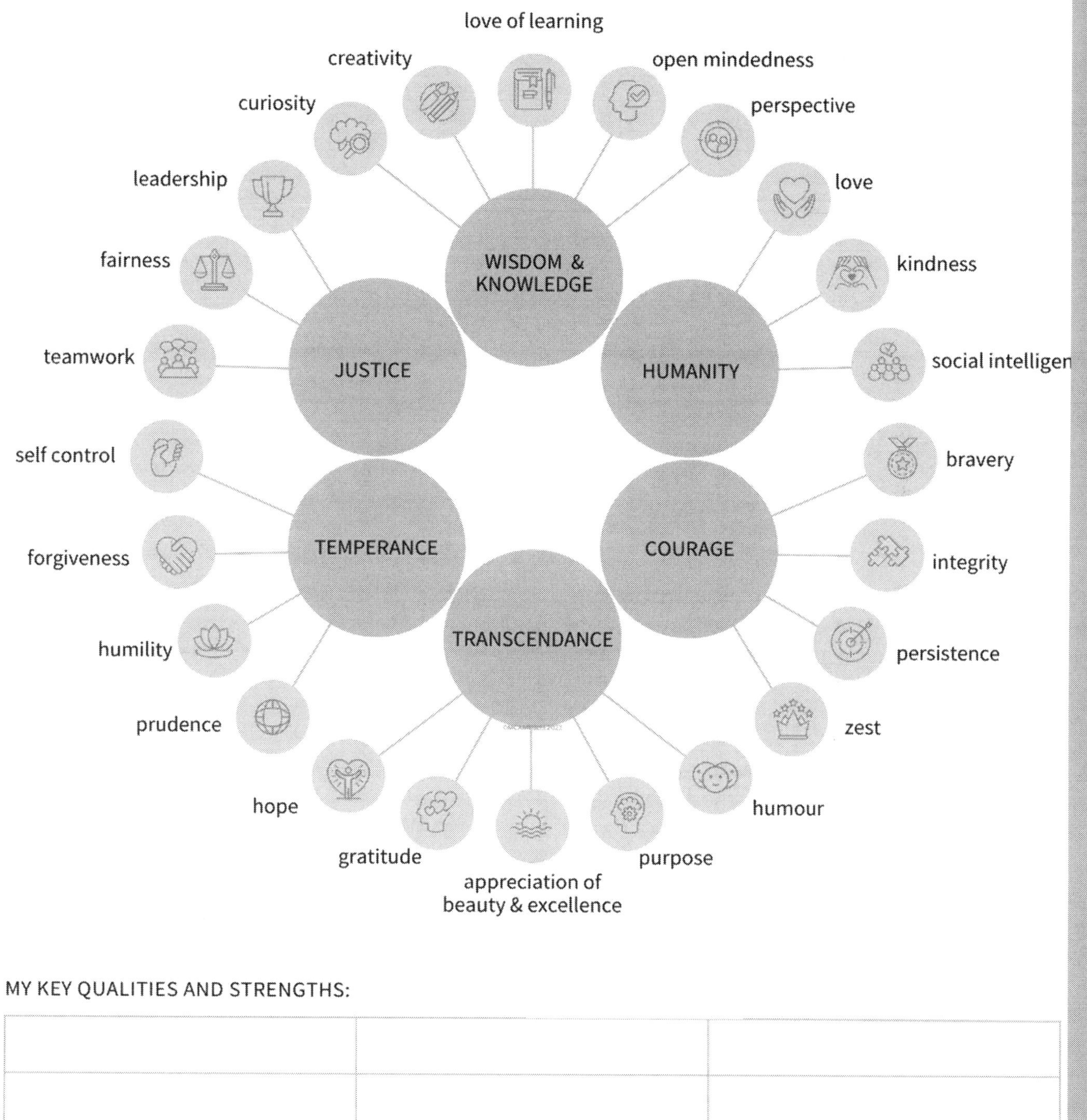

MY KEY QUALITIES AND STRENGTHS:

Day 190 - Believe, & Be Ready!

"Be prepared for action at a moment's notice..."
— Luke 12:35, TPT

BELOVED,

You're fasting, praying, waiting, and trusting, so you should be change-resistant and change-ready if God does something unexpected and unexpected! Suddenly, you meet someone new, fall in love, write a book, receive a promotion, the prodigal returns home, and the doctor declares that there are no sickness symptoms. You are suddenly approved and witness the physical embodiment of what you wished for in the spiritual realm. Believe and be prepared! At the allotted time, God acts abruptly, unexpectedly, and abundantly. God works when it is His time; He is on point, on target, and on time. God can move quickly to heal, assist, redeem, deliver, rescue, promote, rebuild, and restore you. God is unchangeable, yet He wants you to grow and progress in all areas of your life: personally, professionally, cognitively, emotionally, socially, financially, and spiritually. The return of Christ must be your top priority; therefore, pray and prepare. God says, "I'm not just speculating. There is a sense of urgency to all of this. If you're indifferent and complacent, you'll pass up an opportunity. It would help if you were as attentive and alert as a servant waiting for their master to return after a large wedding banquet. You'll put on your shoes and turn on your lamps so you can open the door for Him as soon as He gets home. Be prepared since the Son of Man will appear suddenly." (Luke 12:35-36)."If I leave and construct a house for you, I'll come back and take you to myself, so you may be where I am," Jesus remarked. (Luke 12:40). God can appear anytime to silence your storm or comfort you, His kid. Be expectant: you are not punished but prepared. Suddenly!

God unexpectedly intervenes. He is consistent and constant! He has already assisted you and will do so again. Undoubtedly! You may feel helpless and despondent as you consider your barrenness, disease, weakness, joblessness, desolation, loneliness, and gloom. But the Father asks, "What?" Even if you messed up, the adversary will not be able to prevent what I've planted in you from becoming great. Remember Abraham and Sarah; I summoned him while he was one, blessed him, and created him many. (Isaiah 51:2) Even Sarah gave birth despite her fearfulness and barrenness. Here is your call to believe, and be ready! "*You are blessed because you believed that the Lord would do what he said." (*Luke 1:45, NLT).

AFFIRMATIONS & DECLARATION

Matthew 24:44, NLT, says, *"You also must be ready all the time, for the Son of Man will come when least expected."* I declare, decree, and believe that I am making every effort to be ready for the coming of Jesus Christ in my mind, heart, body, habits, way of life, and means of subsistence. I am carrying out my divine mission. My outlook on life is centered around the Kingdom of God. Jesus has complete control over my life; He is my Lord and Master. My way of life is glorifying God. Pursuing God's plan, meaning, values, and purposes for my life is how I define success. Not the way I begin but the way I conclude, matters. I'm going to the finish line determined, courageous, loyal, and unwavering. Because I have faith, and because I am ready, I will win.

- I am strong, courageous, and worthy of all good things.
- I am ready for any plans of the Lord in my life.
- I am full of peace, love, and happiness because of the Lord.
- I am made ready for what I am preparing for and expecting.
- I will be a dazzling display of the majesty and glory of God.

Isaiah 51:1-2, NLT: "Listen to me, all who hope for deliverance—all who seek the Lord! Consider the rock from which you were cut, the quarry from which you were mined. Yes, think about Abraham, your ancestor, and Sarah, who gave birth to your nation. Abraham was only one man when I called him. But when I blessed him, he became a great nation."

PRAYER

Heavenly Father, I occasionally and too frequently miss the mark, violate Your word, grow weary and impatient with Your timing, misinterpret Your methods, and fall short of doing and seeking Your will. Today, I ask for Your mercy and forgiveness. Help me trust that even the complex processes of my preparation, pruning, plowing and planting season are necessary to promise my meaningful life on earth. Worrying, anxiety, fear, and despair will not add a single day to my life but will take away my joy, power, peace, and hope. You vowed to take me out of the deepest, darkest woods, to set the table for me with a beautiful feast despite and in front of my adversaries. Please enable me to preserve my fearless confidence in You despite what my eyes perceive, the uncertainties, impossibilities, lack, challenges, statistics, enemies' falsehoods, man's knowledge, and emotions of restriction and inadequacy in my circumstances. In Jesus' name, I pray, believe, and be ready, amen.

MY DOPE *faith journal*

Date S | M | T | W | T | F | S

Morning: I feel my emotion! My one-word check-in: ....

DECLARATION

Consider today's verse. I implore the Holy Spirit to reveal His wisdom and truth to me and I declare it over my life.

OBSERVATION

What does the message mean? Lord, help me see it.

PRAYER

What is my prayer request? Lord, I live fully in You.

EMPOWERMENT

How will Your word empower me? Lord, give me the insight to apply my faith to be more significant than my fears.

MY FEARLESS *journey*

Evening: Feel my emotion! My one-word check-up:

What is making me FEEL like this?

What lessons did I LEARNED?

What THOUGHTS did I had?

What prompted my GRATITUDE?

Who did I CONNECTED with?

What brought me JOY?

EVENING PRAYER

WATER:

FRUIT & VEG:

MY MOOD:

My treat for today is:..

Your Qualities & Strengths

Peterson and Seligman describe six virtues and their associated 24 character strengths in Character Strengths and Virtues: A Handbook and Classification. Examine the list to determine your primary qualities and strengths.
Each virtue is anchored in the word of God and should be evident in your life as a believer.
"The Holy Spirit produces a different kind of fruit: unconditional love, joy, peace, patience, kindheartedness, goodness, faithfulness, gentleness, and self-control. You won't find any law opposed to fruit like this." (Galatians 5:22-23, VOICE).

Wisdom and Knowledge
Creativity: coming up with new ways to think about and accomplish things.
Curiosity: an interest in new experiences.
Open-mindedness: thinking about things from various perspectives.
Love of learning: The desire to study new skills and subjects
Perspective: The ability to take a step back and examine one's life events.
Proverbs 2:6 KJV: *"For the Lord giveth wisdom: out of his mouth cometh knowledge and understanding."*

Courage
Bravery: overcoming challenges, not backing down from danger, and expressing the truth.
Integrity: Being honest, authentic, and accurate.
Vitality: Having a positive outlook on life.
Persistence: the quality of continuing despite difficulties.
Psalm 27:14, ESV: *"Wait for the LORD; be strong, and let your heart take courage; wait for the LORD!"*

Humanity
Kindness: doing good things, being helpful, and being generous to others.
Love: The importance of intimate connections
Social intelligence: Being sensitive to the emotions of others.

Justice
Citizenship: Participating in a group effort
Fairness: Treating everyone equally
Leadership: inspiring and empowering a group of individuals.

Temperance
Forgiveness: extending grace and a second opportunity to those you have wronged.
Humility: allowing successes to speak for themselves.
Prudence: being cautious and avoiding unnecessary risks.
Self-control: Managing emotions and behavior

Transcendence:
Appreciation of beauty: Recognizing beauty and quality in one's surroundings.
Spirituality: the belief in the universe's greater purpose.
Seeing the humorous side of life
Hope: wishing for the best in the future
Gratitude: Being grateful for all that one has.

Day 191 - I'm Doing More Than That!

"Many, LORD my God, are the wonders you have done, the things you planned for us. None can compare with you; were I to speak and tell of your deeds, they would be too many to declare."
—Psalm 40:5, NIV

BELOVED,
Sometimes it seems like God isn't answering your prayers because you're asking for too little; you want a son, but He promised a nation. You're manipulating the circumstances to produce Ishmael, but God promised you, Isaac, a promised seed for a nation and generational blessing. He promises to cure you spiritually, psychologically, emotionally, financially, physically, socially, individually, professionally, interpersonally, generationally, and globally. God's function and necessity are to provide you with a loving purpose-partner. Yet, you are dating from a place of low self-esteem, asking from the filters of past, shame, mistakes, brokenness, guilt, and loss, rather than a place of grace, becoming who you are created to be as a royal identity and child of God. Pray from a place of faith, confidence, courage, victory, peace, belongingness, belovedness, security, wholeness, completeness, and hope for a bright, spotless future. You weep for Saul, but God raises and anoints the David in you. You see mistakes when God sees genealogy, the bloodline of Jesus, and a legend for Christ. You weep for Moses, but God proclaims Moses is dead, and He calls you, Joshua, to be strong and courageous as you lead His people to the promised land.
You perceive giants when God sees grasshoppers. You perceive humiliation when God covers your dishonor with His magnificent grace. God sees supernatural involvement in your life, narrative, path, destiny, and legacy to achieve something more prominent, important, significant, and sound. You see loss, lack, and limitation, but God sees limitlessness, newness, creativity, and greatness in you. He challenges you to give Him what's in your hands: the seed, the thought, the idea, promise, purpose, the why, passion, skill, talent, gift, light, little oil, little lunch, little strength, and little faith. God is preparing you for what you're praying, waiting, believing for, and claiming. You're comforted with a lie when God says He loves you with an everlasting love; He'll position you for purpose, bringing you to a Kinsman-Redeemer. Be at the right place and time, and your destiny partner and divine purpose will find you. God views you as the restorer and rebuilder of the past's ruin. You see darkness as a tomb; He considers it a womb, an incubator, and a conception. He calls forth rebirth, fertility, and fruitfulness even in your barrenness and dryness.
When God looks inside-out, He sees a repentant heart, a broken and contrite spirit, a child of the King, a new beginning, a fresh start, and the name, image, and likeness of Christ. You and every season of your life, whether painful, messy, good, wrong, or ugly, are the raw material to the Creator, ingredients in the hand of the Maker, clay in the hands of the Potter, a paintbrush in the hands of the Master painting His masterpiece. These sorrows wounded and pierced the Body of your Savior; the Liberator wore the crown of the throne, leaving evidence of the journey to the cross; Every worry, tear, lie, fear, sickness, and sin are wiped away with the revelation of the nail-scarred hands, piercing, and Blood of a Redeemer. The anxiety due to uncertainty about the future, your seeing things falling apart, being trapped, setbacks, disease, joblessness, grief, loneliness, and humiliation are impacting your fullness of life, and joy shall meet the empty tomb. "This is not that; this is your comeback, rebound, pivot, and reset. I'm doing more than that!"

AFFIRMATIONS & DECLARATIONS
"Yet even amid all these things, we triumph over them all, for God has made us be more than conquerors, and his demonstrated love is our glorious victory over everything!" (Romans 8:37, TPT).

- I am sufficient, empowered, and enough in God. I am blessed and loved by God.
- Forgiveness has been bestowed on me, and I have discovered a new lease on life.
- I am confident that God has a beautiful plan for my life. I am prepared for the next season.

*"But God's amazing grace has made me who I am! And his grace to me was not fruitless. In fact, I worked harder than all the rest, yet not in my own strength, but God's, for his empowering grace, is poured out upon me." (*1 Corinthians 15:10, TPT).

PRAYER
Heavenly Father God, You are my morning glory from the toiling, tears, and pain of night; dawn comes for my restless night, calm in the storm, breath in my lungs, and strength in every struggle. Even in this seemingly hopeless and helpless season, I fearlessly trust You, God. I know my hope is in You, my hope will not be cut short, and that victory has already been won. While I am praying for deliverance from my momentary pain, You have provided for me newness of life, the fullness of joy and greater glory, immeasurable more – an abundant life on earth, eternal life in heaven, dream-like blessing, salvation, redemption, peace, joy, love, hope, significant and massive breakthroughs, uncommon blessings, miracles of healing, healing, new doors of opportunities, promotions, provision for the vision, renewed mindset. I believe when You said, I'm doing more than that! In Jesus' name, I pray, wow me, O Lord, Amen.

MY DOPE *faith journal*

Date S | M | T | W | T | F | S

Morning: I feel my emotion! My one-word check-in: ....

DECLARATION

Consider today's verse. I implore the Holy Spirit to reveal His wisdom and truth to me and I declare it over my life.

OBSERVATION

What does the message mean? Lord, help me see it.

PRAYER

What is my prayer request? Lord, I live fully in You.

EMPOWERMENT

How will Your word empower me? Lord, give me the insight to apply my faith to be more significant than my fears.

MY FEARLESS *journey*

Evening: Feel my emotion! My one-word check-up:

What is making me FEEL like this?

What lessons did I LEARNED?

What THOUGHTS did I had?

What prompted my GRATITUDE?

Who did I CONNECTED with?

What brought me JOY?

EVENING PRAYER

My treat for today is: ....

Finding Your Strengths

By concentrating on the activities you love, this table will assist you in identifying your strengths. Look at the assertions, then finish the table. Think about the activity's primary strength as you compose your replies.

Something you excel at and like doing.
Something you do that inspires you and gives you a sense of vigor.
Something you do that people appreciate.
Something that causes you to lose track of time.

Day 192 - Hold On!

"If you'll hold on to me for dear life," says God, "I'll get you out of any trouble. I'll give you the best of care if you'll only get to know and trust me. Call me and I'll answer, be at your side in bad times; I'll rescue you, then throw you a party. I'll give you a long life, give you a long drink of salvation!"
— Psalm 91:14-16, MSG

BELOVED,
Hold on to God; He will complete His work in you. Wait. Don't abandon Him. You're not done yet, don't confuse the work-in-progress with finish-product. He is always working, incremental, and agile, and this MVP (Minimum Viable Product) is almost done. Be nimble in the palm of His Hand: the Master, Potter, Painter, Maker, Creator, Innovator, Architect, Author, Perfector, Founder, and Redeemer God. It'll happen soon! Don't give up on Jesus! The Father says, "If you cling to me, I'll save you. I'll treat you well if you trust Me. I'll answer if you call, stand by you in need; I'll rescue and joyfully celebrate with you with live long to live fully in My redemption and righteousness! (Psalm 91:14-16). I am your great God! I'm holding you in My Righteous Right Hand. I heard your murmur and SOS, but "Be fearless; I'll help you! (Isa 41:13)."

- **God will complete His work.** When I think about you, I praise God. Exclamations trigger my prayer and praise. I pray gladly for you. I'm glad you've kept believing and preaching God's Message alongside us since you first heard it. I've never doubted that God will finish this fantastic work in you when Christ Jesus returns. (Phil 1:3-6).
- **God wins and has the last word.** Don't panic; pray, wait, and be watchful. The Devil wants to catch you dosing, distracted, doubtful, and dreading. Beware. You're not alone in harsh circumstances. Same for Christians worldwide. Keep the faith, not fear This gracious God, who has an abundance and significant purposes for us in Christ, will soon get you back on your feet. He has the final word, and He says victory! (1 Peter 5:10).
- **God defends you and defeats your foes.** As you have, cling to God. God has ousted a massive army against the adversary, denied every destiny and identity thieves before you as powerless. No one has stood up to you yet. One of you may send a thousand fleeing—God's word. He fights for you. Cover your soul, mind, heart, life, and home in the Blood: Love God with everything in you. (Jos 23:8-11).
- **Be spiritually empowered, matured, strengthened, equipped, and elevated.** Keep your eyes open, stick to your principles, set healthy boundaries, give it your best, be resolute, and love constantly. Stay vigilant and faithful to your beliefs. Be bold. Let clarified vision, limitless love, renewed mindset, immeasurable kindness, and fearless faith drive you. (1 Corinthians 13-14).

Guess what? God isn't done; He's constantly working. He never sleeps or snores; You'll get well fast, yes, wait! The Father says, "Beloved, I've inscribed you on My hands; you are before me. I'm creating anew. Write the vision down; it's true. I've seen your tears and heard your plea; I'll cure you. I'm your Lord. Be fearless; I'm holding your hand. I'll help, wait, trust, believe, grip My hand, and gaze in My eyes!"

AFFIRMATIONS & DECLARATIONS
"After all, it is I, the Eternal One your God, who has hold of your right hand, Who whispers in your ear, 'Don't be afraid. I will help you.'" (Isaiah 41:13, VOICE). My ears are open to the whisper of the Holy Spirit; therefore, I shut out all other voices, noise, confusion, and falsehoods of the enemy. He says, "There is no need to be afraid. I'm here to assist you in the best I can. 'Stay with me! Hold on!'"

- I am convinced and confident that God will make it happen for me. For He who began a good work will see it to completion. I am more than just a conqueror, complete, thriving, holding on to Him!
- I am holding on to faith as my Father's hand firmly grips me. I am thriving! I am holding on not just for me but also for my children, household, family, generation, and legacy of faith. I find refuge under God's wings. God never abandoned me. I hold on in faith anchored in the Faithfulness of my Father.

PRAYER
Heavenly Father, Thank You, Lord, for Your stability and constancy, which enabled me to persevere in the face of adversity, uncertainty, and change. Thank You for working, holding me, returning soon, divinely intervening in my problems, keeping Your promises, breaking through, and bringing out all I trust in Your name. You are forever in my ever-changing situations, conflicts, storms, and crises. Lord, You see everything even if I'm busy and distracted. You notice mess, pain, and mystery. The invaders are swarming. Help! Despite my prayers, fasting, faith, and trust, waiting for deliverance can seem complicated, as if my breakthrough and divine intervention have all been postponed. I feel depressed, lonely, and denied. Friends, relatives, and familiar people abandoned me, so-called lovers left me, and my job rejected me. Deaths, illness, poverty, and rising prices; are all fears that are bad for my health. I'm worried. But God! You're dependable. Yes, I'm clinging to you, Lord. I'm concentrating on Jesus. I ask that You lead, strengthen, and guide me. Help, protect, and assist me in dealing with changes, uncertainty, and obstacles. Lord, You are my Saviour, Helper, Defence, Redeemer, Warrior, Healer, Provider, and Protector. Lord, You are my Hope, Help, Lover, Father, Friend, Savior, and Future. In Jesus' name, I pray, amen.

MY DOPE *faith journal*

Date S | M | T | W | T | F | S

Morning: I feel my emotion! My one-word check-in: ....

DECLARATION

Consider today's verse. I implore the Holy Spirit to reveal His wisdom and truth to me and I declare it over my life.

OBSERVATION

What does the message mean? Lord, help me see it.

PRAYER

What is my prayer request? Lord, I live fully in You.

EMPOWERMENT

How will Your word empower me? Lord, give me the insight to apply my faith to be more significant than my fears.

MY FEARLESS *journey*

Evening: Feel my emotion! My one-word check-up:

What is making me FEEL like this?

What lessons did I LEARNED?

What THOUGHTS did I had?

What prompted my GRATITUDE?

Who did I CONNECTED with?

What brought me JOY?

EVENING PRAYER

WATER:

FRUIT & VEG:

MY MOOD:

My treat for today is: ....

Finding Your Strengths

The following questions can aid in your self-awareness and help you recognize your strengths:

What inspires you?
What are your habits?
How do you interact with others?
What do you think is crucial in life?

Day 193 - Trust God's Re-Direction!

"O Lord, lead me in Your righteousness because of my enemies;
Make Your way straight (direct, right) before me."
— Psalm 5:8, AMP

BELOVED,
Re-direction does not imply rejection. The action of allocating or guiding someone or something to a new or different location or purpose is referred to as re-direction. Re-direction is God's re-positioning. When you're driving and want to get directions from your GPS, you enter your destination, and the GPS then plans, decides, and directs your route. The GPS algorithm can access information ahead of the journey, such as accidents, traffic jams, construction, danger, and detours. It will redirect you if you are lost, misturn, or the intended route unexpectedly changes. God is your spiritual GPS; He knows your goal and has planned your life's journey; He will redirect you if you go off course, shield you from hazards, and let evil plots pass you. When God intervenes and interferes in your life, whether it's a change in employment, relationships, business, finances, or family, He never intended to damage you but rather to redirect you to the best course, best conclusion, and His divine plan, purpose, and promise. Trust God's re-direction, He has the complete picture, information, and knowledge of the ending, starting, and journey, and even when He leads you down a new route, short on specifics, trust His heart, and pray from His character, conduct, and wisdom.

Abram Re-direction and God's Re-Alignment (Genesis 15:1-6)
In a vision, the Lord told Abram, *"Don't be scared. I'll defend you and reward you"* Abram asked God, "What can you offer me? Without a son, my slave Eliezer from Damascus will inherit everything." Abram continued, "You gave me no son; therefore, a slave born in my home will inherit everything." The Lord told Abram, "He won't inherit your possessions. You'll have a son who inherits everything. Then God told Abram to look up. You can't count the stars. Your offspring will be innumerable." Abram trusted God. And God accepted Abram's faith, making him righteous.

Three wisdom keys

1. **Seek God's wisdom and revelation.** In a vision, God revealed to Abram that he should be fearless because He will redirect his life, defend him, and reward him.
2. **Let go of your limiting belief.** Abram considered the natural state and decided to govern the end of his life, saying, "I don't have a son, and my servant will collect everything I own when I die; who will carry on my seed, name, and legacy?"
3. **Trust the All-knowing God.** God had enough knowledge about Abram's life journey and destination, so God corrected him and said, "No, I will redirect your life journey to a new narrative and rewrite the story, destiny, and legacy."

Will you grasp the why and trust my re-direction even if you don't understand how? The Father is saying, "Do not be afraid. I am your Shield and your Protector, your very exceedingly great reward. I will redirect you to protect you and reward you greatly." Trust God's Re-direction!

AFFIRMATIONS & DECLARATIONS
"I hear the Lord saying, "I will stay close to you, instructing and guiding you along the pathway for your life. I will advise you along the way and lead you forth with my eyes as your guide. So don't make it difficult; don't be stubborn when I take you where you've not been before. Don't make me tug you and pull you along. Just come with me!" (Psalms 32:8-9, TPT).

- I am trusting God with every area of my life. I am not lost; I am positioning.
- I am not too old; I am becoming. I am not wandering; I am possessing.
- I am not broken; I am being blessed. I am not losing; I am increasing.
- Everything I need to accomplish my destiny is in me.

PRAYER
Heavenly Father, thank You for guiding, directing, leading, protecting, delivering, and helping me even though You crush my heart to spare my soul. Thank You for giving me second chances when I make mistakes, take the wrong road, disregard Your signals, and reject Your truth, wisdom, methods, and instructions. Lord, pardon me! My former self is gone. I'm sorry, Lord, for settling for second-best, suffering and bringing You humiliation and not glory, always wanting things my way and timing with my limited comprehension and spiritual blindness. Thank You, Lord, for another chance to love, give, transform, rebuild, refocus, and live my divine destiny. Thank You for providing me with spiritual weapons, strategic insight, revelation, and prophetic wisdom to combat the spiritual attacks on me, my children, family, and community. Today, I trust my God's re-direction! In Jesus' name, I pray, amen.

MY DOPE *faith journal*

Date S | M | T | W | T | F | S

Morning: I feel my emotion! My one-word check-in: ....

DECLARATION

Consider today's verse. I implore the Holy Spirit to reveal His wisdom and truth to me and I declare it over my life.

OBSERVATION

What does the message mean? Lord, help me see it.

PRAYER

What is my prayer request? Lord, I live fully in You.

EMPOWERMENT

How will Your word empower me? Lord, give me the insight to apply my faith to be more significant than my fears.

MY FEARLESS *journey*

Evening: Feel my emotion! My one-word check-up:

What is making me FEEL like this?

What lessons did I LEARNED?

What THOUGHTS did I had?

What prompted my GRATITUDE?

Who did I CONNECTED with?

What brought me JOY?

EVENING PRAYER

WATER:

FRUIT & VEG:

MY MOOD:

My treat for today is: ....

Using Your Strengths

Consider the following areas to assist you and provide you with suggestions on how to utilize your strength in new and exciting ways for the next week:

How I'll demonstrate my strength ...

when I'm at home with my family	when I'm working	within my close friendships
while I'm with my pals	when I'm engaged in my hobby	whenever I eat
while I'm by myself	while driving	when I collaborate with others

Day 194 - Never Forget To Be Thankful!

"Let joy be your continual feast. Make your life a prayer. And in the midst of everything be always giving thanks, for this is God's perfect plan for you in Christ Jesus."
— 1 Thessalonians 5:16-18, TPT

BELOVED,
As you wonder, worry, wait, or strive for the things you want, remember to be grateful for what you already have. Cherish and nourish those who adore you. Be cautious not to miss the moon because you are preoccupied with chasing the stars!
Are you thankful no matter what happens? Maybe you have been impacted by the loss of your career or a downturn in your business? Or perhaps you are struggling or recovering from a global or personal health crisis, family, employment, relationship, or financial setback. Or you are impacted by political and social turmoil. Or maybe you've lost your health or a loved one. Such circumstances might be pretty painful. Nonetheless, you have plenty to be thankful for, and there is hope as long as there is life. Jesus is your Living Hope! (1 Timothy 4:10).
Your optimism and thankfulness are effective strategic and spiritual weapons. When you praise, when the enemy expects you to complain, blame God, worry, stress, doubt, and dread, you confound him.
Consider the narrative of Job, who had every reason to be furious yet chose to seek God, pray, praise, and be thankful regardless of the circumstances. The enemy assaulted Job's family, faith, wealth, and health as he sat in his ashes. Job had every right to be furious, bitter, and ungrateful to God; his wounded heart might have damaged his trust, faith, and connection with God. Job's wife even advised him to curse God and give up, saying, "Are you still attempting to keep your integrity? Curse God and die." (Job 2:8-10).
Yet Job is famously remembered and quoted not for his reaction to his wife's ungodly order but his response to God in praise and prayer, despite his pain. *"Though he slay me, yet will I trust in him: but I will maintain mine own ways before him."* (Job 13:15, KJV).
Are you in the ashes today? Will you give in to the enemy's demand, or will you dominate your day with prayer, praise, and gratitude and trade those ashes for beauty? He promises beauty for ashes!
Secular and corporate psychologists profess appreciation of relationships, gratitude, journaling, and self-reflection on the beautiful things in your life, what happened in a day, or what is occurring will promote your health and happiness. Yes, you can train yourself to be happy by being thankful!
1 Thessalonians 5:16-18 provides a golden nugget to do this: "*Rejoice always and delight in your faith; be unceasing and persistent in prayer; in every situation [no matter what the circumstances] be thankful and continually give thanks to God; for this is the will of God for you in Christ Jesus." [AMP].*

AFFIRMATIONS & DECLARATION

- I thank God for allowing me to be born and go through various life situations to experience His goodness, forgiveness, blessedness, and excellence.
  - Every mess I faced turned into a message.
  - Every test I am facing now will turn into a testimony.
- I am grateful for all the big and small blessings God allows me to live a meaningful, significant, and enriched life.
- I am living my divine purpose. I am achieving divine promise and fulfilling divine plan.

PRAYER
Heavenly Father, LORD, I don't want to ask for anything from You today; I want to thank You for everything. Thank You, Lord, for all Your benefits, fruit, gifts, love, peace, never lose, I only win or learn, and You work all things together for good. Lord, thanks for Your guidance, joy, life, grace, mercy, and goodness. It gives me purpose, direction, and insight. Thank You, Lord, that despite my hardships, setbacks, storms, and current conditions, I still thank You because You are Sovereign and Supreme. You fight every conflict, and I'll win. Lord, thanks for Your goodness, compassion, and love. It calms and comforts me. Thank You, Lord, for my Salvation in Jesus Christ, for dying in my place on the cross, accepting all my sin, shame, sickness, and sufferings for past-present-future. I am healed, delivered, redeemed, released, blessed, rescued, and restored. Thank You for Your presence, promise, protection, provision, and power. You pledged never to abandon me, and You are with me. Holy Spirit's resurrection power resides in me, so I embrace thankfully, walk wisely, creatively, intelligently, endure joyfully, and live completely. In Jesus' name, I pray, amen.

MY DOPE *faith journal*

Date S | M | T | W | T | F | S

Morning: I feel my emotion! My one-word check-in:

DECLARATION

Consider today's verse. I implore the Holy Spirit to reveal His wisdom and truth to me and I declare it over my life.

OBSERVATION

What does the message mean? Lord, help me see it.

PRAYER

What is my prayer request? Lord, I live fully in You.

EMPOWERMENT

How will Your word empower me? Lord, give me the insight to apply my faith to be more significant than my fears.

MY FEARLESS *journey*

Evening: Feel my emotion! My one-word check-up:

What is making me FEEL like this?

What lessons did I LEARNED?

What THOUGHTS did I had?

What prompted my GRATITUDE?

Who did I CONNECTED with?

What brought me JOY?

EVENING PRAYER

WATER:

FRUIT & VEG:

MY MOOD:

My treat for today is: ....

365 Journal

Day 195 - Thankful I Didn't Give Up!

If your faith remains strong, even while surrounded by life's difficulties, you will continue to experience the untold blessings of God! True happiness comes as you pass the test with faith, and receive the victorious crown of life promised to every lover of God!
James 1:12, TPT

BELOVED,
It takes much patience to sit and wait. There is nothing worse than having to wait for something or someone. Waiting on God equips you to trust and hope in Him. Everyone desires patience, but no one wants to go through the process of learning and to develop it. While you wait for God to disclose the fulfillment of His promises, you must put your faith and confidence in Him with fearless trust. Waiting is a time of preparation, sandpaper in the finishing process, and your instructor and tutors for faith skills. It also enhances your relationship with God and your capacity to live in the Holy Spirit. There are many teachings in the waiting process to develop Christ-like attributes, gifts, and fruit of the Spirit. The wait is worth it. When you see how the situation works out and the blessings God has in store, you'll be glad you didn't give up. When your viewpoint on things shifts to align with His, you gain a fresh perspective. Despite these faith-shattering tests, there are mind-blowing miracles for you, don't give up!
Keep going; Keep praying! Keep fighting. Keep trusting! Keep waiting! If you feel like you are walking through stormy seas, raging river, or persecution fire, keep going, you are passing through, and this too shall come to pass. Believe in God's promise: When you pass through the deep, stormy sea, you can count on Me to be there. When you pass through raging rivers, You will not drown. When you walk through persecution like fiery flames, you will not be burned; the flames will not harm you. (Isaiah 43:2).
"God will bless you if you don't give up when your faith is being tested. He will reward you with a glorious life, just as he rewards everyone who loves him." (James 1:12, CEV). God got you! He is faithful to His promises. No word of God returns void and unfulfilled. God is not a man, that He should lie, or a son of man, that He should change His mind. Does He speak and not act? (Num 23:19). Does He promise and not fulfill? *"Be brave. Be strong. Don't give up. Expect God to get here soon." (Psalm 31:24, MSG).* Stand on His promise: I will be your God for a Lifetime. I made you, and I am fully accountable and responsible for you. I'll keep holding and carrying you even as you become old and your hair greys! I am your Creator and your Caregiver; I am your Savior and Guardian; I will bring you and save you. (Isaiah 46:4). Proclaim His promise: I am with you and will keep an eye on you no matter where you go. I will return, restore and rebound you in this place one day. I will not leave you until I have completed everything I promised. (Genesis 28:15).
Sometimes, God invites His people to perform great things in the Bible and life with little detail and to trust Him with funding, assistance, and provision for the vision. It may seem like a challenging climb with several barriers. Sometimes not even family and friends believe in your dreams nor understand the assignment and anointing. God's process of manifesting, developing, honing, and preparing you for your purpose might seem bizarre and unpleasant. But God! Do not abandon God. Don't quit. Don't give up on Him due to what appears to be delays, denials, and disappointments. Don't fight the metamorphosis and divine destiny preparation. God knows why, when, and how things work for your good and His glory. He can see the forest from the tree, the fruits, and the bumper crop while the seed is still in the barn. *"So cheer up! Take courage, all you who love him. Wait for him to break through for you, all who trust in him!"* (Psa 31:24, TPT). Trust Him! YOU WILL BE THANKFUL. YOU DIDN'T GIVE UP!

AFFIRMATIONS & DECLARATION
I will lead a disciplined life and not give up, but wait and trust even if the race or road is rough!
"Isn't *it obvious that all runners on the racetrack keep on running to win, but only one receives the victor's prize? Yet each one of you must run the race to be victorious." (*1 Corinthians 9:24, TPT).

- I am thankful to God, for I still have You, although I have experienced much loss in life.
- I am thankful to God for allowing me to see another day of life. I am staying and winning the race.
- I am filled with joy; I am blessed every day; I am not giving up on being thankful each day.

PRAYER
Thank You for never abandoning me. Thank you, Lord, for Your promises in Your Word to take care of me and rescue me; reading it offers pleasure, serenity, comfort, and certainty that You will work things out. I'll exchange my enormous weighty burden in return for Your light yoke. You are the God who sees; You know when I lack strength and faith, rant, and harbor fearful thoughts about You, myself, and others. You know how often I whine about my life, the journey, Your way, Your timing, and my circumstances, yet You still love me. You're faithful while I'm faithless and afraid. I thank You, Lord, for good, bad, and ugly since You work all things for good. I appreciate the choices; You provide me. I choose righteousness, joy, love, and peace. I value my life lessons. Lord, thank You that I'm no longer under condemnation but a child of God. You strengthened and sustained me in the wait. In Jesus' name, I'm glad I didn't quit. I pray, Amen!

MY DOPE *faith journal*

Date S | M | T | W | T | F | S

Morning: I feel my emotion! My one-word check-in: ____________________

DECLARATION

Consider today's verse. I implore the Holy Spirit to reveal His wisdom and truth to me and I declare it over my life.

OBSERVATION

What does the message mean? Lord, help me see it.

PRAYER

What is my prayer request? Lord, I live fully in You.

EMPOWERMENT

How will Your word empower me? Lord, give me the insight to apply my faith to be more significant than my fears.

MY FEARLESS *journey*

Evening: Feel my emotion! My one-word check-up:

What is making me FEEL like this?

What lessons did I LEARNED?

What THOUGHTS did I had?

What prompted my GRATITUDE?

Who did I CONNECTED with?

What brought me JOY?

EVENING PRAYER

WATER:

FRUIT & VEG:

MY MOOD:

My treat for today is: ....

Strengths Tracker

THIS WEEK'S TASK

Choose one of your outlined core competencies. Consider new methods to demonstrate this strength every day for the ensuing week. Studies have linked this activity to greater levels of happiness.

STRENGTH BEING TRACKED: ______________________

	HOW I UTILIZED MY STRENGTH	MY FEELINGS AND THOUGHTS
MONDAY		
TUESDAY		
WEDNESDAY		
THURSDAY		
FRIDAY		
SATURDAY		
SUNDAY		

DAY 196 - 202

Gratitude

Rejoice always, pray without ceasing, in everything give thanks; for this is the will of God in Christ Jesus for you.

— 1 THESSALONIANS 5:16-18, NKJV

Day 196 - Hello... You Matter!

"The Lord your God in your midst, The Mighty One, will save; He will rejoice over you with gladness, He will quiet you with His love, He will rejoice over you with singing."
— Zephaniah 3:17, NKJV

BELOVED,
If you've been knocked down by life to the point where you feel that no one cares about you, it's easy to feel stigmatized, humiliated, and isolated in your suffering. It may seem impossible to start over if your life has been shattered. If you're struggling to overcome depression, anxiety, and the fear of failure, you may feel alone in your suffering. As the devil tempts you with falsehoods and tells you that death is preferable to life, you feel hopeless and unable to resist the devil's temptations. You may think you're just another face in the crowd, but God wants you to know that He has a special place in your heart. Although you may feel helpless and hopeless, God sends His word today to reclaim you as His, to remind you that you matter to Him. In today's environment, it's easy to be swept up in the turmoil and occurrences. The Bible, the blueprint of your life, will remind you that you are not lost nor inconsequential to your loving Heavenly Father and your best friend, Jesus Christ, in this life, situation, or at any given time; Hello, You Matter! You are the King's kid. God refers to you as His Beloved. The phrase '*You Matter*' implies that you are significant, inspirational, relevant, influential, meaningful, and impactful in the eyes of others. So, you matter to God. You're substantial enough to be accepted by God, named by God, created by God, redeemed by God, being significant, vital, noteworthy, and of critical importance in His creation, Kingdom, mission, commission, inheritance, and heritage. You matter to God, the Author of your life story, the Architect of your life, and the Perfector of your faith. You were made by the Creator God and made for God. Your DNA contains His grandeur, wisdom, wealth, prosperity, influence, and dignity. You are a work of art, His masterpiece, and your life counts. You are a *Very Important Person* (VIP); When God created you, He had a divine purpose: fearfully and wonderfully made! You belong to Him! God never stops loving you. He is always redeeming you and doing good with His kindness. Remind yourself of God's truth when feeling lost in the commotion, chaos, condition, and circumstances: personally, generationally, and globally. People and life experiences will try to persuade you that your worth is in question, but God will constantly affirm your value as His beloved child of the most powerful King of the universe. People will insult you, reject you, humiliate you, scam you, fail you, use you, and violate you. They will bring up your history, tag you with numerous labels, and refer to you by your past issues, failures, and flaws, but it is not what they name you that matters but not it's what happens to you, not what you have or don't have; *It is whom you have and to whom you belong; It is what you answer, think, believe, and live;* It is not that you are broken but *what was your experience.* Respond to the revelation, the truth, the light, and love about whom God made you be, the new name He gives you, the new creation He creates in you, the mending of every brokenness; His liberation, calling, and assignment, what God thinks about you, planned for you, and what He has in store for you. *What a lovely destiny and legacy!* A new beginning with a triumphant ending! The devil's malevolent purpose is to murder, steal, and ruin your identity, leaving you to wonder who you are and to whom you belong. You are not your difficulties or faults in the past. You are not your dysfunctional family, nationality, society, or culture's label. You are a child of God, King of the universe; you are necessary to Him, the Most Important, Influential One, God. You matter to One who matters! The God of Creation and Redemption is remaking, rewriting your story, and redeemed you, and singing love songs of joyful deliverance over you! You are royalty! You are a legacy! You are a miracle! You are a masterpiece! You are blessed! You are beautiful! You are radiant! You are created in God's image and likeness! You are His workmanship, magnificence, the apple of His eye, and the splendor of His glory! Hello. You matter!
"*You are altogether beautiful, my darling, beautiful in every way.*" (Song of Solomon 4:7, NLT).

AFFIRMATIONS & DECLARATIONS
- I am loved; God loves me; My God's revelation-truth is my reality. I am coming out of my darkness, hopelessness, fearfulness, negativity, and setbacks. My life matters to God; my life matters to me!
- I am not intimidated by people faking it; I believe in Him and am confident I will see it happen!

PRAYER
Heavenly Father, I pray for Your love and deliverance songs. Amaze my mustard-sized faith as You surprise me with startling breakthroughs and the vast rewards You promise when I seek You and trust You boldly. In the name of Jesus, I hope I will celebrate Your goodness in the land of the living, in my life, my children's lives. In the works of our hands in leadership, relationships, business, career, home, family, and communities, and every family connected. We shall have breakthroughs despite hardships, tribulations, challenges, and temptations. I hope we will experience and become the brilliant exhibition of Your glory in every place You are tearing down, rebuilding, reassembling, reforming, and regenerating. You care about us. Please heal every wound, shatter every evil plan, and unleash demonically hindered blessings, marvels, signs, and miracles. I matter to You, and my life matters to me. In Jesus' name, I pray, amen.

MY DOPE *faith journal*

Date S | M | T | W | T | F | S

Morning: I feel my emotion! My one-word check-in: ______________________

DECLARATION

Consider today's verse. I implore the Holy Spirit to reveal His wisdom and truth to me and I declare it over my life.

OBSERVATION

What does the message mean? Lord, help me see it.

PRAYER

What is my prayer request? Lord, I live fully in You.

EMPOWERMENT

How will Your word empower me? Lord, give me the insight to apply my faith to be more significant than my fears.

MY FEARLESS *journey*

Evening: Feel my emotion! My one-word check-up:

What is making me FEEL like this?

What lessons did I LEARNED?

What THOUGHTS did I had?

What prompted my GRATITUDE?

Who did I CONNECTED with?

What brought me JOY?

EVENING PRAYER

WATER:

FRUIT & VEG:

MY MOOD:

My treat for today is: ....

Why I'm Grateful

I am grateful to be myself because

I am grateful for my family because:

I am grateful for my friends because

Something that happened this past week that I am grateful for was...

Day 197 - Freedom Of Forgiveness!

"Jesus said, "Father, forgive them, for they don't know what they are doing."
And the soldiers gambled for his clothes by throwing dice."
— Luke 23:34, NLT

BELOVED,
Forgiveness is a process, and it may not be easy to forgive and let go after all that has happened, but it is a decision that provides freedom, serenity, and inner strength, and it is worth the effort. Let go of the past, but hold on to the hope in God that they will not steal your present or future since your soul deserves serenity. Grace from God is enough. Today, your focus is on the freedom of Forgiveness. Jesus says, "*If you forgive people when they sin against you, then your Father will forgive you when you sin against Him and when you sin against your neighbor. But if you do not forgive your neighbors' sins, your Father will not forgive your sins.*" (Matthew 6:14-15, VOICE). Forgiveness is a "process or action to being forgiven, forgiving oneself and forgiving others." According to psychologists, Forgiveness is a choice to let go of hatred, bitterness, or revenge against a wrongdoer, regardless of the violation, the apology, or whether they earn it. According to the Bible, Forgiveness is God's commitment not to hold your trespasses against you but to offer you kindness, grace, and love through confession, repentance, and faith in Jesus Christ as our Lord and Savior. Unforgiveness opposes God's mercy. Marianne Williamson once said, "*Unforgiveness is like drinking poison and waiting for the other person to die.*" Bitterness, fear, wrath, fury, and retribution result from unforgiveness. Forgiveness liberates you. Observe that you don't fall short of God's favor and that no bitterness wells up to afflict yourself and others. (Hebrews 12:15). "*Do to others as you would have them do to you.*" (Luke 6:31). When you forgive, you overcome the spirit of fear, the core cause of wrath, worry, revenge, and bitterness.
Allow God's love to heal, liberate, restore, revive, and rejuvenate you."*Count yourself lucky, how happy you must be— you get a fresh start, your slate's wiped clean. Count yourself lucky—God holds nothing against you, and you're holding nothing back from him." (Psalm 32:1-2, MSG)*. Forgiveness releases God's goodness; unforgiveness is a sign of weakness that leads to deep-seated animosity. Forgiveness is for your whole person's healing: spiritual, emotional, social, financial, mental, and physical wellness. So, let go, on with your life. Forgiveness is finding light at the end of the tunnel after learning to live without an apology and closure. Forgiveness doesn't reverse the past or erase the violation but offers a fresh start, new chances, lessons learned, and a strong testimony of grace. So, knowing God will forgive you swiftly, forgive others immediately. As Jesus showed, forgiving is the greatest manifestation of divine love. The Kingdom of God and the rules for Forgiveness are explained in the parables of Matt 18:23-35; Jesus explains the expectation of Believers to show Forgiveness to others just as He has forgiven us of our multitude of sins. He commands you to forgive those who have harmed you and strive to forgive others as God has forgiven you. (Matt 6:14-15). Forgiveness is an expression of love and humility. Unforgiveness is a sin; rooted in hatred, pride, and fear. Forgiveness is freedom. Choose to be forgiven by God, forgive yourself, and forgive others.

AFFIRMATIONS & DECLARATIONS
- Today, I choose to let it go; no apology is needed or necessary; it is that my soul needs serenity!
- I seek God's forgiveness and receive His mercy, forgiveness, and freedom. I am cleansed from all guilt.
- I choose to forgive myself and ask that others whom I offended may release me.
- I choose to forgive others, cancel their debt, and heal; no longer will I see through the lens of my pain. God has so much more in store for me. I am forgiven and have forgiven. I am free, peaceful, and joyful.

PRAYER
Lord, I appreciate Your kindness, compassion, goodness, grace, and forgiveness. You rescued me from despair, anguish, sin, humiliation, and grief with flawless love and mercy. Thank You for sending Jesus as a sin-sacrifice and atonement so I might experience forgiveness, redemption, restoration, and reconciliation. Lord, forgive me for my previous sins, failures, defects, doubts, and fear. Lord, release me from toxic fear, false pride, wrath, rage, bitterness, unforgiveness, disobedience, and grudge. Lord, show me your kindness and humility so I may forgive others. Lord, help me forgive those who have wronged me. Your love and strength allow me to live freely despite others' hatred, abuse, violation, and rage. Lord, teach me the dangers of unforgiveness and bitterness. It harms my relationships, thinking, habits, behavior, character, and culture. Please help me be patient with individuals I pray for and not give up so fast, just as You are patient with me. Today I am forgiven, and I forgive. In Jesus' name, I pray, amen.

MY DOPE *faith journal*

Date S | M | T | W | T | F | S

Morning: I feel my emotion! My one-word check-in: ______

DECLARATION

Consider today's verse. I implore the Holy Spirit to reveal His wisdom and truth to me and I declare it over my life.

OBSERVATION

What does the message mean? Lord, help me see it.

PRAYER

What is my prayer request? Lord, I live fully in You.

EMPOWERMENT

How will Your word empower me? Lord, give me the insight to apply my faith to be more significant than my fears.

MY FEARLESS *journey*

Evening: Feel my emotion! My one-word check-up:

What is making me FEEL like this?

What lessons did I LEARNED?

What THOUGHTS did I had?

What prompted my GRATITUDE?

Who did I CONNECTED with?

What brought me JOY?

EVENING PRAYER

WATER:

FRUIT & VEG:

MY MOOD:

My treat for today is: ....

Gratitude Prompts

Which insights are you grateful you learned?

What are you most thankful for in your present life right now?

Which moments of your day brought you joy?

What are your favorite activities?

What about this season do you love?

Which books have you read that have left an impression on you?

What are you most excited about?

Who makes you smile?

What kind of climate do you prefer?

Which countries are you most thankful to have visited?

What are your favorite foods?

What skills do you possess that make you grateful?

Day 198 - I'm Awake, Blessed, Grateful!

"All my heart will give thanks to You, Eternal One. I will tell others about Your amazing works. I will be glad and celebrate You! I will praise You, O Most High!"
— Psalm 9:1-2, VOICE

BELOVED,
Spiritual, emotional, financial, social, and mental wellness are all equally vital and impact your physical health. As a result, the practice of Naturopathic Doctors is appealing since it considers the whole person's optimal health. It would be ideal if you received frequent examinations, guidance, and monitoring on all elements of your well-being, making behavioral adjustments to improve your lifestyle so that you may live your best life to the fullest in every dimension of wellness. Remember to schedule regular check-ups with your family doctor for preventative care and investigate the social, behavioral, and biological influences on your physical health as part of a periodic check-up of your whole health.
If you were sick and went to a hospital emergency department, you would be triaged to assess the urgency and criticality of your condition and determine the treatment plan for health care and cure.
Also important is your self-care strategy; how frequently do you do emotional, mental, or spiritual check-ups? One of the 365 Live Fearlessly journey's cornerstones is to feel your feelings and give a one-word check-in. Make self-discovery and emotional awareness a daily habit. One-word check-in helps you become self-aware, honest, and expressive of your emotion. Immerse yourself in worship, praise, conversation, prayer request, the message, and God's word, and allow the Holy Spirit to change the narrative and shift the stressful environments, negative energies, minds, attitudes, and feelings. Thanks for checking for a spiritual assessment. Here are the results from the evaluation:

Phase 1: Diagnostic, Data Collection, Discovery
This spiritual check-up is for you.
- Awake? ✅
- Blessed? ✅
- Grateful? ✅

Phase 2: Finding and Recommendation
- God is not finished yet; He is still working and is there for you; Your future will outperform your past. This day is the Lord's day; rejoice! Be diligent in praise and have an attitude of gratitude!

Phase 3: Prescription, Prophetic Insights, & Self-Care Strategies
- Pray persistently, pray all the time no matter what. Take prayer and thanksgiving always.
- "*Pray, and keep praying. Be alert and thankful when you pray." (Colossians 4:2, VOICE).*

Phase 4: Spiritual Analysis & Biblical Confirmation
- ✅ I am awake and alert. I rise in grandeur because my light has come, and God's brightness now streams from me! Attention! Darkness covers the globe and the nations, but God arises on me, and His splendor comes over me! I am radiant! (Isaiah 60:1).
- ✅ I am blessed beyond measure. I've been showered with incredible grace till I overflowed with confidence and love for Jesus, the Risen King and Anointed One! (1 Timothy 1:14).
- ✅ I am grateful, peaceful, and cheerful, deserving of love, serenity, tenderness, kindness, happiness, holiness, and healthy relationships. I am always happy, constantly praying, worshipping, and thanking God for everything. This mindset is how God wants me, His child, to live fully. (Ps 138:1-2).
- ✅ I am blessed by a faithful Father famous for His faithfulness! I know the LORD, my God, is God because He maintains His promises and diligently watches over His word. Even if I'm unfaithful, He remains faithful; He cannot deny Himself. The Lord is reliable and will establish and protect me. As I confess my sins, He will forgive and cleanse me from the past, present, and future sins.

Phase 5: Affirmation, Declaration, & Prayer for Fearless Faith to Rebound
- ***I AM AWAKE.*** *"Awake, O sleeper, and arise from the dead, and Christ will shine on you." (Ep 5:14).*
- ***I AM BLESSED.*** *May God bless you; glance upon you and grant favor and serenity. (Num 6:24-26).*
- ***I AM GRATEFUL.*** *Always express gratitude for this is God's will for you in Christ Jesus. (1 The 5:18).*

PRAYER
Heavenly Father, Great Physician, I am awakened to a new day. You called me to arise, rejuvenate, and thrive. I appreciate You for helping me recognize Your divine purpose, plan, and promises in my life as a new beginning. As I come alive to Your presence, I stop looking around and start focusing on Jesus and within myself. As You restore my spiritual blindness, I can see Your joy, peace, love, and righteousness; Your gospel, grace, kindness, and gifts are still intact, freely available, and designed specifically for me. Thank You for the new mindset, miracles, and mercies today. In Jesus' name, I pray, Amen.

MY DOPE *faith journal*

Date S | M | T | W | T | F | S

Morning: I feel my emotion! My one-word check-in: ....

DECLARATION

Consider today's verse. I implore the Holy Spirit to reveal His wisdom and truth to me and I declare it over my life.

OBSERVATION

What does the message mean? Lord, help me see it.

PRAYER

What is my prayer request? Lord, I live fully in You.

EMPOWERMENT

How will Your word empower me? Lord, give me the insight to apply my faith to be more significant than my fears.

MY FEARLESS *journey*

Evening: Feel my emotion! My one-word check-up:

What is making me FEEL like this?

What lessons did I LEARNED?

What THOUGHTS did I had?

What prompted my GRATITUDE?

Who did I CONNECTED with?

What brought me JOY?

EVENING PRAYER

WATER:

FRUIT & VEG:

MY MOOD:

My treat for today is: ....

Gratitude Quiz

I recognize and appreciate the pleasant things that come my way.

- Never
- Sometimes
- Often

I'm happy with what I've got.

- Never
- Sometimes
- Often

I appreciate how privileged I am to access necessities such as food, clothing, and shelter.

- Never
- Sometimes
- Often

I am grateful for my physical health.

- Never
- Sometimes
- Often

I reflect on difficult circumstances to help me realize how blessed I am.

- Never
- Sometimes
- Often

I consider others who have less fortunate circumstances than I do.

- Never
- Sometimes
- Often

I keep in mind all the advantages and chances I have.

- Never
- Sometimes
- Often

Day 199 - I Will Be With You!

"Behold, I am with you and will keep [careful watch over you and guard] you wherever you may go, and I will bring you back to this [promised] land; for I will not leave you until I have done what I have promised you."
—Genesis 28:15, AMP

BELOVED,
Human promises have often been broken, aspirations destroyed, and faith shattered. Still, when God pledged that He would be with you, it was a covenant promise and relationship, a paternal commitment, fatherhood accountability, a confidant friendship, and a Promise-keeping God's trustworthiness. God: "I will be with you!" You can count on that promise to stand the test of time. God is always there for you whatever you confront, whether now or in the past. With confidence, you may face today and the days ahead, knowing that it isn't about who left you but is always with you. When you're between a rock and a hard place, The Promise-keeping, Covenant-Fulfillment, Faithful Father, *Friend-that-Sticks-Closer-than-a-Brother*, Redeemer, Immanuel: God is with us, Way-Maker, and Creator, He says, *"I will be with you!"*
The Father's promise to you - I am with you from the promise (start) through the journey (amidst) to its fulfillment (end). I am with you; always, I will protect you wherever you go; one day, I will return you to this place. I will not leave you until I have fulfilled all of my promises to you. (Genesis 28:15). Be fearless. I am with you from the beginning when it all began; I redeemed you, I called you by name, you are mine, no matter what you face in this lifetime, season, I will be there with you through the storms, flood, burning furnace, between a rock and a hard place, for I am your God, personally, intimately. I paid the total price for you. You are mine; That's how important you are to me and how much I adore you! (Isa 43:1-4). Your heart needed a Lover. Your mind needed the Prince of Peace, your soul needed a Savior, your life required a Divine Surgeon, your rock bottom needed a Rock of Safety, your solitude required a Friend, your emotions needed the necessary tranquility and rest, your body required Great Physician's healing touch, your loneliness required the Companionship of a friend and your vision required Provision. Your orphanage and fatherlessness needed a Father. Your brokenness needed a Repairer of the ruins; you needed a fresh start, the stability, safety, and security of Everlasting Love. I'm your Father and Friend. I'll be there for you. Be strong. You are coming out of that fire, and not even smoke will smell on you. I will be with you! I am in the fiery furnace with you; We are walking through fire; The flames will not scorch you. It will not burn you nor set you ablaze. You will not look like what you went through; The fire will purify you, not devour you. The fire will refine you. The fire is hot, but the *hotter the battle*, the sweeter the blessings. Just know you are coming out like fine gold. You are a diamond! Be courageous! Jesus says, 'I'm calling you out of the boat to come and walk on water with me. You are a water-walker! 'Take courage! It is I. Don't be afraid.' Come out of the boat. You are a water-walker! In My Presence, water will not drown you. No more self-doubt, limiting belief; keep your eyes on Me. I am your God! Beneath you are My everlasting arms to catch you if and when you fall. I will be with you! (Matt 14:27-32).

AFFIRMATIONS & DECLARATIONS
I am expressing my gratitude for all the good fortune, commendations, congratulations, blessings, happiness, success, and glory to my Miracle-working, Game-changing, Chain-breaking, Way-making, and Covenant-manifesting God. God is speaking to me today, assuring me that He will always be with me. Today, I am relying on God's word.

- I am enough and valuable to God. I am blessed with all spiritual blessings. The Lord of the breakthrough is with me. All my walls are coming down! I am breaking through and breaking out!

PRAYER
Heavenly Father, thanks for Your advice. Lord, forgive me for rushing Your plans; instruct me when to slow down and keep my eyes on You when You ask me to walk on water. I must quit underestimating Your supernatural powers to empower my talents and listen to the enemy's falsehoods driving my anxieties, weaknesses, and failures. God's ways are perfect. Your goodness, pleasure, and grace are appreciated. You know me best. You know my troubles, concerns, storms, furnaces, hopes, and desires. You know how much I want out of my battle, predicament, setback, self-doubt, selfishness, self-sabotaging attitude, sickness, and other folly. You know my dreams, goals, and intentions. You know the journey is challenging; therefore, I can't go without You. I need Your enthusiasm and courage to conquer my fears.
Lord, heal my blindness, deafness, muteness, sickness, barrenness, darkness, loneliness, faithlessness, fruitlessness, and brokenness. You don't know how unhappy I'll be if this doesn't happen, but I want what You desire for me, as You planned it and executed it. Give me nevertheless-faith, even-if-faith, Your-will-be-done-as-it-in-heaven-faith; I know You love me. I'll brag about God's faithfulness to my enemies. If He slays me, I'll believe. You have a plan. Lord, don't let my desires and desperation cloud Your will, manner, and time. If my willingness and timing don't match Your intentions for me, put up a roadblock. You will be with me, in Jesus' name, amen.

MY DOPE *faith journal*

Date S | M | T | W | T | F | S

Morning: I feel my emotion! My one-word check-in: ....

DECLARATION

Consider today's verse. I implore the Holy Spirit to reveal His wisdom and truth to me and I declare it over my life.

OBSERVATION

What does the message mean? Lord, help me see it.

PRAYER

What is my prayer request? Lord, I live fully in You.

EMPOWERMENT

How will Your word empower me? Lord, give me the insight to apply my faith to be more significant than my fears.

MY FEARLESS *journey*

Evening: Feel my emotion! My one-word check-up:

What is making me FEEL like this?

What lessons did I LEARNED?

What THOUGHTS did I had?

What prompted my GRATITUDE?

Who did I CONNECTED with?

What brought me JOY?

EVENING PRAYER

WATER:

FRUIT & VEG:

MY MOOD:

My treat for today is: ....

5 Ways to Gratitude

1 Write a daily journal to remind yourself of the positive things in your life.

2 Remember the difficult situations you've been through and concentrate on what you've learned from them.

3 Use your senses and be grateful for the ability to touch, see, smell, taste, and hear.

4 Use appreciative gestures such as smiling, saying thank you, and sending gratitude letters.

5 Utilize visual clues that function as reminders to inspire feelings of thankfulness.

Day 200 - The Joy Of Worship!

Nehemiah said, "Go and enjoy good food and sweet drinks. Send some to people who have none, because today is a holy day to the Lord. Don't be sad, because the joy of the Lord will make you strong."
—Nehemiah 8:10, NCV

BELOVED,
You enjoy good news, and it brings you joy; may the One who delivers the truth ignite your delight and blessing and overtake the fake news that sap your happiness. True worship is the sentiment or display of respect and reverence for God. It is based on whom God is to you in this situation, what God has done for you, and not hindered by what you are going through. Worship is based on God's divine nature, character, and conduct - His plan, purpose, and promises. Show awe-inspiring devotion and admiration for God by bringing Him honor, love, and glory in your worship despite your feeling of fear. You experience joy, inner strength, peace, and hope in worship as you rejoice in His presence. Your testimony brings joy to your worship. Can you testify of the divine intervention of God in your past and this day? *"This is the day the Creator God has made; let us celebrate and be happy today."* (Ps 118:24). *"This day is holy to our Lord. Do not grieve, for the joy of the Lord is your strength."* (Neh 8:10).

In Genesis 37, 39-45, there was a conspiracy to assassinate Joseph, an agreement for minor acts of injustice, all in an attempt to disrupt his divine purpose and end his destiny. But no one could stop God's purpose for his life.No demon, no devil, no one can stand in the way of God's perfect plan and meaning in your life. *"For the LORD of hosts has purposed, and who will annul it? His hand is stretched out, and who will turn it back?"* (Isaiah 14:27, ESV). Joseph went from the pit to Pharoah's household as a slave, the wrongful accusation of Potiphar's wife that sent him to prison, and the interpretation of the dream by the cupbearer, who promised to remember him but forgot him. But not God; you saw how God used and worked all things together for good. One day, God orchestrated a situation for Joseph to bring his gift before Pharoah, and there was a 24-hour turnaround; he woke up in prison and went to sleep that same day in the palace as a Prime Minister. You will find a similar sentiment in Romans 8:28: *God works all things together for good.* Even the most wicked intentions can be turned into good for His dedicated followers by God. There is joy in your worship; go and make a joyful noise.

Do you know the magnificence and marvels of the Way-Maker, Healer, Redeemer, and Creator God? Can you argue you wouldn't have succeeded without God? Can you boldly testify, Jesus, You are my soul's lover, raised me out of the desolate pit, and set my feet on a rock; I found You at rock bottom and My storm anchor? Can you disclose God's battle scars that show you survived when the adversary believed it was over? Can you recall your praise testimonies and bring joy to your worship?

AFFIRMATIONS & DECLARATIONS
Today, I testify of the goodness and greatness of my God. When this evil world rejects me, humiliates me, falsely accuses me, and makes me sick, psychologically, emotionally, and physically. When I am alone with my God in solitude, He is my Solace. I proclaim that the Lord will not abandon me. Your loving loyalty, O LORD, encourages me when I remark, *"My foot is sliding."* When I'm overwhelmed by anxiety, worries, fears, anger, and pain, Your comfort soothes my spirit.
"When anxiety overtakes me and worries are many, Your comfort lightens my soul." (Ps 94:19, VOICE).

- I would never have made it without my God.
- I am stronger, braver, more intelligent, better, and wiser. I am overtaken with pleasure, joy, and awe.
- I am overjoyed because I will receive a large reward in Heaven.

Psalm 16:11, TPT: "Because of you, I know the path of life, as I taste the fullness of joy in your presence. At your right side, I experience divine pleasures forevermore!"

PRAYER
Heavenly Father God, thank You for Your precious word that reminds me of Your grace, goodness, and greatness. Let the truth about the gospel fill my heart with wisdom, understanding, the beauty and majesty of Jesus, and the power of the Holy Spirit energize, equip, empower, and enable me. Today, I choose to share my testimony and gratitude, choose joy, and increase my faith over every fear. Lord, You created me, as my Maker, Creator, and Redeemer God, to live fully, by the power of Your joy, and as our Risen King, Your rule of grace frees me from our fear, emotions, troubles, and darkness, and as my Redeemer, You release me. May I be found by You ready to embrace the change, my new creation, my new identity, renewed mind, new vision, transformed character, fearless faith, limitless belief to worship You in spirit and truth every day of the Lord? Please, draw my heart, home, hands, head, habits, and nations to You as we exalt and honor Jesus. In the righteousness and zealousness of my faith, by the grace and all for the glory of God, in Jesus' name, I pray, Amen.

MY DOPE *faith journal*

Date S | M | T | W | T | F | S

Morning: I feel my emotion! My one-word check-in: ____________

DECLARATION

Consider today's verse. I implore the Holy Spirit to reveal His wisdom and truth to me and I declare it over my life.

OBSERVATION

What does the message mean? Lord, help me see it.

PRAYER

What is my prayer request? Lord, I live fully in You.

EMPOWERMENT

How will Your word empower me? Lord, give me the insight to apply my faith to be more significant than my fears.

MY FEARLESS *journey*

Evening: Feel my emotion! My one-word check-up:

What is making me FEEL like this?

What lessons did I LEARNED?

What THOUGHTS did I had?

What prompted my GRATITUDE?

Who did I CONNECTED with?

What brought me JOY?

EVENING PRAYER

WATER:

FRUIT & VEG:

MY MOOD:

My treat for today is: ....

THIS WEEK'S TASK

Feeling Grateful

Consider and select three things you are grateful for each day of the week..

	GRATITUDE 1	GRATITUDE 2	GRATITUDE 3
MONDAY			
TUESDAY			
WEDNESDAY			
THURSDAY			
FRIDAY			
SATURDAY			
SUNDAY			

Day 201 - I Am His!

"See what kind of love the Father has given to us, that we should be called children of God; and so we are."
—1 John 3:1, ESV

BELOVED,
There is much power in the knowledge, revelation, prophetic insight, wisdom, understanding, belief system, and most importantly, a sense of belongingness and belovedness of these three simple words. *"I AM HIS!"* A sense of belonging refers to social wellness and the desire for "the human emotional need to associate with, love and intimacy, be accepted by others, have friends and family, and be a part of a social group or community." Everyone has a sense of belonging to be socially connected, loved, and in happy, healthy relationships. According to Abraham Maslow's Hierarchy of Needs theory having a sense of belonging has a significant impact on your behavior and motivation; it is the third level of need (a total of five levels) after satisfying your basic physiological needs (food, clothes, water, shelter, rest, health, and procreation) to move to the next dimension and fulfill your safety needs (protection, stability, security, wellness, and financial provision). Unfortunately, many of God's children remain in toxic relationships and unhealthy and harmful situations to pacify rather than satisfy their need to belong because of poor self-esteem, low self-worth, and a lack of self-confidence. God is your Great Sheperd, a faithful Provider, and a loving Protector, meeting your needs (every level); you shall have no lack. He is your Heavenly Father and a Friend that sticks closer than a brother. You are a partaker in His royalty, heritage, and inheritance of His kingdom; He is your God, and you are His. Today, God has given His message to reassure you of His loyalty and your identity and nobility and to repair the false construct of your love and sense of belonging.
The Revelation
- Identity - You must know who you are!
- Belongingness - You must have faith in Whom you belong!
- Connection - You must understand the roles and responsibilities of the covenant relationship.
- Belovedness- You must believe in His redemptive love for your divine rebirth and restoration.
- Becoming - You have a high change resilience, be change-ready rather than change-resistant!

AFFIRMATIONS & DECLARATIONS
God, Himself, said it – *You are mine!* This truth is His promise to me. I know whom God says I am! I walk in authority, love, liberation, power, dominion, miracles, and favor. My Father says, "They shall be Mine; I am the Lord." (Numbers 3:13b). "*Listen, Jacob, to the One who created you, Israel, to the one who shaped who you are. Do not fear, for I, your Kinsman-Redeemer, will rescue you. I have called you by name, and you are mine.*" (Isaiah 43:1, TPT). Therefore I affirm:
- I am a child of God.
- I am a prototype of Jesus.
- I am made in His image and likeness.
- I am growing in favor of God and man, like Jesus.
- I am His masterpiece, and I have The Master's peace: "He is mine, and I am His!"

"My beloved is mine and I am His... I belong to my beloved and he belongs to me... I belong to my beloved, and his desire is for me."
- Song of Solomon 2:16, 6:13, 7:10

PRAYER
Heavenly Father God, thank You for this truth, revelation, wisdom, knowledge, understanding, and prophetic insight. Lord, thank You for taking me under Your wing as a change-ready and well-learned disciple, repairing me, rebranding me as Your own, and reclaiming me in Your grace.
I'm Yours, and You're mine! It's good to be strong and fearless as I navigate the power dynamics, politics, unfairness, battles, lies, fears, and challenges of this life journey to be comforted by the revelation, truth, and light that *I'm Yours.* Today, however, I am reminded that the most gratifying, meaningful, fulfilling, defining, transformational, and the most significant belonging in my life is simply this: *I belong to You; I am His!* May I live in the freedom of Your love, the wisdom of Your grace, exploring the sweet spot where my **p**urpose, **i**dentity, **l**egendary, and **l**egacy integrate, His **PILL** that cures all my wounds of the past that blurred my vision? Let this transition be my conversion story that collides and synchronizes with Your rhythm of goodness, grace, and timing, causing waves of Your glory on earth, revealing that *I am His* and pleasing You in all I do. I pray in Jesus' name, Amen.

MY DOPE *faith journal*

Date S | M | T | W | T | F | S

Morning: I feel my emotion! My one-word check-in: ____________

DECLARATION

Consider today's verse. I implore the Holy Spirit to reveal His wisdom and truth to me and I declare it over my life.

OBSERVATION

What does the message mean? Lord, help me see it.

PRAYER

What is my prayer request? Lord, I live fully in You.

EMPOWERMENT

How will Your word empower me? Lord, give me the insight to apply my faith to be more significant than my fears.

MY FEARLESS *journey*

Evening: Feel my emotion! My one-word check-up:

What is making me FEEL like this?

What lessons did I LEARNED?

What THOUGHTS did I had?

What prompted my GRATITUDE?

Who did I CONNECTED with?

What brought me JOY?

EVENING PRAYER

WATER:

FRUIT & VEG:

MY MOOD:

My treat for today is: ....

MASLOW'S HIERARCHY OF *needs*

Maslow's Hierarchy of Needs is a five-tier model of human needs, portrayed as hierarchical motivational levels within a pyramid. Each person must meet the lower-level needs they can attend to higher-level requirements.

Affirm **Philippians 4:19, AMP**:
"And my God will liberally supply (fill until full) your every need according to His riches in glory in Christ Jesus."

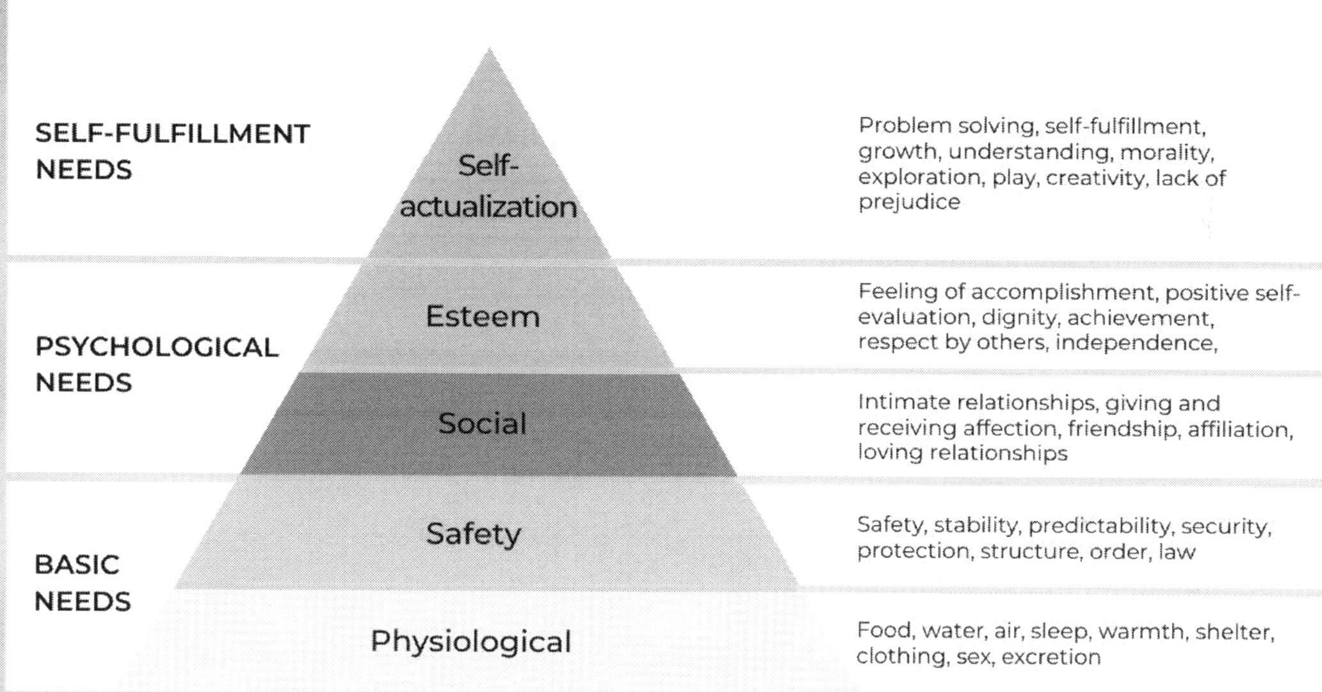

How are you currently meeting these demands, requirements, and needs?

What could you do to address these demands, if you aren't already doing so?

Day 202 - This Day!

"The steadfast love of the Lord never ceases; his mercies never come to an end; they are new every morning; great is your faithfulness."
—Lamentations 3:22-23, ESV

BELOVED,
Start your day with the 3C Routine: **C**ommand the day, **C**ommit everything to God, and **C**onverse with God, self, and others. Listen for God's soft, still voice; His sheep know His voice. Prayer is a two-way conversation. Ask and wait for His revelation of what His word says about you, your situation, His promises, plans, and purpose for you. Then retell yourself with positive self-talk and affirmations, oppose the lies and liar, Satan, and cancel the fears with the declaration of scriptures over your life and every circumstance. Finally, put prayer and praise on it, and seal the deal with faith. Be very present this day, not worried about yesterday or anxious about tomorrow. Release the jail doors of yesterday's mistakes and the steering wheels to an unknown future to a God who knows everything and paid the full wage for freedom from every captivity and circumstance. Declare that today is the day of deliverance, uncommon favor, breakthrough, peace, joy, and new beginnings. "*So no wonder we don't give up. Even though our outer person gradually wears out, our inner being is renewed daily. We view our slight, short-lived troubles in the light of eternity. We see our difficulties as the substance that produces for us an eternal, weighty glory far beyond all comparison because we don't focus our attention on what is seen but on what is unseen. For what is seen is temporary, but the unseen realm is eternal." (*2 Corinthians 4:16-18, TPT).
"Faith says before you get there, He is already there." Take the Bible, the compass, the playbook, the manual for your masterpiece, the blueprint book of life, and learn more about the character and conduct of the Master, His attributes, and actions. Pray from His heart of love, compassion, and goodness. Believe everything He thinks about, says about, created for, and prepares for you. The journey may be rough sometimes, but He promises to get you there safely and blessed at the appointed time. *"This is the day the Lord has made. Let us rejoice and be glad in it."* (Psalm 118:24, CSB)

AFFIRMATIONS & DECLARATIONS
In the name of Jesus, I declare that all chains are broken. My shackles have been destroyed, and my God has lavished His anointing on me. Devil, you must take your hands off my life today. On this day, the Lord removes the heavy burden from my shoulders and breaks off the yoke of bondage from my neck because of the heavy anointing upon you! (Isaiah 10:27, TPT).

- I arise to meet this day, fearless and faithful.
- I walk into this day utterly free. I walk by the Spirit in faith and not by sight.
- Every yoke and burden is broken and removed from me on this day.
- I am prepared for this day. I am renewing my mindset, faith, and vision.
- I am a new creation with a new character that aligns with my calling.
- I am ready for God to pour every new blessing, benefit, reward, more grace, peace, and joy unto me on this day.
- I let go and trusted God.; O Lord, revive me; I'm craving more of You today!

"So it will be In that day that the burden of the Assyrian will be removed from your shoulders and his yoke from your neck. The yoke will be broken because of the fat."
— Isaiah 10:27, AMP

PRAYER
Heavenly Father, Thank You for always having a place for me under Your wings, in Your plan, purpose, promises, and heart. Lord, thank You for inviting me into an abundant life on earth and eternal life in heaven, to live fully in the confidence of being loved, wanted, accepted, desired, chosen, known, purposed, cleansed, redeemed, and celebrated.
I am overjoyed to know that I am Yours, and today, You have made it to save, deliver, provide, protect, and bring me out of trouble; therefore, I am exceedingly glad in it! Lord, grant me the opportunity to experience the kind of deep connections, engagement, relationships, social networks, and community for which I was designed, gifted, and prepared to thrive, be happy, and prosperous. Lord, I give You praise, glory, and thanksgiving, for You alone are worthy, O Lord! This day is Your day, You made it, and therefore it is my day of joy, victory, and peace in Jesus' name; I pray, Amen.

MY DOPE *faith journal*

Date S | M | T | W | T | F | S

Morning: I feel my emotion! My one-word check-in: ____________________

DECLARATION

Consider today's verse. I implore the Holy Spirit to reveal His wisdom and truth to me and I declare it over my life.

OBSERVATION

What does the message mean? Lord, help me see it.

PRAYER

What is my prayer request? Lord, I live fully in You.

EMPOWERMENT

How will Your word empower me? Lord, give me the insight to apply my faith to be more significant than my fears.

MY FEARLESS *journey*

Evening: Feel my emotion! My one-word check-up:

What is making me FEEL like this?

What lessons did I LEARNED?

What THOUGHTS did I had?

What prompted my GRATITUDE?

Who did I CONNECTED with?

What brought me JOY?

EVENING PRAYER

WATER:

FRUIT & VEG:

MY MOOD:

My treat for today is:..

Daily Gratitude

Something that made me happy today

One person I am grateful to

One thing I did today for myself

One thing I am excited about

One thing I'm not going to take for granted

One challenging lesson I'm glad I learned

DAY 203 - 209

Give To Others

"

Don't hold back—give freely, and you'll have plenty poured back into your lap—a good measure, pressed down, shaken together, brimming over. You'll receive in the same measure you give.

— LUKE 6:38, VOICE

Day 203 - What If?

"He always comes alongside us to comfort us in every suffering so that we can come alongside those who are in any painful trial. We can bring them this same comfort that God has poured out upon us."
—2 Corinthians 1:4, TPT

BELOVED,
What if your affliction is the *'burning bush'* God is using to get your attention for Him to release His divine nature and glory? His affection, anointing, assignment, alignment, abundance, and advancement?
When God was ready to elevate Moses, He got His attention with a burning bush.
What if this situation, in its severity, urgency, complexity, ambiguity, and seeming impossibility, is your burning bush, causing you to pause in the wilderness and look to God for help? Your **PILL**, the transforming process that will collide with your **p**urpose, **i**dentity, **l**egendary, and **l**egacy, synced with the timetable of Heaven, and produce waves on earth, globally and generationally?
Sometimes, you wander off the path that God has ordained and predestined for you, and as a loving Father, God allows a *'burning bush'* to get your attention so you can seek Him, serve Him, trust Him, and carefully follow His word and ways. Confess it *"Before I was afflicted, I went astray, but now I keep Your word and seek Your ways."* Maybe you used to get lost all the time before you were humbled, but now you realize the wisdom, knowledge, and truth in His words. Flowing from God's generosity and goodness, everything He does is a work of art of miracles and majesty; He will show the strength, beauty, light, and liberation of His lovely words and works.
Or is it because you are so devoted to believing and doing what God says that others fabricate stories about your character or the enemy so relentlessly destroying your calling, character, conduct, and career? (Psalm 119:67-69). But God! He wastes nothing! Muster up your even-if faith, saying what-if the devil intended to harm, kill, steal, and destroy, then welcome to the glory-showdown for Jesus comes to bring the fullness of joy and newness of life; nothing can stop God's faithfulness and promises for victory and abundance. The devil is a liar!
"What then? If some did not believe or were unfaithful [to God], their lack of belief will not nullify and make invalid the faithfulness of God and His word, will it? Certainly not! Let God be found true [as He will be], though every person be found a liar, just as it is written [in Scripture', 'That You may be justified in Your words, And prevail when You are judged [by sinful me.'" (Romans 3:3-4, AMP).

AFFIRMATIONS & DECLARATIONS
I declare, "*even in the unending shadows of death's darkness, I am not overcome by fear. Because You are with me in those dark moments, near with Your protection and guidance, I am comforted.*"
(Psalm 23:4, VOICE).

- I open myself to the calling of God and His work in me.
- God is the architect of my life and the author of my glory.
- He promises that my story ends in victory if I stay connected to Jesus. God cares for me.
- I submit to His will, way, time, plan, promise, and purpose in my life.
- I pay attention to and obey His instructions and directives.

"Even when your path takes me through the valley of deepest darkness,
fear will never conquer me, for You already have!
Your authority is my strength and my peace.
The comfort of Your love takes away my fear.
I'll never be lonely, for You are near."
– Psalm 23:4, TPT

PRAYER
Heavenly Father God, Lord, forgive me for manipulating Your will when I want my way and my expected time to be correct. Lord, I let go and let You, God, have Your way and Your perfect will; whatever Your plan and purpose are, Lord, by Your grace, use me for Your glory. Lord, I can't do, confront it, endure it, get through it, face it, fight it or win it without You. Have Your way Lord in my life, living, livelihood, by Your grace, manifest and transform me into a dazzling splendor of Your glory. Lord, use my setbacks, brokenness, sickness, loneliness, barrenness, wilderness, joblessness, and insufficiency. Even my disobedience, shame, humiliation, rejection, wrongful accusation, failure, and everything that the enemy intended to harm me to turn all things around for my good and Your glory, a favorable outcome for me as a blessing to Your kingdom, my purpose, identity, legend, and legacy in Jesus' mighty name, I pray, Amen.

MY DOPE *faith journal*

Date S | M | T | W | T | F | S

Morning: I feel my emotion! My one-word check-in: ______________________

DECLARATION

Consider today's verse. I implore the Holy Spirit to reveal His wisdom and truth to me and I declare it over my life.

OBSERVATION

What does the message mean? Lord, help me see it.

PRAYER

What is my prayer request? Lord, I live fully in You.

EMPOWERMENT

How will Your word empower me? Lord, give me the insight to apply my faith to be more significant than my fears.

MY FEARLESS *journey*

Evening: Feel my emotion! My one-word check-up:

What is making me FEEL like this?

What lessons did I LEARNED?

What THOUGHTS did I had?

What prompted my GRATITUDE?

Who did I CONNECTED with?

What brought me JOY?

EVENING PRAYER

WATER:

FRUIT & VEG:

MY MOOD:

My treat for today is:..

Random Acts of Kindness Ideas

- Remove weeds and put flowers in an underutilized public space.
- Place the exact change for a snack in the vending machine's change slot.
- Take a package of cookies to your local fire station or a police station.
- If someone is unable to pay their debt, forgive it.
- When you've completed a fantastic book, put it somewhere public for someone else to find.
- Overtip a server or leave a hefty tip for the pizza delivery person.
- Place coins on the roadway for others to see.
- Give a street musician a tip.
- Visit a nursing facility to brighten the day of an old individual who does not receive many visits.
- Assist a senior citizen with their garden.
- Cook supper for a friend, buy groceries or meals online and send them to a friend as a gift.
- Allow someone who looks to be rushing to cut ahead of you in line.
- Take a buddy to lunch and pay attention to them.
- Give your extra laptop to an older person you know who is housebound.
- Leave little scraps of paper with encouraging comments in library books.
- Purchase a few extra bags of dog food and donate them to a local animal shelter.
- Perform a chore for another member of your household.
- Donate sanitary goods to a women's shelter in your community.
- Make cookies for your mailman or woman.
- Invite someone along to a holiday dinner with your family.
- Allow another vehicle to merge in front of you.
- Give a compliment to someone.
- Volunteer in a soup kitchen.
- Offer to babysit for busy parents so they can have some alone time.
- Purchase surplus groceries and donate them to a local food bank.
- Donate craft items to a deserving school.

Day 204 - God's Speed!

"Then he said to me, Fear not, Daniel, for from the first day that you set your heart to understand and humbled yourself before your God, your words have been heard, and I have come because of your words."
—Daniel 10:12, ESV

BELOVED,
God's timing is perfect and right. He is on target and at the appointed time. Your expectations must be synchronized, aligned, and coincide with God's perfect timing and loving ways.
God is wise, just, and patient. He knows everything. He is present everywhere and always at work for us. Nothing catches God by surprise. He declares the end at the beginning; Alpha and Omega God.
You may think God didn't answer your prayers as expected. But God is saying I heard the first time. He is always at work and hears, sees, and knows you.
You need to learn to trust Him! You may have approached the throne of grace boldly, seeking help in your time of time. You may be waiting desperately, praying, fasting, and trusting God for a breakthrough, healing miracles, deliverance, restoration, and blessing.
The revelation in response to your request is given. (Daniel 10:12), and He is speaking to you today: God says, I heard you the first time you humbled yourself and prayed. I listened to your prayer on Day 1 and answered, but there is spiritual warfare for your breakthrough.
Believe and receive because you will win despite the spiritual warfare for your breakthrough!
"Do not be afraid, my beloved child. From the very first day that you began to pursue understanding and humble yourself before your God, your words have been heard. I have been sent in response to what you've said." (Daniel 10:12, VOICE)

AFFIRMATIONS & DECLARATIONS
"And He changes the times and the seasons; He removes kings and raises up kings; He gives wisdom to the wise. And knowledge to those who have understanding." (Daniel 2:21, NKJV). The Lord will raise me to a position of respect, favor, and abounding glory. He'll defeat my adversary, force him to fess up, and shower me with blessings. As a result, the Lord delights in being generous and gracious to me, and He glorifies himself by showing compassion to me. The Lord is a righteous God; those who wait for him and hope in Him are happy. (Isaiah 30:18).

- I am trusting the Lord with all my heart.
- I surrender all my burdens to Him.
- I am strong and courageous.
- I am living for God, not for man.
- I seek first the Kindom of God and His righteousness.
- I have a future filled with hope.

"The Lord is not slow to fulfill his promise as some count slowness, but is patient toward you, not wishing that any should perish, but that all should reach repentance."
– 2 Peter 3:9 ESV

PRAYER
Father God, Thank You for the seasons of miracles, signs, wonders, and manifestations in my life of Your works, grace, and blessings. Give me Your revelation as You reveal what is in my heart, prepare my character for what I am praying for to be ready to handle the answered prayers, and deliver promises appropriately when they arrive and become my reality.
Please help me rejoice as I will be patient in prayer, perseverance, positivity, endless gratitude, courageous peace, confident joy, limitless love, fearless faith, and prophetic insight to strengthen my endurance and not give up.
Father God, help me keep my eyes on You consistently, amplify my listening skills to hear Your still small voice, and give me the strength, tenacity, and determination it takes to override my thoughts, fears, and feelings. When I am weak and challenged by my environment, the people around me and my circumstances give up, give in, and put off the actions. I need to take You at Your word, be still, wait, trust, and stay in synchrony with You in Jesus' name.
Thank You for Your infinite wisdom, favor, grace, honor, loving-kindness, and promise to answer my prayers timely and perfectly in Jesus' name; I pray, Amen.

MY DOPE *faith journal*

Date S | M | T | W | T | F | S

Morning: I feel my emotion! My one-word check-in: ____________

DECLARATION

Consider today's verse. I implore the Holy Spirit to reveal His wisdom and truth to me and I declare it over my life.

OBSERVATION

What does the message mean? Lord, help me see it.

PRAYER

What is my prayer request? Lord, I live fully in You.

EMPOWERMENT

How will Your word empower me? Lord, give me the insight to apply my faith to be more significant than my fears.

MY FEARLESS *journey*

Evening: Feel my emotion! My one-word check-up:

What is making me FEEL like this?

What lessons did I LEARNED?

What THOUGHTS did I had?

What prompted my GRATITUDE?

Who did I CONNECTED with?

What brought me JOY?

EVENING PRAYER

WATER:

FRUIT & VEG:

MY MOOD:

My treat for today is: ....

365 Journal

Day 205 - God's Got This!

"Therefore do not worry about tomorrow, for tomorrow will worry about itself. Each day has enough trouble of its own."
—Matthew 6:34, NIV

BELOVED,
God's got this. He is with you, He is in you, and He is fighting for you!
Luke 1:37 confirms this truth: nothing is too challenging, complex, chaotic, or complicated for God.

- "For with God, nothing shall be impossible." [KJV]

God holds all power, every strength you need to win this battle, and all love you need to satisfy every need as you belong to Him. Psalm 62:11 -12 says, *"Once God has spoken; twice have I heard this: that power belongs to God, and that to you, O Lord, belongs steadfast love. For you will render to a man according to his work."*
When David was on the run for his life, he penned this psalm. His adversaries were declaring that they intended to depose him as king and were on the prowl for ways to get rid of him. But the man, known as a man after God's own heart, made his way beneath God's wings with the assurance that certainly God's got this!
As you journey through this life, you're just going to have periods in your life when you're under assault from your adversaries. Like David, you must have unshakeable and fearless faith because you have a safe place to go in God's presence, power, and comfort of His love. God is our refuge and strength, a close powerful, present friend in challenging times. The Father says, "You're not alone; I'm here to help. Don't fear, don't stress, don't get disheartened; I have your back. Everything is in order, and everything will turn out OK. Yes, it will. Repeat it until you believe it, *'God's got this!'*"

AFFIRMATIONS & DECLARATIONS
Affirm, declare, and believe these eight God's truths in your heart, your head, and in the atmosphere.
"Listen to my testimony: I cried to God in my distress, and he answered me. He freed me from all my fears!" (Psalms 34:4, TPT)
My Heavenly Father says,

1. I will go ahead, and I got your back.
2. Even in your darkness, My light dawns!
3. Don't be obsessed with money but live content with what you have, for you will always have My presence.
4. Do not yield to fear, for I am always near.
5. Renew your mindset and declare My power, presence, promise, and Providence.
6. The same Resurrection Power that rose Jesus from the dead is living inside you.
7. I am your God, present among you, a strong Warrior there to save you.
8. Don't you ever think for one moment that you are alone, and I have abandoned you, for I have arrived ahead of you to prepare you for the miraculous blessings and the benefits I have promised you?

I agree and affirm:

- Every day, I get closer to Jesus.
- I am never alone because God is by my side every day.
- I am forgiven and never forsaken.
- God has loved me since before the creation of the world.
- Nothing can separate me from the love of the Lord.

"He alone is my safe place; his wraparound presence always protects me.
For he is my champion defender; there's no risk of failure with God.
So why would I let worry paralyze me, even when troubles multiply around me?"
—Psalm 62: 2, TPT

PRAYER
Lord, Thanks for Your faithfulness; I adore and honor You; I know You got this! I declare that You are trustworthy, gracious, powerful, and loving and that Your Kingdom will last forever. Thank You for being with me, protecting me, healing me, and providing me with everything I require. Please help me love and serve You, practice self-love, and care for others faithfully. Give me the grace to follow Your instructions, persist in You, and resist the desires of the flesh. Allow Your Holy Spirit to empower me and equip me to wait and interact with You in a trustworthy manner. Allow my thanksgiving sacrifices to satisfy You, magnify Your name, and enable me to provide consistent services to You so that I may be called, prepared, and qualified to receive Your blessings. In Jesus' name, I pray, Amen.

MY DOPE *faith journal*

Date S | M | T | W | T | F | S

Morning: I feel my emotion! My one-word check-in: ....

DECLARATION

Consider today's verse. I implore the Holy Spirit to reveal His wisdom and truth to me and I declare it over my life.

OBSERVATION

What does the message mean? Lord, help me see it.

PRAYER

What is my prayer request? Lord, I live fully in You.

EMPOWERMENT

How will Your word empower me? Lord, give me the insight to apply my faith to be more significant than my fears.

MY FEARLESS *journey*

Evening: Feel my emotion! My one-word check-up:

What is making me FEEL like this?

What lessons did I LEARNED?

What THOUGHTS did I had?

What prompted my GRATITUDE?

Who did I CONNECTED with?

What brought me JOY?

EVENING PRAYER

WATER:

FRUIT & VEG:

MY MOOD:

My treat for today is: ....

Health Advantages of Kindness

According to research, doing acts of kindness and making others feel good is associated with more powerful emotions of well-being.

enhances social relationships and support networks, resulting in a genuine sense of belonging

Being mindful of our actions of compassion boosts emotions of happiness and joy.

offers a more optimistic view of one's situation

helps to a happier community

boosts self-esteem, self-confidence, and optimism

minimizes feelings of loneliness and isolation

Day 206 - Bigger, Better & More Rewarding

"You shall give to him freely, and your heart shall not be grudging when you give to him, because for this the Lord your God will bless you in all your work and in all that you undertake."
—Deuteronomy 15:10, ESV

BELOVED,
Your current season or history may prevent you from seeing, thinking, and believing God's promises for much more, infinitely beyond, and more extraordinary. There may be many things that point to doom and gloom. Still, God says, "I beg to differ," promising an increase, enlargement, expansion, multiplication, exponential growth, and limitless advancement despite all the evidence to the contrary: personal experiences, mistakes, statistics, experts, political leaders, and bosses. "What you are isn't defined by what others think of you; it's defined by what I do. "Now to Me who can carry out My divine plan and do exceedingly abundantly more than you could ever ask or imagine, infinitely more than your most fervent prayers, hopes, or desires, according to My Holy Spirit's power at work within you. (Eph 20: 3). I, the Lord, will bless you with more extensive, significant, and rewarding. I will reveal the wisdom, strategies, direction, and plan to accomplish your purpose, calling, and destiny to complete His will and manifest His glory in you as a Kingdom Builder."
The story is told in John 21:1-13, *'Jesus and the Miraculous Catch of Fish.'* The disciples have been toiling until Jesus arrived and stepped on the scene - where miracles happen! So *"Jesus said to them, 'Children, do you have any fish [to eat along with your bread]?' They answered, 'No.' And He said to them, 'Cast the net on the right-hand side of the boat (starboard), and you will find some." So they cast [the net], and then they were not able to haul it in because of the great catch of fish. Then that disciple (John) whom Jesus loved (esteemed) said to Peter, 'It is the Lord!'"* (John 21:5-7, AMP). Today, face the challenge and change, obey His instructions and follow His direction. Faithfully, cast your net to the other side of fear and expect immeasurably more, overflow abundance, a supernatural breakthrough! They did, and they saw the miraculous fish catch with their own eyes as the net broke! Simon Peter was returning to his old way of making a living. Life had shifted, and Simon Peter faced a new era. Jesus, whom He journeyed as his disciples, was crucified, and now the uncertainty of what the future holds is all Peter can discern. Peter decided to go fishing, and others joined him. But remember, Jesus had called Peter and Andrew to follow Him from 'fishermen' and said He would make them 'fishers-of-men.' The entire journey as they followed Jesus from *The Great Call* to *The Great Crucification* was the preparation process for *The Great Commission* to go and make disciples. You must lift your lids off a limitless God and fearlessly trust His directions as you faithfully throw your nets on the other side of fear. When we are about to give up, stop and seek His Spirit and listen for Him speaking to us. May Jesus appear and offer us a peek of what He has in store for us: Bigger, *Better, and More Rewarding!*

AFFIRMATIONS & DECLARATIONS
"I will instruct you and teach you in the way you should go; I will counsel you [who are willing to learn] with My eye upon you. Do not be like the horse or like the mule which have no understanding, Whose trappings include bridle and rein to hold them in check; otherwise, they will not come near to you.
Many are the sorrows of the wicked, but he who trusts in and relies on the Lord shall be surrounded with compassion and lovingkindness." (Psalm 32:8-10, AMP).

- I am trusting God. He will bring it together for me more prominent, better, and more rewarding than I prayed, asked, worked, dreamed, or imagined.
- God's plan for my significance is greater than the standard of success set by the world around me.
- My success comes from doing God's will to the best of my ability.

PRAYER
Father God, Thank You for giving me a bigger, better, and more rewarding life, promise, hope, future, and destiny. You are the King of kings and Lord of lords, and every good and perfect gift comes from You. In exchange for my commitment to You, You have promised that Your plans will be successful and more significant. My success will come from aligning my plans with Yours, acknowledging Your Presence, aligning and accepting Your word, embracing Your Spirit, and fearfully obeying Your word. Please help me sense Your Spirit and listen to Your voice as You guide me with wisdom to faithfully cast my net on the other side of fear (the right side of the boat). Lord, grant me victory in everything I do and in every situation I am in by Your grace and all for Your glory. To this day and always, may I be filled with joy, peace, honor, humility, patience, and favor by the love of Father, Son, and Holy Spirit, as well as by their tenderness, faithfulness, and loving-kindness? Through Jesus Christ, our Lord, Amen.

MY DOPE *faith journal*

Date S | M | T | W | T | F | S

Morning: I feel my emotion! My one-word check-in: ....

DECLARATION

Consider today's verse. I implore the Holy Spirit to reveal His wisdom and truth to me and I declare it over my life.

OBSERVATION

What does the message mean? Lord, help me see it.

PRAYER

What is my prayer request? Lord, I live fully in You.

EMPOWERMENT

How will Your word empower me? Lord, give me the insight to apply my faith to be more significant than my fears.

MY FEARLESS *journey*

Evening: Feel my emotion! My one-word check-up:

What is making me FEEL like this?

What lessons did I LEARNED?

What THOUGHTS did I had?

What prompted my GRATITUDE?

Who did I CONNECTED with?

What brought me JOY?

EVENING PRAYER

WATER:

FRUIT & VEG:

MY MOOD:

My treat for today is: ....

365 Journal

Please make a list of all of your *big audacious goals* and write them down. Joy comes from making goals and imagining what God has in store for you, and this inspires you to believe that your life will be even better, bigger, better, and more rewarding.

"Bring all who claim me as their God, for I have made them for my glory. It was I who created them." (Isaiah 43:7, NLT)

Day 207 - God Is Faithful!

"No one will be able to stand against you as long as you live. For I will be with you as I was with Moses. I will not fail you or abandon you."
—Joshua 1:5, NLT

BELOVED,
God is faithful! You may have faith in God's faithfulness to guide you through the process of becoming the unique person He intended you to be. God is a dependable source of provision and a caring defender. Your creation and existence have a purpose, significance, and importance because of God's faithfulness. Your confidence in God's unwavering and faithful love will never disappoint you. His steadfast love for you is infinite. You are complete in the sufficiency and faithfulness of Christ-sufficiency and Christ-completeness that fill you up to the brim. God's faithfulness guarantees your salvation, sanctification, purity, and pardon for your transgressions. Your fearless trust is anchored on God's faithfulness through your faith-filled prayer. With God's Holy Spirit around and dwelling in you, you may experience His faithfulness in the power, stability, protection, and provision.
In God's book, your entire life has already been written, and your story finishes in victory for His glory. Do not give up on yourself by re-reading the same chapter or staying on the same page after experiencing disappointment but accept the transition from the road you're currently on to something new. You may rely on God's faithfulness to close the gap. Help you get to where you need to go in life. Don't lose hope in your faithful Heavenly Father. Do not give up on your destiny, narrative, and legacy just because you are tired, disappointed, and irritated at the moment. Your God is reliable, trustworthy, and dependable. It's well-known that your God is faithful. As the Author, every day of your life has already been recorded, and He is faithful to carry out and complete each one. Don't let yourself become stuck at the point of disappointment. Don't waver from your course. Keep clinging on. Do not give up on your future because you are exhausted, disappointed, and irritated.

- God is faithful, even when you're faithless, since He can't lie, die, or deny Himself. (2 Tim 2:13).
- God is faithful to create a way out of every test and deal with the tester. He will offer a way out of every temptation, difficulty, and pain. He's the Waymaker. You've faced no temptation that others don't face. God is faithful; He won't let you be tempted beyond your capabilities, but He will provide a way out so you can endure it. (1 Cor 10:13).
- God is faithful to forgive you always. If you admit your transgressions, God proves He is faithful and righteous by ignoring and purging you from your wrongdoing. (1 John 1:9).
- God is faithful. Despite everything, the Lord is faithful and keeps His promises; He will uphold and defend you from the evil one. (2 Thessalonians 3:3).
- God is forever faithful. The Almighty God is the One True God. He is an authentic, reliable, and trustworthy God who maintains His vows for a thousand generations. He loves those who love Him, receives and reciprocates His love, and obeys His instructions and mandates! (Deu 7:9).
- God is a faithful Father, always truthful and perfect. God's love is always sincere and flawless. God isn't a man and never lies. No need to retract, repent, take back, or not honor what He stated. (Num 23:19).

AFFIRMATIONS & DECLARATIONS
"The Lord says, *"I love justice, and I hate oppression and crime. I will faithfully reward my people And make an eternal covenant with them."* (Isaiah 61:8 GNB)

- In Christ, I find myself. He faithfully rewards me and binds His vow with a contractual agreement.
- I have faith that the Lord will make all things new. I will experience God's faithfulness, no fear!
- I have courage because I know He stands by me. Will, my trust in Him, will never disappoint me.
- I am kept and rescued when tempted; God is faithful, and He will help me endure through temptations.
- I am sure and fearless; God is faithful and keeps His promises in my life.
- I am not alone; God will never abandon me; I am victorious, and God will never let me down.

PRAYER
Father God, Thank You because my sins have been forgiven because of the work of Jesus. It is a miracle of grace and generosity that I will never take for granted. As I grow in grace, may it inspire me to be more forgiving, patient, and forgiving of others? Thank You for carrying us through the turbulence of deep waters, the raging fires of trials, and the agony of brutal losses. I am constantly aware of how much I rely on You, Your grace, Your strength, and Your power to get us through even the most challenging days. Thank You for being there for me. During this season, please help me to keep your focus on You first. Lord, I ask for Your supernatural protection today, personally and globally. Lead me away from temptation and assist me in fleeing the presence of potentially harmful activities or influences. When I am weak, help me look for strength and remember Your faithful love; You want the best for me. In Jesus' name, I pray, Amen.

MY DOPE *faith journal*

Date S | M | T | W | T | F | S

Morning: I feel my emotion! My one-word check-in:

DECLARATION

Consider today's verse. I implore the Holy Spirit to reveal His wisdom and truth to me and I declare it over my life.

OBSERVATION

What does the message mean? Lord, help me see it.

PRAYER

What is my prayer request? Lord, I live fully in You.

EMPOWERMENT

How will Your word empower me? Lord, give me the insight to apply my faith to be more significant than my fears.

MY FEARLESS *journey*

Evening: Feel my emotion! My one-word check-up:

What is making me FEEL like this?

What lessons did I LEARNED?

What THOUGHTS did I had?

What prompted my GRATITUDE?

Who did I CONNECTED with?

What brought me JOY?

EVENING PRAYER

WATER:

FRUIT & VEG:

MY MOOD:

My treat for today is: ....

Volunteering

When you put your confidence in God's constancy, even a small act of kindness may have a significant impact. Feed whole nations with your little lunch. God is faithful! Volunteering is a beautiful way to help others, and getting engaged may be extremely helpful to your well-being. According to research, volunteering and charitable activities increase positive emotions of self-esteem, social connectedness, joy, and well-being. Here are some ways you may get involved:

1. Offer to contribute to your children's school or childcare. Alternately, volunteer at a local creche or youth organization.

2. Use your abilities to educate others - for example, you may provide painting, musical instruments, dancing, or cuisine.

3. Participate in a local gardening/tree-planting initiative that cares for animals to help safeguard your local ecosystem.

4. Visit an older person at home or a nursing facility. If this isn't an option, think about calling a more senior person you know for a talk.

5. As a mentor, provide others who are having a hard time with your knowledge and assistance. Share with them internet tools and support networks.

6. In your neighborhood, organize a fundraising activity like a cake sale, a fun run, or a talent show. Whatever you decide, enjoy yourself.

Day 208 - Good Riddance; Rest with God!

"Then, because so many people were coming and going that they did not even have a chance to eat, he said to them, Come with me by yourselves to a quiet place and get some rest."
—Mark 6:31, NIV

BELOVED,
Good riddance means to show pleasure at being liberated from a difficult or unpleasant person or situation. *"You're fired - and good riddance!"* (Isa 22:19, MSG). Today, you will learn the gift of farewell as you will tell your old life, old sins, old ways of living, behaving, and being, old toxic relationships, old dead-end situations, sinful life: Good riddance! Past, pain, fear, humiliation, anxiety, depression, mental disorder, disease, poverty, and living in your carnal flesh: Good riddance as you rest and relax with God. In the name of Jesus, repent and confess. Jesus forgives, delivers, and redeems you from everything that had you under lockdown in sin, shame, sickness, sorrow, and struggle. When Jesus releases you, don't return to what or who He rescued from, He whom the Son set free is free indeed. John 5:1–15 tells us Jesus told the paralytic by the Pool of Bethesda, and John 8:3–11) suggests that Jesus told the woman caught in adultery: 'Go and sin nor more!' It would be foolish to return to the thing that broke and hurt you after Jesus has mended you and made you well and whole to live fully. Only a lunatic do the same thing repeatedly and expects new results. *"As a dog returns to its vomit, so a fool repeats his foolishness?"* (Pro 26:11). This same scripture applies to repentance. True repentance occurs when a person is not only cleansed of sin but also ceases to commit it. In 2 Peter 2:20-22, the apostle Peter alludes to the same adage in Proverbs 26:11. *"If they've escaped from the slum of sin by experiencing our Master and Savior, Jesus Christ, and then slid back into that same old life again, they're worse than if they had never left. Better not to have started out on the straight road to God than to start out and then turn back, repudiating the experience and the holy command. They prove the point of the proverbs, 'A dog goes back to its own vomit' and 'A scrubbed-up pig heads for the mud.'" (MSG).*
Has God violently rescued you from a situation you knew was not the best for you but were not strong enough to leave? Has God redeemed you from a life of sin, slavery, and struggle, but at times you long for the 'floss' and the followers? The Children of Israel cried out to God in the land of their oppression and enslavement at the hands of the Egyptians. The Israelites continued groaning due to their enslavement and called out to be freed from captivity. Their cries for rescue reached God. When God observed the condition that the people of Israel were in, He was compelled to intervene. God collaborated with Moses to bring the Israelites to safety. Yet, in Numbers 11:4-23, the Israelites complained that what they had in Egypt was better. *"The rabble among them [who followed Israel from Egypt] had greedy desires [for familiar and delicious food], and the Israelites wept again and said, 'Who will give us meat to eat? We remember the fish we ate freely and without cost in Egypt, the cucumbers, melons, leeks, onions, and garlic. But now our appetite is gone; there is nothing at all [in the way of food] to be seen but this manna.'"* (Num 11:4-23, AMP). If God rescued you from 'Egypt,' don't long for the good old days of slavery and bondage but trust God during the transition, transformation, wilderness, and preparation seasons as He leads and heals you through the pain of your process into your divine purpose and the promised land.
"The one who remains defiant after repeated reprimands will suddenly be shattered, and there will be no remedy for him." (PROVERBS 29:1, VOICE).

AFFIRMATIONS & DECLARATIONS
"Be still before the Lord and wait patiently for him; fret not yourself over the one who prospers in his way, over the man who carries out evil devices!" (Psalm 37:7, ESV)

- I am redeemed. My God rescues me. The Lord gives me strength and peace. God loves me.
- I am not by myself. My God sees my struggle and will save, sustain, and support me.

PRAYER
Father God, thank You for reminding me through Your Word that You have given me the ability to be brave, strong, confident, control my thoughts, trust You, believe in myself, and move forward. When my thoughts and emotions feel out of control and fearful, I ask that You grant me a clear and peaceful mind, quietness of my heart, and comfort of my soul. I am grateful for all of the good things You have given me in my life and the reckless and redemptive love. Lord, I need You to help me find peace, joy, ability, inner strength, resilience, grit, and comfort in You. You are the beginning and end of everything. Take it, Lord, if it is not of You! As I move forward, Lord, allow me to find the divine strength I need from You and the confidence and courage to head back to the valley to lift and lead Your children to their deliverance. In Jesus' name, I muster up my mustard-sized seed faith and declare good riddance; I rest with God, in Jesus' name, Amen.

MY DOPE *faith journal*

Date S | M | T | W | T | F | S

Morning: I feel my emotion! My one-word check-in: ....

DECLARATION

Consider today's verse. I implore the Holy Spirit to reveal His wisdom and truth to me and I declare it over my life.

OBSERVATION

What does the message mean? Lord, help me see it.

PRAYER

What is my prayer request? Lord, I live fully in You.

EMPOWERMENT

How will Your word empower me? Lord, give me the insight to apply my faith to be more significant than my fears.

MY FEARLESS *journey*

Evening: Feel my emotion! My one-word check-up:

What is making me FEEL like this?

What lessons did I LEARNED?

What THOUGHTS did I had?

What prompted my GRATITUDE?

Who did I CONNECTED with?

What brought me JOY?

EVENING PRAYER

WATER:

FRUIT & VEG:

MY MOOD:

My treat for today is: ....

Let go of the things that are stifling your progress. Reflect on your life and release everything keeping you from resting in Christ, walking away from things that aren't good enough for you, which steal your energy, light, love, health, and soul. God will not withhold marvelous things from you. 'Good riddance-you're fired!'

Affirm it: I deserve wellness, happiness, inner strength, and peace of mind.

Day 209 - Let's Pray

"In the same way, prayer is essential in this ongoing warfare. Pray hard and long. Pray for your brothers and sisters. Keep your eyes open. Keep each other's spirits up so that no one falls behind or drops out."
—Ephesians 6:18 MSG

BELOVED,
Come on, let's pray! Have you prayed about it as much as you have worried and whined about it? God said you have not because you asked not. When you ask, ask with the right motive, not selfish desires but being kingdom-minded, God's will, His righteousness, seeking His kingdom first. Most of the time, you can change the course of your life with something as simple as a prayer! You would be surprised what one prayer can do. When you stop worrying and decide to worship. When you stop panicking and choose to praise. When you stop grumbling and disobeying Him, confess, repent, cast all cares and concerns unto Him, and seek His forgiveness, mercy, grace, and compassion. When you stop cussing and decide to release all cares and worries upon God. When you stop venting and decide to prophesy the word of God, what He says about you, think of you, identify you, and name you, in store for you, planned, promised, and purposed for you. When you take your hands off the steering wheels, let go, let God handle the journey, and take complete control.
Stop talking about your problems, and start praying for the promises of God! Let's pray His word.
Let's cry out to God in tears with a broken spirit and a contrite heart. God will not despise your sacrifices. The sacrifice of God's desire is a broken spirit. O Lord, You will not reject a broken and repentant heart. He hears your prayer for life, living, livelihood, family, career, relationships, household, future, spiritual growth, wisdom, leadership, and personal development. He responds with transformation for an excellent quality of life, long life, wholeness, wellness, peace, joy, provision, protection, health, and righteousness. Let's pray fervently and earnestly, for the prayer of a righteous man is powerful and effective. (James 5:16).

AFFIRMATIONS & DECLARATIONS

1. *"Hear my prayer, O Lord, and attend to my needs, this humble prayer for I am oppressed and weak, in which I express my pain and grievances to my Eternal and Sovereign God, my Heavenly Father. Hear my prayer, O Lord, and let my cry for help come to You! Hear my prayer, O Lord, and let my cry come unto thee. Hear me, O Eternal One, hear my prayer! Hear my lonely, desperate cry for help. Do not hide from me when my days are filled with anguish; Lend Your ear to my wailing, and answer me quickly when I call."* **(Psalm 102:1-4, VOICE)**
2. *"Hear my prayer, O LORD! Lord, listen to all my tender cries. Read my every tear, like liquid words that plead for your help. I feel all alone at times, like a stranger to you, passing through this life just like all those before me."* **(Psalm 39:12, TPT)**
3. *"Hear my prayer, O Lord, give ear to my supplications: in thy faithfulness answer me and in thy righteousness. Lord, you must hear my prayer, for you are faithful to your promises. Answer my cry, O righteous God! Eternal One, I come to You in prayer. Hear me out; I plead with You. Lend an ear to my requests. In Your faithfulness and justice, respond to my pleas."* **(Psalm 143:1, VOICE)**

- I am surrendering everything to God, who strengthens me. I am praying to God, who hears me.
- I am helped; God is helping me. I am prayed and prepared—my prayers performed by Jesus Christ.

James 5:16, AMPC: *Confess to one another, therefore, your faults (your slips, your false steps, your offenses, your sins) and pray [also] for one another, that you may be healed and restored [to a spiritual tone of mind and heart]. The earnest (heartfelt, continued) prayer of a righteous man makes tremendous power available [dynamic in its working].*

PRAYER
Father God, I thank You, Lord, for Your tremendous wisdom. I know little, yet I am thankful to serve the All-knowing God. My heart has been crushed due to my immoral impulses, selfish agenda, mistakes, or circumstances beyond my control. I have tried hiding my humiliation, fear, depression, anxiety, worry, anger, feelings of failure and the future, and negative emotions from You. Would You please pardon me for how I have previously acted, thought, doubted, self-condemned, or slandered others? My broken heart has broken my faith in You, but I can no longer sustain myself. I need Your divine intervention, wisdom, love, presence, and hope. I appreciate Your understanding of my life, mind, soul, heart, and life choices better than I do. God, in Your good pleasure, cause me to prosper, build up, revive, bless my broken heart, renew my peace of mind, joy, inner strength, and comfort my soul. LORD, You are near the brokenhearted; You save the contrite in spirit. Lord heal me as I am brokenhearted, sick, hurting, afraid, and bind up my wounds. For Jesus, when You enter the scene, miracles happen! I return to You in prayer, repentance, thanksgiving, and petition. I bring my concerns and confessions and return to You, LORD.
Take away all my iniquity and receive me graciously, that I may present the fruit of my lips. (Hosea 14:2). I thank You for Your rescuing grace in the person of Your Son, Jesus Christ. I thank You for using the Holy Spirit to revive my dead heart and giving me the strength to persevere when I am tempted to give up. Renew my thoughts and provide me with confidence in You. In Jesus' mighty name, I pray. Amen.

MY DOPE *faith journal*

Date S | M | T | W | T | F | S

Morning: I feel my emotion! My one-word check-in: ....

DECLARATION

Consider today's verse. I implore the Holy Spirit to reveal His wisdom and truth to me and I declare it over my life.

OBSERVATION

What does the message mean? Lord, help me see it.

PRAYER

What is my prayer request? Lord, I live fully in You.

EMPOWERMENT

How will Your word empower me? Lord, give me the insight to apply my faith to be more significant than my fears.

MY FEARLESS *journey*

Evening: Feel my emotion! My one-word check-up:

What is making me FEEL like this?

What lessons did I LEARNED?

What THOUGHTS did I had?

What prompted my GRATITUDE?

Who did I CONNECTED with?

What brought me JOY?

EVENING PRAYER

WATER:

FRUIT & VEG:

MY MOOD:

My treat for today is: ....

Giving to Others

WEEK OF KINDNESS

Choose an act of kindness to perform on each day of the week. In the table, note what you did and how it made you feel. You pray and physically help, be the hands and feet of Jesus this week.

	WHAT YOU DID	HOW IT MADE YOU FEEL
MONDAY		
TUESDAY		
WEDNESDAY		
THURSDAY		
FRIDAY		
SATURDAY		
SUNDAY		

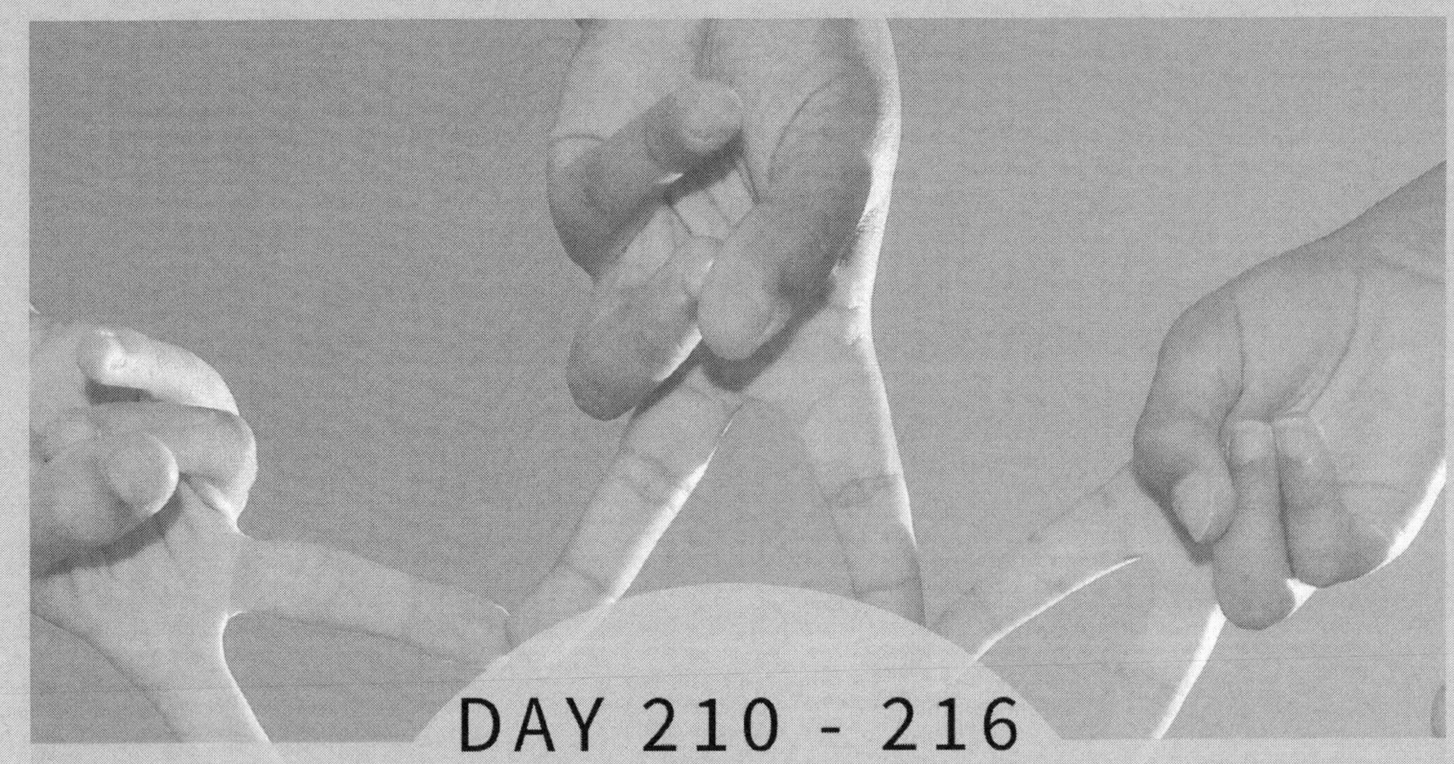

DAY 210 - 216

Connect With Others

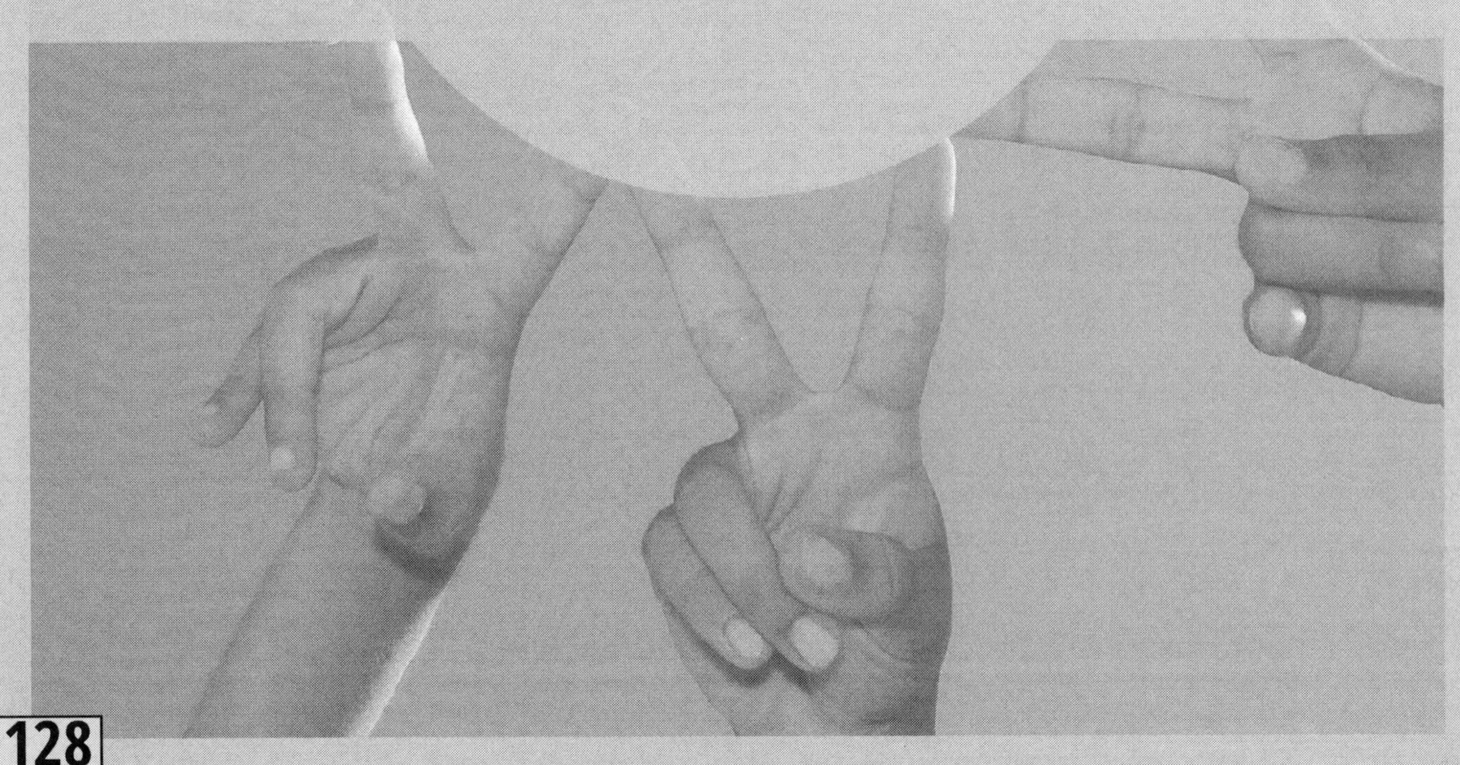

“

They worshiped together at the Temple each day, met in homes for the Lord’s Supper, and shared their meals with great joy and generosity—all the while praising God and enjoying the goodwill of all the people. And each day the Lord added to their fellowship those who were being saved.

— ACTS 2:46-47, NLT

Day 210 - I Choose Joy

"Consider it pure joy, my brothers and sisters, whenever you face trials of many kinds, because you know that the testing of your faith produces perseverance."
—James 1:2-3, NIV

BELOVED,
With all the happenings around globally and personally increased joblessness, financial troubles, recession, depression, anxiety, mental disorders, sickness, failing relationships, family crisis, divorce, untimely death of loved ones, and many devastating situations, happiness is fleeting, BUT JOY is internal! "We cannot cure the world of sorrows, but we can choose to live in joy." —Joseph Campbell.

Did you realize there's a distinction between joy and happiness.?

Happiness – 'the motivating condition or characteristic of happiness, vents or experiences in your life might externally drive happiness. It is an evaluation of how you feel about your life. It includes pleasure, contentment, satisfaction, cheerfulness, gladness, delight, good spirits, enjoyment, self-love, and well-being as assessed over time.'

Joy is an inspired and inner feeling of great pleasure that creates contentment, delight, strength, and peace. *"The joy of the Lord is my strength."* (Nehemiah 8:10[b], KJV)

So as a believer, you cultivate joy to boost your happiness. The word of God tells you to rejoice amid hardships and transitions because these events prepare you for greater glory, awe-inspiring victories, and speechless joys. 1 Peter 1:6, NLT, says, "*So be truly glad. There is wonderful joy ahead, even though you must endure many trials for a little while.'*

Happiness is fleeting! Such satisfaction is externally motivated and depends on events and happenings around you! Happiness is influenced by experiences and tracked throughout time.

Joy is an internally generated and inspired sense of immense pleasure, delight, satisfaction, and peace. Joy makes happiness a choice. Joy is now, at any time, no matter what, rejoice; His joy is your strength. Joy is the fullness of life, being present in His presence, mindful of His reckless love, engaged and connected to Christ, hopeful in His arrival for the fullness of joy, abundance, and life forever more. Your joy is not an event but eternal. Your joy is found in a personal relationship and intimacy with the Lord. Your joy brings change-resilience and is not hampered by the conditions of your circumstances but by Your confidence in the compass and compassion of Christ.

AFFIRMATIONS & DECLARATIONS
The only way to show my gratitude and reverence for God is to offer Him the worship that pleases His heart while also expressing my admiration and adoration for Him. Since I have received my rights to an unshakeable kingdom, unspeakably joy, fearless faith, new identity, and limitless love, I am grateful and glorify God with the purest worship and courageous joy that impresses His heart while also expressing the awe and respect that I have for Him. My God is holy, consuming fire in my eyes! (Hebrews 12:28-29).

- I am not hopeless. My hope is in God.
- This trouble is temporary; This too shall pass; My joy is internal and eternal!
- I am built for this. I was created for such a time as this.

"Since we are receiving our rights to an unshakable kingdom we should be extremely thankful and offer God the purest worship that delights his heart as we lay down our lives in absolute surrender, filled with awe. For our, God is a holy, devouring fire!"
—Hebrews 12:28-29, TPT

PRAYER
Father God, Lord, I turn to You for solace when things are rough. When heavy burdens burden me, You raise me with confident joy and give me cause to hope for a better and brighter future. As a consequence of You, my heart is filled with delight, joy, and contentment. Everything that happens, in my opinion, is part of Your plan. While battling my problems, I know You will support and guide me through anything that comes my way. I know that whatever occurs today will find and fill me with Your eternal joy, hope, and peace. Thank You for Your joy and pleasure, which are strength, stability, mindset, vision, and safety. Thank You for Jesus and the shelter and serenity You provide to me as I place my confidence in You as my Rock of Salvation. I pray that as You send me out from here, I will have a joyful expectation of what You will do in me and that You will be near me in my journey and walks of life. Thank You for the delight in Your presence because You alone are my constant hope, and the fullness of joy that will endure forever is found in Your right hand! Lord, may Your joy, love, wisdom, hope, and peace fill my heart, knowing that the joy of the Lord is my strength, health, happiness, and hope. I pray in Jesus' name, Amen!

MY DOPE *faith journal*

Date S | M | T | W | T | F | S

Morning: I feel my emotion! My one-word check-in:

DECLARATION

Consider today's verse. I implore the Holy Spirit to reveal His wisdom and truth to me and I declare it over my life.

OBSERVATION

What does the message mean? Lord, help me see it.

PRAYER

What is my prayer request? Lord, I live fully in You.

EMPOWERMENT

How will Your word empower me? Lord, give me the insight to apply my faith to be more significant than my fears.

MY FEARLESS *journey*

Evening: Feel my emotion! My one-word check-up:

What is making me FEEL like this?

What lessons did I LEARNED?

What THOUGHTS did I had?

What prompted my GRATITUDE?

Who did I CONNECTED with?

What brought me JOY?

EVENING PRAYER

WATER:

FRUIT & VEG:

MY MOOD:

My treat for today is: ....

Some Advice For Making Social Connections

Maintain eye contact

Be yourself

Pay attention and participate.

Schedule quality time together.

Show love and compassion

Ask questions for clarity

Be authentic

Aim for more in-depth discussions.

Provide help

Listen carefully

Smile

Be honest

Day 211 - It Is Your Season & Time!

"Let us not become weary in doing good, for at the proper time we will reap a harvest if we do not give up."
—Galatians 6:9, NIV

BELOVED,
It may appear hopeless if you're nearing the ending or conclusion of anything, but God tells you that the old must die for the new to be born. Stop thinking of the darkness only as a tomb, a place of death, and instead think of it as a womb, a place of birth and transformation. Although the change process may be interpreted in various ways, one of the most common is that it can be misunderstood as painful, fearful, hopeless, and the end. On the other hand, God can transform what appears to be death into a new life and lack into limitlessness. You can count on God's favor, grace, and goodness when things get tough. Because of God's power, even the worst circumstances may be used to your advantage and benefit.
Your season and time for the turnaround have finally arrived! Every one of us has had to face or cope with the various seasons in our life at some point. Regardless of your age: whether you are young or elderly, you have all had to meet or deal with certain obstacles and transitions in your life. Regardless of your marital status: if you're single, waiting, taken, complicated, married, widowed, or divorced, you've had to confront or cope with changing seasons or challenging times. These situations allow you to encounter His abundant blessings in your life. You experienced God's divine intervention in your past seasons to rescue, sanctify, and fill you with the Holy Spirit's joy, peace, grace, love, and strength. It makes no difference to your nationality, demographic factors, whether rich or poor, educated or uneducated; you had to face or cope with various seasons in your life. The point is that you faced and overcame inevitable storms and seasons in your life. You go through transitions in life, but God promised to be with you, get you through it, and reward you with His love. You may be experiencing or adapting to a specific season in your life right now. Rest assured, you are coming out. It is your season and time to be blessed. God's word in Ecclesiastes 3:1-22 says that for everything, there is a season and a time for every matter under heaven; for 'time and chance happen to them all.' (Ecclesiastes 9:11).

AFFIRMATIONS & DECLARATIONS
But I trust in You, O LORD; I declare, "You are my God. My time, season, future, and this day are in your hands; deliver me from the hands of my enemies, from those who pursue me."
I declare that God changes the times and seasons; He removes kings and establishes them. He gives wisdom to the wise and knowledge to the discerning. He is changing my situation, story, and season.

- I am ready to flourish.
- I am prepared for abundance.
- I am positioned for greatness. I believe in myself and God.

"He sets in motion the times and the ages; He deposes kings and installs others; He gives wisdom to the wise and grants knowledge to those with understanding."
—Daniel 2:21, VOICE

PRAYER
Father God, please enable me to trust You and Your timing. I tend to become irritated, worried, anxious, sight-sighted, doubtful, impatient, and take issues into my own hands. Please, Holy Spirit, alter this element of my heart, mind, life, choices, behavior, and personality. Lord, teach me to trust and believe in Your perfect timing, excellent and perfect gifts, and perfect will. I pray for patience, appreciation, and recognition that Your methods, missions, and mandates are more impressive than mine. I'm not always a patient person spoiled by the fast-food, microwave prep, and instant download mentality of this culture. Would You please help me become more personally developed and spiritually matured in this area and remember that I am a citizen of heaven? Thank You for being the living hope in my hopelessness, patience with my impatience, compass, and compassion along my life's journey, and serenity, shelter, strength, and safe place as I face my situations and storms. Would You please assist me in having faith because You are faithful? Give me the confidence and courage to trust Your word, ways fearlessly, will, and time.
In the name of Jesus, I declare change, speak life, and announce this a new season, a new attitude, a new beginning, new worship, a new outlook, a new wine skin and fresh fine, and a fresh anointing for a new day. In the name of Jesus, I declare that God accomplishes all His plans and promises for me from this day forward; my breakthrough shall be major. My season of mediocrity, barely scraping by, limitation, need, bitterness, sickness, darkness, wilderness, brokenness, cashlessness, helplessness, hopelessness, and loneliness is ended. God is rewriting my narrative. It's the start of a new beginning; I am restored; this is my time and season! I pray in Jesus' name, Amen!

MY DOPE *faith journal*

Date S | M | T | W | T | F | S

Morning: I feel my emotion! My one-word check-in: ____________________

DECLARATION

Consider today's verse. I implore the Holy Spirit to reveal His wisdom and truth to me and I declare it over my life.

OBSERVATION

What does the message mean? Lord, help me see it.

PRAYER

What is my prayer request? Lord, I live fully in You.

EMPOWERMENT

How will Your word empower me? Lord, give me the insight to apply my faith to be more significant than my fears.

MY FEARLESS *journey*

Evening: Feel my emotion! My one-word check-up:

What is making me FEEL like this?

What lessons did I LEARNED?

What THOUGHTS did I had?

What prompted my GRATITUDE?

Who did I CONNECTED with?

What brought me JOY?

EVENING PRAYER

WATER:

FRUIT & VEG:

MY MOOD:

My treat for today is: ....

Conversation Prompts

What I realized was...

I learned that ...

I'd want to emphasize...

This makes me consider...

This reminds me of ...

Could you please show me?

This makes me think of...

Could you elaborate on what you mean?

I'm astonished by...

This brings to mind something else...

I agree with you because ...

I noticed that ...

Day 212 - God Says, "I AM..."

"God said to Moses, "I am who I am. This is what you are to say to the Israelites: 'I am has sent me to you.'"
—Exodus 3:7-14, NIV

BELOVED,
Today as you travel along what seems like a dark, unfamiliar life path, can you hear His soft, still voice in the clutter of your worries, fear, anxiety, busyness, chaos, confusion, and frustration? Have you cast your cares and concerns unto Him? Have you sought Him, His wisdom, and His strength? In Exodus 3:7-14, there was divine intervention, and The Lord said to Moses, "I've witnessed my people's suffering in Egypt. I've heard them sobbing because of their enslavers, and I care about them. I've come to rescue them from the Egyptians and deliver them to a pleasant, spacious place with milk and honey... "Moses said to God, "Suppose I go to the Israelites and say to them, 'The God of your fathers has sent me to you,' and they ask me, 'What is his name?' Then what shall I tell them?" God says, "I am who I am."

The Father says I know your current situation and condition but do you know who I AM?
"Who am I to you? I AM, The GREAT I AM! I am your Joy and Strength! I am your Peace!
No one comes to the Father except through Me. Jesus says I am the Way, Way-Maker, Revelation, Resurrection, Truth, Source, Light, Strength, Vine, Door, and the positive energy, provision, protector, and the miraculous healing power of your life. If you remain connected to me, abide in Me and I in you, you will bear great fruit. I am more than able to help, heal, bless, keep, sustain, deliver, provide, protect, restore, comfort, redeem, and rebuild you! Whatever you need, ask, request, dream, desire, imagine, think according to my word. I can, and I will do it! God says, "I AM...."
And I am here with you, and You are mine! It has been accomplished, conquest completed, and victory abounding! I am Alpha and Omega, the beginning and the ending. I will give water to all who are thirsty. As my gracious gift, they will continuously drink from the fountain of living water. "

AFFIRMATIONS & DECLARATIONS
I thus announce that because I trusted in Jesus, God has now found me acceptable in His sight, and I have been redeemed, granted with salvation, peace, joy, love, wellness, and prosperity.

- I am the King of King's child.
- I am remarkably made. I am redeemed. I am fearless. I am held in the arms of God.
- Christ is my strength, and I am filled with joy.

"Our faith in Jesus transfers God's righteousness to us, and he now declares us flawless in his eyes." This means we can now enjoy true and lasting peace with God because of what our Lord Jesus, the Anointed One, has done for us.
—Romans 5:1, TPT

PRAYER
Father God, Lord, help me discover faith, love, hope, and patience amid morning's confusion, anxiety, irritation, oppression, opposition, and turbulence.
Give me the desire, determination, and discipline to experience Your presence, see You, hear You, praise You, communicate with You, and worship You. And when I do, I beg you to grant me an encounter, draw me deeper, give me a more profound experience, meet me in the valley, close every gap between where I am and where I ought to be with You in my life, my calling, purpose, and vision. "Because Jesus died for my sins, I am no longer separated from God. I live in close union with him." (Romans 5:10). Would you please equip and empower me so my hope, faith, love, peace, health, wealth, wellness, wholeness, and joy improve considerably? Would you please reveal the revelations, prophetic insights, wisdom, and more profound ways of who You are? Would you give me an even better than my most excellent understanding of what I thought I am in You, would be, and what I mean to you? Please give me the confidence to know that You're the GREAT I AM!
Lord, I'm sure the devil wants to hinder, distract, and keep me trapped, fearful, anxious, worried, and too busy to spend time with you. Could You please help me live like your beloved child of royalty, legacy, significance, elegance, and excellence? As heir of Your Kingdom, your precious child, and co-heir with Christ, help me to believe, abide, adore, and connect in You rather than struggle and stress so that I might live calmly, righteously, abundantly, and joyously. In the name of Jesus, I pray, Amen.

MY DOPE *faith journal*

Date S | M | T | W | T | F | S

Morning: I feel my emotion! My one-word check-in: ____________

DECLARATION

Consider today's verse. I implore the Holy Spirit to reveal His wisdom and truth to me and I declare it over my life.

OBSERVATION

What does the message mean? Lord, help me see it.

PRAYER

What is my prayer request? Lord, I live fully in You.

EMPOWERMENT

How will Your word empower me? Lord, give me the insight to apply my faith to be more significant than my fears.

MY FEARLESS *journey*

Evening: Feel my emotion! My one-word check-up:

What is making me FEEL like this?

What lessons did I LEARNED?

What THOUGHTS did I had?

What prompted my GRATITUDE?

Who did I CONNECTED with?

What brought me JOY?

EVENING PRAYER

WATER:

FRUIT & VEG:

MY MOOD:

My treat for today is: ....

THIS WEEK'S TASK

Making A Social Connection

Focus on creating one new social connection each day. Mention the social connection you formed and how it made you feel in writing.

	WHAT YOU DID	HOW IT MADE YOU FEEL
MONDAY		
TUESDAY		
WEDNESDAY		
THURSDAY		
FRIDAY		
SATURDAY		
SUNDAY		

Day 213 - Proper Correction, A Bridge To Growth!

"For the moment all discipline seems painful rather than pleasant, but later it yields the peaceful fruit of righteousness to those who have been trained by it."
—Hebrews 12:11, ESV

BELOVED,
You grow and continuously improve with corrective feedback, self-awareness, self-reflection, self-assessment, self-accountability, and self-education for continuous self-improvement and lifelong learning. Several methods are available for personal growth and leadership development — SWOT analysis and 360-degree evaluations are practical personal mastery tools for learning how to request, receive and provide constructive criticism. A SWOT analysis is a planning technique that helps you identify your strengths, weaknesses, opportunities, and threats to overcome obstacles and identify opportunities. A 360-degree review is a procedure in which you solicit and receive feedback on your performance, abilities, attitude, and contributions from peers, colleagues, friends, and family. The 360-degree feedback mechanism gathers input on your performance from all corners of the community, allowing you to uncover your blind spots for improvement. God has 360-degree awareness of you, yet His love is still limitless. He knows your strengths, weaknesses, opportunities, and threats, He knows the greatness within you, and the challenges you are facing are tactics, tools, tutors, and teachers that He is singing to provide proper correction as a bridge to grow, cross over, and become whom He created you to be. The Lord disciplines those whom He loves. God never condemns, but God convicts you of your sins, evil thoughts, and wrong-doings. He loves us too much to see us settle for mediocrity or ordinary life. Proverbs 3:12 says,*" For the LORD corrects those he loves, just as a father corrects a child in whom he delights."* (NLT). Your development and growth cost you something, hefty tuition, don't miss the lessons, don't skip class, grow through the storm, and realize it is not punishment but preparation. Hebrews 12:6 says,

- *"For the Lord's training of your life is the evidence of his faithful love. And when he draws you to himself, it proves you are his delightful child."* (TPT).
- *"For the LORD disciplines those he loves, and He punishes each one he accepts as his child."* (NLT).

AFFIRMATIONS & DECLARATIONS
My Father says**,** Remember that I made you develop, evolve, transform, and become greater. You constantly think there must be more; believe me, there is."*...And I know that same faith continues strong in you. This is why I remind you to fan into flames the spiritual gift God gave you when I laid my hands on you. For God has not given us a spirit of fear and timidity, but of power, love, and self-discipline."* (2 Tim 1:5-7 NLT). What would you d,o, and whom would you be if you were not afraid, angry, anxious, and walked by faith rather than feelings? I lovely correct you. Whoever spares the rod and spoils the child dislikes their children; whoever loves them disciplines them. (Prov 13:24). *"Whoever loves discipline loves knowledge, but he who hates reproof is stupid."* (Prov 12:1, ESV).

- I cheerfully receive my correction as a bridge to growth. I consider it joy through it all. God has taught me how to live a disciplined and successful life through His guidance. Through the Holy Spirit, I have power, love, and self-discipline.
- God protects me, and I am not afraid of corrections, challenges, struggles, or problems. Because God loves me, I can walk with confidence today.

Proverbs 12:1, ESV: *"Whoever loves discipline loves knowledge, but he who hates reproof is stupid."*

PRAYER
Heavenly Father, Lord, I thank You for working in me and providing me with the desire, discipline, and resolve to accomplish what You want in and for me. Thank You from the bottom of my heart for the wisdom, instruction, knowledge, and understanding that Your word has challenged and transformed. You're the Potter, and I'm the clay in Your hands. Could You kindly shape me in the way You see fit? You discipline me, Lord, because You love me. Would You please assist me in breaking the cycle of sin, mediocrity, toxicity, complacency, defiance, and disobedience and choosing to be a disciplined, well-learned child, servant, and disciple? Thank You for never condemning me but rather convicting and correcting me. I praise and worship Your Name for Your unfailing and unconditional love, compassion, faithfulness, wisdom, and limitless promotion because Your Name backs up all of Your promises. You respond to my prayers immediately and offer me hope, joy, serenity, wholeness, and a wealthy future. Thank You for granting me power and confidence, inspiring and elevating me to greatness. I am becoming and living my purpose because You are preparing, promoting, and placing me in a noble position by Your grace and glory. I pray in Jesus' name. Amen.

MY DOPE *faith journal*

Date S | M | T | W | T | F | S

Morning: I feel my emotion! My one-word check-in: ______

DECLARATION

Consider today's verse. I implore the Holy Spirit to reveal His wisdom and truth to me and I declare it over my life.

OBSERVATION

What does the message mean? Lord, help me see it.

PRAYER

What is my prayer request? Lord, I live fully in You.

EMPOWERMENT

How will Your word empower me? Lord, give me the insight to apply my faith to be more significant than my fears.

MY FEARLESS *journey*

Evening: Feel my emotion! My one-word check-up:

What is making me FEEL like this?

What lessons did I LEARNED?

What THOUGHTS did I had?

What prompted my GRATITUDE?

Who did I CONNECTED with?

What brought me JOY?

EVENING PRAYER

WATER:

FRUIT & VEG:

MY MOOD:

My treat for today is: ....

SWOT *analysis*

You can manage your weaknesses, take advantage of your chances, and deal with any threats using a personal SWOT analysis. "Search me, O God, and know my heart: try me, and know my thoughts." (Psalm 139:23, KJV).

STRENGTHS

What are you good at? What features about myself do you like? What praise do other people give you?

WEAKNESSES

What would you change? What do you keep out of? What flaws do people perceive in you? What could you improve upon?

OPPORTUNITIES

What opportunities are there for you? What trends are there that you might take advantage of? Is there anything going on in your area?

THREATS

What dangers may you face? What difficulties or hurdles do you face? What are the tendencies that are working against you?

Day 214 - God Has Ordered Your Restoration!

"For I will restore health unto thee, and I will heal thee of thy wounds, saith the Lord; because they called thee an Outcast, saying, This is Zion, whom no man seeketh after."
—Jeremiah 30:17, KJV

BELOVED,

Although life has its ups and downs, you don't want to spend your entire existence on earth stuck in a valley or a wilderness. Demonic powers, generational curses causing bad breaks, poverty, disease, ungodly soul ties, and spiritual warfare can all hinder your breakthrough and deliverance. Let's petition the throne of grace today for your health, wellness, wholeness, and financial breakthrough, a supernatural restoration that only God Almighty, Himself can give. Lord, You said in Your Word that we have not because we asked not. You are imploring You for health, healing, and financial success even if it takes a miracle, gaining access to open windows and portals of heaven for You to pour out such blessing that there will not be enough room to receive.

The Father says, "You can hold Me accountable to My Word. Today, I remind you that I am Your God, I am aware of My accountability and responsibility as your Faithful Provider and Loving Protector and your entitlement as My child, and it warrants the expectations of My performance in alignment with My Will, Word, and Ways. I am Your Father God; there is no fatherlessness in My kingdom, only limitless. I am not a man, so I do not lie. I am your God, who forgives all your iniquities, binds up your wounds and broken heart, and heals all your diseases, defeats, and disorders. There is undoubtedly a future hope for you, and your children and confidence will not be cut off. I, God, will reward you for this; your hope will not be disappointed. You know that I, God am faithful to keep My covenant and loving-kindness to those who love Me and keep My commandments. If you are reading this, this is My confirmation for your health, wellness, and financial success before this month ends in Jesus' name."

AFFIRMATIONS & DECLARATIONS

Lord, my humiliation will be replaced by a twofold share, and my embarrassment will be replaced by eternal joy at my significant favor and fortune. My inheritance in my land doubles for all my troubles, and I shall have double pleasure. (Isaiah 61:7). Lord, I pray for my friends and family, I release every offense, and just as you turned Job's captivity around when he prayed for his friends, so shall you turnaround my situation and restore unto me double for my trouble just as you gave Job twice as much as he had before all his misfortune. (Job 42:10).

- In Christ, I find myself.
- God uniquely created me, and He will restore me.
- I've been healed and restored to my original creation, my former self.
- I am made in the image and likeness of my God.
- I am blessed with God's favor and understanding.

"And after you have suffered a little while, the God of all grace, who has called you to his eternal glory in Christ, will himself restore, confirm, strengthen, and establish you."
—1 Peter 5:10, ESV

PRAYER

Father God, Thank You, Lord, for everyday life, living, livelihood, righteousness, wisdom, and the blessings You've bestowed upon me. Abba Father, I beg Your pardon and pray that You will restore to me the years that the locusts devoured, my health and wellness, my finances, freedom, joy, peace, love, laughter, family, career, business, and the years that I stupidly squandered by Your mercy and grace. I am delighted You have ordered my restoration, and today I take it back by force. For eternity's sake, I begin to live my life as You would like me to live it now and forever. I am restored and its manifestation time. I will also praise You with the harp for Your faithfulness, O my God; I will sing praises to You with the lyre, O Holy One of Israel.

Thank You, Lord, for issuing a command that has been published to bless me, restore me, rebuild me, reclaim me, rebound me to prosperity, health, wellness, righteousness, peace, joy, love, influence, affluence, worship. And so shall it be, as spoken and written this day, in Jesus' mighty name! In Jesus' name, I pray, praise, and proclaim these prophetic utterances, AMEN!

MY DOPE *faith journal*

Date S | M | T | W | T | F | S

Morning: I feel my emotion! My one-word check-in: ……………………

DECLARATION

Consider today's verse. I implore the Holy Spirit to reveal His wisdom and truth to me and I declare it over my life.

OBSERVATION

What does the message mean? Lord, help me see it.

PRAYER

What is my prayer request? Lord, I live fully in You.

EMPOWERMENT

How will Your word empower me? Lord, give me the insight to apply my faith to be more significant than my fears.

MY FEARLESS *journey*

Evening: Feel my emotion! My one-word check-up:

What is making me FEEL like this?

What lessons did I LEARNED?

What THOUGHTS did I had?

What prompted my GRATITUDE?

Who did I CONNECTED with?

What brought me JOY?

EVENING PRAYER

WATER:

FRUIT & VEG:

MY MOOD:

My treat for today is:...

365 Journal

Day 215 - I am Waiting, Not Wailing!

"Yet the Lord longs to be gracious to you; therefore he will rise up to show you compassion. For the Lord is a God of justice. Blessed are all who wait for him!"
—Isaiah 30:18, NIV

BELOVED,
God asked you to wait, not to wail, whine and worry. Waiting is hard work, especially when God asks you to do it. Often, it is filled with worry, anxiety, distress, bitterness, and anger, so much so that we, with our limited knowledge, decide to help out the Only Wise God. God expects us to wait actively, to worship, and not worry while we wait. Faith without work is dead. He wants to rest in Him as He works on our behalf. The waiting season is crucial to our spiritual growth, character transformation, change readiness, and purpose-fitness. God uses WAIT to train your rebound faith muscles, build grit, and change resilience. You must wait patiently on God to see how the matter will turn out. Waiting is actively trusting a trustworthy God. You will not grow weary nor faint.
The Father says, "Wait, my child, until you learn how the matter turns out…."
In the book Rebound Faith: Chayah, the author explained her significant losses during her 5-family court battle, she cried out to God during the waiting season, and God, the King of the Universe, gave her word of promise and encouragement in 2 Kings 8:6 of the Shunammite Woman's restoration. *"The king asked the woman about it, and she told him. Then he assigned an official to her case and said to him, 'Give back everything that belonged to her, including all the income from her land from the day she left the country until now.'"*(NIV). God wastes nothing, no pain, tears, or waiting season; He promised and orders restoration despite the pain of the process; God shall steal your show and showcase you as a dazzling display of His glory, splendor, magnificence, and majesty. Noami coached Ruth, saying, *"Wait, my daughter, until you learn how the matter turns out, for the man will not rest but will settle the matter today."* (Ruth 3:18, ESV). God has placed divine authority and anointed an official in charge of your case, and they will not rest until they restore and favor you. All you have to do now is wait!

AFFIRMATIONS & DECLARATIONS
Here are 12 things God is saying to you during the wait.

- God says I promise to renew your strength, mindset, vision, and faith when you wait upon Me.
- God says I will guide and direct you as you wait patiently and actively on Me.
- God says, trust me. Allow me to clear the path and make the way straight for you.
- God says there is a time for everything and a season for every activity under the heavens.
- God says I have you wait, so you, neighbors, friends, families, co-workers, church people, pastors, and enemies will know that I did it!
- God says this wait is to hone your faith to trust Me completely.
- God says, wait actively, not anxiously!
- God says, during this wait, let this hope burst forth within you, releasing a continual joy.
- God says, I am teaching, training, and developing you to wait in confidence during this wait.
- God says the wait is not because I am delayed.
- God says what seems like a delay is not denial. I said wait, no need to wail.
- God says, I wish to be generous to you, and so I wait on high for Him compassion on me; for me, the Lord is a God of justice; how happy are those who seek, trust, and wait on and in Him.

I don't mind waiting on God; I am waiting for God joyfully, prayerfully, and thankfully, not wailing.

PRAYER
God, the Father, Thank You for enabling Your steadfast Word to take root in my heart and anchor my mind, thoughts, self-talk, and deeds. Thank You, Father, for always being with me, especially during my waiting season. I am convinced you have something great in store for me because of Your past performance, conduct, and character, and You are the same unchanging God. Your promises to me, Your child, are numerous, precious, perfect, and priceless, and I desire to stand, kneel, rest, and be comforted by my faith in them. I choose to connect with you and abide in You every step of the way, day by day, precept by precept, moment by moment, throughout my life's journey.
In Jesus' name and by your grace, my reward for my waiting, my testimony, transformation, restoration, healing miracles, financial breakthrough, deliverance, and exceptional benefits will bring the ultimate glory of Your holy name, Christ Jesus. Amen.

MY DOPE *faith journal*

Date S | M | T | W | T | F | S

Morning: I feel my emotion! My one-word check-in: ____________________

DECLARATION

Consider today's verse. I implore the Holy Spirit to reveal His wisdom and truth to me and I declare it over my life.

OBSERVATION

What does the message mean? Lord, help me see it.

PRAYER

What is my prayer request? Lord, I live fully in You.

EMPOWERMENT

How will Your word empower me? Lord, give me the insight to apply my faith to be more significant than my fears.

MY FEARLESS *journey*

Evening: Feel my emotion! My one-word check-up:

What is making me FEEL like this?

What lessons did I LEARNED?

What THOUGHTS did I had?

What prompted my GRATITUDE?

Who did I CONNECTED with?

What brought me JOY?

EVENING PRAYER

WATER:

FRUIT & VEG:

MY MOOD:

My treat for today is: ....

Tips For Making Social Connections

Maintain eye contact

Listen carefully

Pay attention

Schedule quality time together

Show love and compassion

Ask questions for clarity

Be honest

Aim for deeper level conversations

Provide help

Be yourself

Smile

Be authentic

Day 216 - I sought Him & He Sustained Me!

"And my God will supply every need of yours according to his riches in glory in Christ Jesus."
—Philippians 4:19, ESV

BELOVED,
Are you in a tight spot? Do you ever find yourself in a precarious position? Do you think you've had enough of bad news, bad break-ups, *bad mind,* bad company, and bad breaks in your life, even after a seeming victory? Do you ever feel like you're continuously fleeing from danger, opponents, adversity, assaults, and attacks even from those in your inner circle, family, and friends? Are you seeking God to sustain and shelter you?
In 1 Samuel 21:10-15, David ran from Saul to the enemy's camp and pretended to be insane as an escape plan. David fled Saul the same day and went to Achish, Saul's enemy. The king's servants asked, 'Isn't this David, whom they cheered said he rules the land. They sang and danced about him, right? Saul and David both killed thousands.' When David heard what others were saying about him, he feared what Achish, king of Gath, might do, so he changed his behavior to act silly and appear mad. He scratched the city gates with his nails and drooled into his beard. Achish said, 'See? Can't you tell he's nuts? Why is he in my house? Did you think I didn't have enough insane people?'
In Psalm 34, God protected David while he feigned to be mad to flee from Abimelech. David praised God for providing for him, sustaining him, and getting him out of a tight spot: *"God met me more than halfway; He freed me from my anxious fears. Look at Him; give Him your warmest smile. Never hide your feelings from Him. When I was desperate, I called out, and God got me out of a tight spot. God's angel sets up a circle of protection around us while we pray."* (Psa 34:4-7, MSG)
As you seek God in the valley, He shows up as your Shepherd, shifting you from a valley of despair to a valley of hope. He restores your soul, leads you along the path of righteousness, and sustains your shalom (peace of mind, tranquility, well-being, health, and prosperity), joy, protection, provision, strength, and hope. He gives you all you need to be whole, well, and complete, breaking free from any force that would try to keep you captive, chaotic, and confused.
— God is sustaining and strengthening you: Shepherd, Strength, Shield, Shalom, and Shelter
— God is supplying you with all your provision and protection needs from His wealth and wisdom,
— God is restoring your joy as you rejoice and trust in Him!

AFFIRMATIONS & DECLARATIONS
"I sought the Lord [on the authority of His word], and He answered me, And delivered me from all my fears. They looked to Him and were radiant; Their faces will never blush in shame or confusion. This poor man cried, and the Lord heard him And saved him from all his troubles. The angel of the Lord encamps around those who fear Him [with awe-inspired reverence and worship Him with obedience], And He rescues [each of] them." (Psalm 34:4-7, AMP).

- God is protecting me. The name of Jesus saves me, and His blood covers me.
- My God lovingly protects and faithfully sustains me. God loves me limitlessly.
- In my weakness, God's power shines the brightest in me, for me, and through me.
- I was saved by grace, not by works so that I might do good deeds.

"O taste and see that the Lord [our God] is good; How blessed [fortunate, prosperous, and favored by God] is the man who takes refuge in Him. O [reverently] fear the Lord, you, His saints (believers, holy ones); For to those who fear Him, there is no want. The young lions lack [food] and grow hungry, But they who seek the Lord will NOT require any GOOD thing."
— Psalm 34:8-10, AMP

PRAYER
Heavenly Father, Almighty God, King of the Universe. I exalt You above all my fears, troubles, situations, and afflictions and exchange my heavy burdens for the light and easy yoke of Jesus. I stand on Your WORD today for answered prayers, supernatural deliverance, breakthroughs, healing miracles, and blessings. Under your wings, I seek safety, security, shelter, sincerity, and strength.
Thank You, LORD! Indeed, I sought You, and You sustained me! Surely Your goodness and mercy shall follow me, and Your unfailing love will pursue me, all the days of my life, and I shall dwell securely in the house of the Lord forever, in Jesus mighty and matchless name, I pray and praise. AMEN!

MY DOPE *faith journal*

Date S | M | T | W | T | F | S

Morning: I feel my emotion! My one-word check-in: ____________

DECLARATION

Consider today's verse. I implore the Holy Spirit to reveal His wisdom and truth to me and I declare it over my life.

OBSERVATION

What does the message mean? Lord, help me see it.

PRAYER

What is my prayer request? Lord, I live fully in You.

EMPOWERMENT

How will Your word empower me? Lord, give me the insight to apply my faith to be more significant than my fears.

MY FEARLESS *journey*

Evening: Feel my emotion! My one-word check-up:

What is making me FEEL like this?

What lessons did I LEARNED?

What THOUGHTS did I had?

What prompted my GRATITUDE?

Who did I CONNECTED with?

What brought me JOY?

EVENING PRAYER

WATER:

FRUIT & VEG:

MY MOOD:

My treat for today is: ....

365 Journal

DAY 217 - 223

Be Active

“

So since we stand surrounded by all those who have gone before, an enormous cloud of witnesses, let us drop every extra weight, every sin that clings to us and slackens our pace, and let us run with endurance the long race set before us.

— HEBREWS 12:1, VOICE

Day 217 - God's Favor Shall Honor You!

"The LORD will guide you always; he will satisfy your needs in a sun-scorched land and will strengthen your frame. You will be like a well-watered garden, like a spring whose waters never fail."
—Isaiah 58:11, NIV

BELOVED,
They say, "Favor is not fair. God's favor is a force!" The favor of God is undeserved, unmerited, and *free grace*, a powerful force and source of the *dunamis power* of God. Favor is given to you, His child, to achieve supernatural blessings, divine covering, wellness, and elevation of the *whole person*, your mind, body, soul, life, living, and livelihood. *"He did this that He might clearly demonstrate through the ages to come the immeasurable (limitless, surpassing) riches of His free grace (His unmerited favor) in [His] kindness and goodness of heart toward us in Christ Jesus."* (Eph 2:7, AMPC).
God's favor breaks human understanding, protocols, reasonings, hierarchical structures, qualification criteria, global boundaries, geographical borders, age, generation, timezone, family status, bank account, budget, statistics, reports, science, biology, mathematics, and historical trends. God's favor is indeed a divine force or power. It brings unexplained honor not based on titles, degrees, monetary standing, budget, social status, nationality, gender, race, fame, name, and family background but God's free grace. *"For it's by God's grace that you have been saved. You receive it through faith. It was not our plan or our effort. It is God's gift, pure and simple. You didn't earn it; not one of us did, so don't go around bragging that you must have done something amazing."* (Eph 2:8, VOICE). It doesn't matter how long or often you have been overlooked, rejected, denied, wrongfully accused, abused, humiliated, abandoned, or terminated in the name of Jesus; God's favor shall honor you. *"So can't you see? Now is the time to respond to his favor! Now is the day of salvation!"* (2 Cor 6:1-2, TPT). LORD, you bless the righteous; you surround them with your favor as with a shield.
"But let them all be glad, those who turn aside to hide themselves in you. May they keep shouting for joy forever! Overshadow them in your presence as they sing and rejoice. Then every lover of your name will burst forth with endless joy. Lord, how wonderfully you bless the righteous. Your favor wraps around each one and covers them under your canopy of kindness and joy." (Psa 5:12, TPT)

AFFIRMATIONS & DECLARATIONS
I am working for and waiting in My God, and He will bless, favor, and honor me, NOW! Since I am God's child and coworker, I serve, obey, and seek Him and will not take His marvelous grace for granted, allowing His favor to influence, impact and inspire my life. My God has heard to me, at the time of His favor, and the day I needed salvation, He came suddenly and supernaturally to my help.

- I decree that my season of failure and frustration is over. Things are about to change!
- I am walking into a season of favor and honor in Jesus' name.
- God will make me into a great nation.
- I am favored, wise, admirable, anointed, appointed, adored, and attractive.
- God will publicly bless me and make me whole, wise, famous, healthy, and wealthy.
- I am blessed to be a blessing, a channel of benefit to others, a financial pillar, and a steward.

"For it is by free grace (God's unmerited favor) that you are saved (delivered from judgment and made partakers of Christ's salvation) through [your] faith. And this [salvation] is not of yourselves [of your own doing, it came not through your own striving], but it is the gift of God."
—2 Corinthians 6:1-2, TPT

PRAYER
Lord, You are holy and righteous. You are lovely and deserve to be praised greatly. You are worthy, Lord, and Your dominion endures for all generations. You are the All-Powerful God, the only true and living God. You are the supreme ruler of heaven and earth. Forever is Your kingdom, glory, and power. Lord, please show me Your ways, teach me Your paths, and guide me in the truth. Come, Holy Spirit, spiritually empower, motivate and inspire me as I meditate on the Word day and night to gain truth, wisdom, righteousness, favor, prosperity, peace, joy, love, honor, and long life. Teach me humility and the fear of the Lord, for these are the beginnings of wisdom. I beg You to favor and bless my life, children, home, family, career, finances, and relationships. Lord, protect me and set an excellent example for our enemies. Fill my heart with Your joy, Lord, and guide my steps. In Jesus' name, I pray, Amen!

MY DOPE *faith journal*

Date S | M | T | W | T | F | S

Morning: I feel my emotion! My one-word check-in: ....

DECLARATION

Consider today's verse. I implore the Holy Spirit to reveal His wisdom and truth to me and I declare it over my life.

OBSERVATION

What does the message mean? Lord, help me see it.

PRAYER

What is my prayer request? Lord, I live fully in You.

EMPOWERMENT

How will Your word empower me? Lord, give me the insight to apply my faith to be more significant than my fears.

MY FEARLESS *journey*

Evening: Feel my emotion! My one-word check-up:

What is making me FEEL like this?

What lessons did I LEARNED?

What THOUGHTS did I had?

What prompted my GRATITUDE?

Who did I CONNECTED with?

What brought me JOY?

EVENING PRAYER

WATER:

FRUIT & VEG:

MY MOOD:

My treat for today is: ....

How To Walk 10000 Steps

- When you have a few minutes, take a walk around your house.
- Put the clothes away one load at a time.
- While walking, listen to a podcast.
- When you're on the phone, take a walk.
- Place your car as far away from the business as possible.
- Make use of a step counter.
- Between errands, take a walk.
- Include walking in your commute.
- Children should be walked to school.
- Leave your workplace to go for a stroll during your lunch break.
- If you get there early to an event, go for a little stroll.
- Instead of using the elevator, use the steps.
- Invite a walking companion to join you.
- At the supermarket, circle all the aisles.
- Pick a restroom on a different level.
- Take your family for a stroll.
- Watch a box set while jogging on a treadmill.
- Set a one-minute walk reminder for every hour.
- While you're walking, have meetings.
- Get off the bus or train early if you're using it.

Day 218 - You Shall Finish Strong!

"I press on to reach the end of the race and receive the heavenly prize for which God, through Christ Jesus, is calling us."
—Philippians 3:14, NLT

BELOVED,
You are constantly reminded that your tale will end in triumph. What's more, you're perplexed about how and when things will pick up after this apparent impossibility of disaster, whether it's due to anything you did wrong or something that happened through no fault of your own. Why would this catastrophe and defeat in your personal life, health, financial well-being, and professional success positively impact personal connections, family life, plans, or aspirations? But God has planned an inflection point for the rebound, so shatter whatever fears you may have, every humiliation should be broken, break down every barrier, and sever any ties to the past. Bring an end to the generational curses of failure, disease, poverty, and addiction passed down through your bloodline, family, and generations in the name of Jesus. Your story is different; you are a history-changer and chain-breaker. It doesn't matter how it has started or is going right now. "Finishing is better than starting. Patience is better than pride." (Ecclesiastes 7:8, NLT). Declare that you shall finish strong. Think again if you ever doubted God's ability to achieve more than you ever thought possible. Rather than shoving you about, He achieves it through His Spirit's gentle activity within you. As a result of supernatural intervention, you will restart, be energized, and end with a bang! So change the narrative and speak life and victory:
"Lord, you are so good to me, so kind in every way and ready to forgive, for Your grace fountain keeps overflowing, drenching all Your devoted lovers who pray to You. God, won't You pay attention to this urgent cry? Lord, bend down to listen to my prayer. Whenever trouble strikes, I will keep crying out to You, for I know Your help is on the way." (Psalm 86:5-7 TPT).
In the name of Jesus, You Shall Finish Strong! You serve an infinite and limitless God. He gives you the tools and resources to restart and finish strong. He sends tutors, coaches, and mentors to help you along the way, to be His feet and hands. Announce over your life today that you can do all things through Christ who strengthens you, and your finishing shall be better than starting, and you are patient to wait on God.

AFFIRMATIONS & DECLARATIONS
To run the course of life with elegance, you must be determined. "I race straight for the divine invitation of attaining the high goal and obtaining the victory-prize through the anointing of Jesus," Philippians 3:14 reads. You'll finish strong!
Write out the vision, divide it into attainable goals, and stay focused on the goal rather than the process. Change the process while keeping the goal in mind. You will finish strong!

- Today is the first day of my new beginning. I am empowered to start and equipped to endure.
- I eliminate procrastination, self-doubt, fear, impostor syndrome, fixed thinking, and restricted belief.
- I seek God to strengthen my faith and joy. I have the authority to begin.

"I'm not saying that I have this all together, that I have it made. But I am well on my way, reaching out for Christ, who has so wondrously reached out for me. Friends, don't get me wrong: By no means do I count myself an expert in all of this, but I've got my eye on the goal, where God is beckoning us onward—to Jesus. I'm off and running, and I'm not turning back."
—Philippians 3:12-14, MSG

PRAYER
Abba, Father God, Thank You for always being there for me, for Your patience, loving-kindness, unconditional loyal love, and for allowing me to call out to You when I needed it.
It amazes me that the Sovereign God, Lord of the Universe, would pursue me, plan for me, provide for me, help me, lead me, fight for me, protect me, take the time to listen to me, and care about what I have to say even when I fail Him so many times.
Father, please bless me with more grace, wisdom, strength, and faith to keep me on the right path, run this race with endurance, keep the confidence in You, and equip and empower me to get started, keep going, and finish strong. Would You please give me the strength to be stronger, the courage to be more courageous, the hope to be hopeful, and the encouragement to endure and keep going? Nothing is impossible nor too complicated for You and with You, my God. I believe that through Christ, who strengthens, empowers, elevates, and educates me, I can accomplish anything, and I shall finish strong by His grace and all for His glory. In Jesus' name, Amen.

MY DOPE *faith journal*

Date S | M | T | W | T | F | S

Morning: I feel my emotion! My one-word check-in: ....

DECLARATION

Consider today's verse. I implore the Holy Spirit to reveal His wisdom and truth to me and I declare it over my life.

OBSERVATION

What does the message mean? Lord, help me see it.

PRAYER

What is my prayer request? Lord, I live fully in You.

EMPOWERMENT

How will Your word empower me? Lord, give me the insight to apply my faith to be more significant than my fears.

MY FEARLESS *journey*

Evening: Feel my emotion! My one-word check-up:

What is making me FEEL like this?

What lessons did I LEARNED?

What THOUGHTS did I had?

What prompted my GRATITUDE?

Who did I CONNECTED with?

What brought me JOY?

EVENING PRAYER

WATER:

FRUIT & VEG:

MY MOOD:

My treat for today is:..

How Exercise Can Increase Happiness

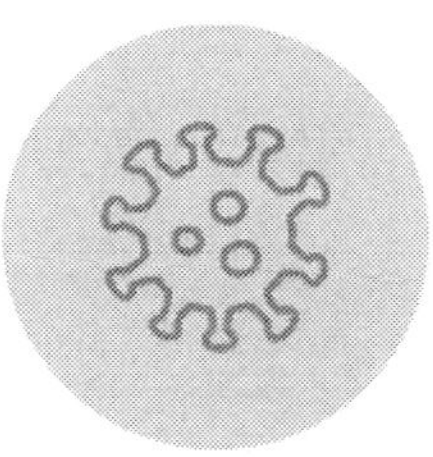

IMPROVES IMMUNITY

The less often you are to become unwell, the stronger your immune system is.

CONFIDENCE BOOST

You feel quite accomplished, which increases your confidence.

LOWERS ANXIETY

The benefits of exercise include improved mood and less anxiety.

LIVE LONGER

prevents cognitive aging and increases longevity

ENERGY BOOST

Happier emotions are more prevalent when one has more energy.

REDUCES STRESS

Exercise and training assist your body in adjusting to stress.

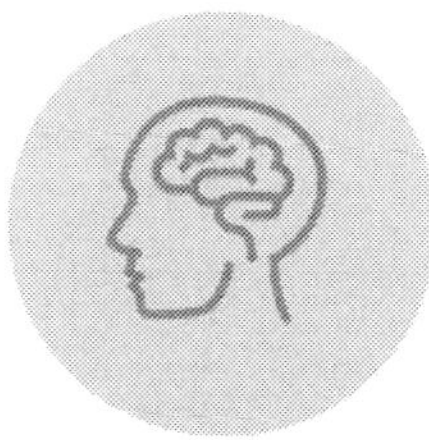

INCREASES DOPAMINE

Dopamine is linked to positive emotions like joy and happiness.

BETTER SLEEP

Regular exercise enhances the quality of sleep.

HEALTHY EATING

Encourages healthy eating for the benefit of both your body and you.

Day 219 - You Serve An Influential God

"Many are the plans in the mind of a man, but it is the purpose of the Lord that will stand."
—Proverbs 19:21, ESV

BELOVED,

You may be saying; I replied, "*But my work seems so useless! I have spent my strength for nothing and to no purpose. Yet I leave it all in the LORD's hand; I will trust God for my reward*" (Isaiah 49:4, NLT).

The truth is you serve an influential God. When it comes to marketing, "influencer" is a term that is frequently used to describe someone who has the power to influence prospective consumers through sharing or advocating products or services on social media. As a result, you may believe that my social media capital does not measure up, as I do not have photographs with celebrities or strong social capital, nor do I have the opportunity to hear about promotions and investments before they are made public. When compared to the knowledge of knowing Jesus as your personal Lord and Savior, Apostle Paul would argue that they are all worthless."*Yes, everything else is worthless when compared with the infinite value of knowing Christ Jesus my Lord. For his sake I have discarded everything else, counting it all as garbage, so that I could gain Christ.*" (Philippians 3:8, NLT). You are weak and unable to accomplish anything unless you have a strong relationship with Him. Only those prepared to answer God's call are called and commissioned to go. Jesus said, "*You have not chosen Me, but I have chosen you and I have appointed and placed and purposefully planted you, so that you would go and bear fruit and keep on bearing, and that your fruit will remain and be lasting, so that whatever you ask of the Father in My name [as My representative] He may give to you.*" (John 15:16, AMP). As a result of God's favor, grace and power, you'll be able to do things that no human influencer can. In a matter of seconds, God can flip the tables and deliver promotions, new creations, and more incredible marvels of transforming your fine wine right out of the water.

Pastor John Hagee, once said, *"Stop saying, 'I don't know the right people!' Do you know God? He's rather influential on this planet!"*

Do you know your God?

He is your Source: Savior, Strength, Strong-Tower, Salvation, Strength, and Shalom! There is nothing too tricky nor impossible with God. He has a significant influence on everyone and everything. He has great plans and beautiful promises for you and your future. He is the King of the Universe. He is the Creator and Redeemer God. You serve an influential God, All-Powerful, All-knowing, Almighty God. So stop thinking, "I don't know the right people." How great is the power of the Blood? You are the righteousness of God.

He is your Abba Father. You have access to His throne of grace through Jesus, Redeemer God. He is your personal Lord and Savior, where you will always find help, wisdom, divine intervention, truth, and everything you need in life, living, and livelihood. You are a significant person (VIP) to the Most Influential Person. **Indeed, you serve an influential God!**

AFFIRMATIONS & DECLARATIONS

You got His words and promises from a Promise-Keeping, Covenant-Fulfillment God.
Beloved, In the name of Jesus, I declare. Indeed, You Are A Light for the Nations!
Stand on His unfailing loyal love.
Know that you are chosen and predestined
Walk into the plans God has for you and your future.
Seek His joy and His destiny-plan
Indeed, You serve an Influential God!

- God amazingly creates me.
- I will not be afraid of evil.
- God gives me strength.
- I am blessed with every kind of spiritual blessing.

"But the Lord's plans stand firm forever; his intentions can never be shaken what joy for the nation whose God is the Lord, whose people he has chosen as his inheritance. The Lord looks down from heaven and sees the whole human race."
—Psalm 33:11-13 NLT

PRAYER

Abba, Father, Creator, and Redeemer God, You are very influential and promised to take care of me. Lord, I confess Your words over my life. Thank You for loving me, choosing me, and using me as splendor and grandeur to show Your glory and faithfulness. I believe. I receive, and I activate the manifestation and fulfillment. In Jesus' mighty and matchless name, I pray. Amen.

MY DOPE *faith journal*

Date S | M | T | W | T | F | S

Morning: I feel my emotion! My one-word check-in: ____________

DECLARATION

Consider today's verse. I implore the Holy Spirit to reveal His wisdom and truth to me and I declare it over my life.

OBSERVATION

What does the message mean? Lord, help me see it.

PRAYER

What is my prayer request? Lord, I live fully in You.

EMPOWERMENT

How will Your word empower me? Lord, give me the insight to apply my faith to be more significant than my fears.

MY FEARLESS *journey*

Evening: Feel my emotion! My one-word check-up:

What is making me FEEL like this?

What lessons did I LEARNED?

What THOUGHTS did I had?

What prompted my GRATITUDE?

Who did I CONNECTED with?

What brought me JOY?

EVENING PRAYER

WATER:

FRUIT & VEG:

MY MOOD:

My treat for today is: ....

Day 220 - You're A Victorious Warrior!

"For every child of God defeats this evil world, and we achieve this victory through our faith."
—1 John 5:4, NLT

BELOVED,
Whether you know it or not, you're continuously engaged in a spiritual battle. The Devil may devour anyone since he has an evil desire to murder, steal, and destroy. Because he has little remaining time, he is prone to rage. You are a victorious warrior, a legend in Christ's service, and an obedient soldier in God's complete armor when you show up to the battleground every day. When the going gets tough, you're ready for anything. However, Jesus cautioned you that you will encounter difficulties in your journey here on earth, but that you need not be afraid since you have already won, and our triumph is eternal! In the Book of Job, Satan begged and pleaded with God to allow him to touch God's servant, Job. When you are devoted to God, Satan has to go through God to get to you, God's child, saint, servant, and anointed one.
The Lord asked the Devil, "Where have you come from?" The Devil then replied to God, "From wandering the world and walking on it." The Lord asked Satan, "Have you thought and meditated about My servant Job? For there is no one like him on the face of the earth, a pure and upright man who reveres God with awe and abstains from and turns away from evil because he adores God because he regards Me as his God." The Devil said to God, "Does Job worship, fear, and love God for nothing?" (Job 1:7-9). Satan has to seek permission from God to touch you. God will not give you more than you can endure, and when tempted, you are equipped to win, and God has made a way of escape. God watches over you to be victorious, so stay strong when life happens! As you prepare for this new day, put on the Whole Armor of God; introduce your pain and the enemy's plot to God's power, and plan takes authority in Jesus' name.
God has revealed seven tactics in Ephesians 6:10-18 and an attack plan for this fight. You're a victorious warrior! Put on the whole armor of God daily. Let the weakling say, 'I am a warrior, not a worrier.' You are a genuine warrior; you are not immune to fear; you are inspired by faith, ignited by His Spirit, and battle regardless. Use these strategic and spiritual weapons, and you must win!

1. — A belt of truth
2. — The breastplate of righteousness
3. — Shoes the gospel of peace
4. — Shield of faith
5. — Helmet of salvation
6. — The sword of the Spirit, the word of God
7. — Prayer and supplication

Three Strategic and Prophetic Insights.

- You must put on the complete armor of God to face the fight and confront the battle.
- You must fight to the finish, battle till the end, don't give up! Never back down. Stand firm; don't stop striking the enemy until wholly destroyed.
- You must understand that you are fighting a spiritual battle for your blessings, answered prayers, delivered promises, mind, seed, soul, heart, life, home, children, and destiny to capture your purpose, identity, legend, and legacy.

AFFIRMATIONS & DECLARATIONS
"The Lord will march out like a champion, like a warrior he will stir up his zeal; with a shout, he will raise the battle cry and will triumph over his enemies." (Isaiah 42:13 NIV).
"You show steadfast love to thousands, but you repay the guilt of fathers to their children after them, O great and mighty God, whose name is the Lord of hosts." (Jeremiah 32:18 ESV).

- I am on the winning team with the Champion Defender.
- I am clothed, armed, dangerous, and fully armored.
- I am destroying the band of raiders. I shall recover it all, big and small.
- I am coming out undefeated, with the plunder and spoils of the battle.

"And may your name be honored forever so that everyone will say, "The Lord of Heaven'sHeaven's Armies is God over Israel!" And may the house of your servant David continue before you forever."
—2 Samuel 7:26 NLT

PRAYER
Almighty God, I pray earnestly and put on the full armor. I overcome everything trying to overtake and overwhelm me in Jesus' name. By Your grace and all for Your glory, O Lord, I thank You for the victory. In Jesus' name, I have the strategies to fight. In Jesus' might and matchless name, I pray, praise, and proclaim these prophetic utterances. Manifest, fulfill, and perform your victory, O Lord, Amen.

MY DOPE *faith journal*

Date S | M | T | W | T | F | S

Morning: I feel my emotion! My one-word check-in:

DECLARATION

Consider today's verse. I implore the Holy Spirit to reveal His wisdom and truth to me and I declare it over my life.

OBSERVATION

What does the message mean? Lord, help me see it.

PRAYER

What is my prayer request? Lord, I live fully in You.

EMPOWERMENT

How will Your word empower me? Lord, give me the insight to apply my faith to be more significant than my fears.

MY FEARLESS *journey*

Evening: Feel my emotion! My one-word check-up:

What is making me FEEL like this?

What lessons did I LEARNED?

What THOUGHTS did I had?

What prompted my GRATITUDE?

Who did I CONNECTED with?

What brought me JOY?

EVENING PRAYER

WATER:

FRUIT & VEG:

MY MOOD:

My treat for today is: ....

Day 221 - Let's Pray For Each Other!

Rejoice always, pray continually, give thanks in all circumstances; for this is God's will for you in Christ Jesus
-1 Thessalonians 5:16-18, NIV

BELOVED,

Let's pray for each other. First, pray for self-compassion, kindness, and goodness to overflow from you so that you might be light-seeds of righteousness to others. Even when facing your storms or ascending out of your valley, you might become so consumed with the problems that you forget to help others, intercede, or volunteer. In your mind, your lunch is a pittance compared to the needs of a nation. Keep your head above water despite your exhaustion, frustration, and humiliation. As you figure out your assignment, your friends and family may have been critical of you, and it appears their dependence has failed you; pray! However, be kind, show compassion for yourself, and be patient with others since we all go through difficult times. Pray for your loved ones, and pray for the church. You should pray for your career but also your coworkers, your home but also neighbors, and your entire city. Pray for your business and the needs of clients, customers, and staff; Pray for your family, including your children and the others who live in your home. Pray for health, wisdom, joy, salvation, favor, and peace for yourself, your loved ones, and the world; Your church, boards, pastors, leaders, congregation, and the places where you get your spiritual nourishment should be on your prayer list. God governs all authority, so pastors, leaders, and influencers should be held accountable to Him. To be an intercessor, a disciple, an advocate, an evangelist of God's favor, grace, and love, pray for yourself to give your change and struggles to God.

Connect with a group of believers and share your experience, praise reports, and prayer requests to build a stronger relationship with God. Be a safe place for others as you learn to manage your emotions and grow personally and spiritually. Apply God's promises in your prayers. Everyone can see the dirt in others, the one to call out the gold. (Proverbs 11:27). Observe God's whispers and flashes of people in your thoughts, and pray for them when you see or think of them. Make a special effort to remember the younger generation in your prayers. You need to pray for fatherhood and identity in our modern society, for marriages, families, and children. Pray that God's grace and power should be seen and experienced in these challenging times. Proverbs 11:25 says, "*The generous will prosper; those who refresh others will themselves be refreshed.*" Pray that God would use you to establish His kingdom, not to serve your interests at the expense of others, but to serve as a financial pillar, steward of His grace, and conduit for His gifts. Pray for a blessing that will spread like wildfire and last forever. Pray for all Christians and unbelievers to be saved. Even amid your trials, you are blessed with the increase, multiplicity, healing of your wounds, and breakthroughs like Job, after he prayed for his friends, despite it all. "*When Job prayed for his friends, the LORD restored his fortunes. In fact, the LORD gave him twice as much as before!*" (Job 42:10, NLT). May the power of the Holy Spirit and the authority of Jesus Christ be at work in you.

Make a prayer list today and write at least five names for whom you will pray this week. Continue to add to this list. Pray specifically for their unique needs, salvation, and hope in their situation. Leave a word of encouragement, scripture, or quote in the newsfeed of Chayah Club and share or tag someone to bring hope. Be encouraged and stay prayed up! Receive 3 John 1:2, *"Beloved; I pray that in every way, you may succeed and prosper and best in good health physically, just as I know your soul prospers spiritually."*

AFFIRMATIONS & DECLARATIONS

Lord, let my heart be enlightened, so I may see the hope You called me to and Your magnificent inheritance in the saints. (Eph 1:18). I thank my Father, who has qualified me to inherit His holy people's kingdom of light. He saved me from darkness and brought us into His Son's kingdom. (Col 1:12-13). When I pray, hear my humble petitions. Yes, hear me from above and forgive me and the land. (2 Chr 6:21). I am a child of God and an heir of Your kingdom. I am God's chosen one, holy and deeply loved. I am a new creation. God loves me and others. I am self-compassionate and show kindness to others. I have an enormous love for God, self-love, and brotherly love. 2 Chron 7:14, ESV says, "*if my people who are called by my name humble themselves, and pray and seek my face and turn from their wicked ways, then I will hear from heaven and will forgive their sin and heal their land.*" Lord, I repent and seek Your divine intervention.

PRAYER

Father God, in the name of Jesus, I pray Your word over my life, my friends, communities, cities, and our families. May God grant us from the riches of His glory to be strengthened, healed, protected, provided for, and promoted. I pray that we may be filled up throughout our beings, minds, hearts, and lives to all the fullness of God so that we may have the most decadent experience of God's presence in our lives, wholly filled and flooded with God Himself. I love You and thank You for uniting and connecting me in Chayah Club and with Christ and allowing me to live, spiritually grow, and be divinely connected to You. I choose not to love the world or its things, I am co-crucified with Christ, and I crucified my carnal flesh, worldly standards, and all of its passions. Lord, I offer my body as a living and holy sacrifice, clarify my vision, receive Your redemptive love and show compassion as I bear abundant Fruit of the Spirit, and I choose to renew my mind by the living Word of God. By so doing, I will be able to prove that the will of God is good, acceptable, and perfect for me and all my friends, families, and believers. In Jesus' name, I pray, Amen.

MY DOPE *faith journal*

Date S | M | T | W | T | F | S

Morning: I feel my emotion! My one-word check-in: ______________________

DECLARATION

Consider today's verse. I implore the Holy Spirit to reveal His wisdom and truth to me and I declare it over my life.

OBSERVATION

What does the message mean? Lord, help me see it.

PRAYER

What is my prayer request? Lord, I live fully in You.

EMPOWERMENT

How will Your word empower me? Lord, give me the insight to apply my faith to be more significant than my fears.

MY FEARLESS *journey*

Evening: Feel my emotion! My one-word check-up:

What is making me FEEL like this?

What lessons did I LEARNED?

What THOUGHTS did I had?

What prompted my GRATITUDE?

Who did I CONNECTED with?

What brought me JOY?

EVENING PRAYER

WATER:

FRUIT & VEG:

MY MOOD:

My treat for today is: ....

365 Journal

Make a list of at least five people you'll be praying for this week. Please keep adding items to this list. Be precise in your prayers for their individual needs for salvation and hope. You may post a message of hope on the Chayah Club's newsfeed and share it with others.

THIS WEEK'S TASK

Be Active

Endeavor to be physically active for 30 minutes each day. Describe the action you took and how it made you feel in writing.

	WHAT YOU DID	HOW IT MADE YOU FEEL
MONDAY		
TUESDAY		
WEDNESDAY		
THURSDAY		
FRIDAY		
SATURDAY		
SUNDAY		

Day 222 - Are You Checking IF God Can?

"And truly Jesus did many other signs in the presence of His disciples, which are not written in this book; but these are written that you may believe that Jesus is the Christ, the Son of God, and that believing you may have life in His name."
—John 20:30-31, NKJV

BELOVED,
Are you checking if the Unchanging God, All-Powerful, Promise-Keeping, Covenant-Fulfillment, Creator, Redeemer God is still faithful? Are you checking up on God, monitoring that thing you left in God's hand? Jesus is looking at you, saying, "Will you trust Me? Do you believe in Me? Didn't I tell you that if you believe in Me, you will see God unveil His power?"
A personal story: My children frequently ask me to pray for them. They would come to my door almost every day and tell me, "Mom, God hasn't replied." Never if God can, but that He hasn't answered yet! When I am traveling, they will text me and say, "Mom, did you pray, but God hasn't yet replied?" Check-ins with God have been some of my life's most profound and intimate experiences and faith journeys with my boys. I would use the *'pree'* to pray: Lord, I know there are many requests before You, but please prioritize their prayer requests. You don't need to give them everything; most importantly, it's an opportunity to learn to rely entirely on You and put all of their fears, needs, worries, and anxieties in Your capable hands." I love it when God says, "Wait, I've got something better in store." After they had waited and hoped, He delivered *immeasurably more than-you-asked-or-imagined*. As for myself and my family, we'll be serving God. I'm leaving behind a legacy of faith revival! As a reminder today, God has not forgotten you and His hands are not too short to reach you. He is at work even now. He's working it out for you.
Checking in with God is perfectly acceptable, and you may be assured that He is aware of your presence when you do so. His promises and goals will be made clear to you. Join us as we learn to be in tune with God's work. As God uses you to spread His grace, love, and glory over the world, you'll be in sync with the beat of heaven.
In John 11:38-40, all hope was dashed as Lazarus was dead. Jesus asked, Didn't I say if you trust in Me, you'll witness God's power? Jesus then went to the tomb, a cave with a stone covering its entrance. "Roll away the stone," Jesus said. Martha cried, "But Lord, he's been dead four days—his corpse is decaying!" Jesus asked her, "Didn't I say if you trust in me, you'll witness God's power?"
The Father says, "You must believe in Me, and rivers of live water will flow from you. Believe you will receive anything you pray for in My will, and it will be yours. Without faith, it would be not easy to please Me, for you approach Me in confidence, believing I am the truth and that I reward those who seek Me with passion and power. With your double, you believe after seeing Me, but those who haven't seen Me but have believed in Me will be blessed even more. Those who accepted Christ and His name became God's children. Rid your language from asking If I can? Believe, and all is possible. Learn from *Mark 9:23-24:* "What do you mean 'if'?" asked Jesus. Believers can do anything. Like the boy's father shouted, 'I believe, Lord; assist my small faith! Help my unbelief, Lord!'"

AFFIRMATIONS & DECLARATIONS
I eliminate every IF God can and believe that My God promises, *"If I hold on to Me, I'll save you. If I trust Me, I'll take good care of you. I'll rescue you, then throw you a party; I'll grant you a long life, a long cup of salvation."* (Psalm 91:14-16). Whoever hears My message and believes Him who sent Me has eternal life. He's gone from death to life and isn't judged. (John 5:24). I can make grace abundant to you so you can abound in every good work. (2 Corinthians 9:8)."

- God's love pours through me; He will never leave me.
- God has a good plan for my life. God's 'liquid-love' is always lavishing me thoroughly.

PRAYER
Father God, Thank You for reminding me that nothing is too difficult or impossible for You to handle. Forgive me for questioning You, prying or peeping rather than praising You through the pain of the process, introducing my pain to Your power, and keeping my eyes looking at Jesus to manifest my purpose. Would You please help me trust You and believe You can do the impossible in my life even when journeying through the deepest, dark, and long waiting season? Lord, I know that You are working for me right now; I believe that You will finish the work You started with me. I fearlessly seek and trust You, and I believe in myself. O Lord, please heal me from spiritual blindness, deafness, and muteness, and give me the faith, desire, and ability to see, hear, and talk to You. I pray that I will dig deeper and deeper into You. Therefore I will see the manifestation of miracles, signs, and wonders, the revelation of Your love, word, power, and majesty in my (PILL) **p**urpose, **i**dentity, **l**egend, and **l**egacy. In Jesus' name, Amen.

MY DOPE *faith journal*

Date S | M | T | W | T | F | S

Morning: I feel my emotion! My one-word check-in:

DECLARATION

Consider today's verse. I implore the Holy Spirit to reveal His wisdom and truth to me and I declare it over my life.

OBSERVATION

What does the message mean? Lord, help me see it.

PRAYER

What is my prayer request? Lord, I live fully in You.

EMPOWERMENT

How will Your word empower me? Lord, give me the insight to apply my faith to be more significant than my fears.

MY FEARLESS *journey*

Evening: Feel my emotion! My one-word check-up:

What is making me FEEL like this?

What lessons did I LEARNED?

What THOUGHTS did I had?

What prompted my GRATITUDE?

Who did I CONNECTED with?

What brought me JOY?

EVENING PRAYER

WATER:

FRUIT & VEG:

MY MOOD:

My treat for today is: ....

365 Journal

Would it be amazing when God....

Day 223 - Today Is The Day, U-Power-Up!

"But I am going to take off your chains and let you go. If you want to come with me to Babylon, you are welcome. I will see that you are well cared for. But if you don't want to come, you may stay here. The whole land is before you—go wherever you like."
—Jeremiah 40:4, NLT

BELOVED,
Even if life isn't perfect, you have a perfect God to help you through it all. He uses everything (the good, the terrible, and the ugly) in your life for His benefit and the glory of His name. As a result, we've come to believe that everything in your life has a purpose since you're God's devoted lovers called to carry out His design, divine plan, and purpose. (Romans 8:28). Let this hope spring inside you to power you up, unleashing a constant gladness; keep going, even when things are tough, for God is always there for you. (Romans 12:12) Be encouraged, no matter where you are today. Believe and be spiritually empowered. Today is the day that *you power up!* **God is saying,**
"But today, I'm freeing you, releasing you from your shackles. How long you've been chained; I free you from the chains on your hands today. It doesn't matter how long you've been bound; today, you are loosened. You may have been held back, setback, or encountered a roadblock, but I'm going to let you go and come back from every blockage, barrier, and burden. You are free from your chains, captivity, and circumstances. This day is when you break free, break out, and break through. Today is your day of liberation, U-power-Up!"
Are you acting, thinking, and stating that you are enslaved when God has already set you free? According to the songwriter Bob Marley, it would help if you freed yourself from mental slavery in Redemption Song.
"Emancipate yourselves from mental slavery. None but ourselves can free our minds."— Bob Marley
Are you burdened by burdens for which Christ has already paid the price and penalty for the pardon and purity of your sins, laying down His life as an atonement to set you free and give you new life?
Najwa Zebian once said, *"These mountains that you are carrying, you were only supposed to climb."*
Faith without work is dead, and talk is cheap, and God has not given you a fearful spirit but power from the Holy Spirit and authority in the name of Jesus.
"The kingdom of God is not a realm of grandiose talk; it is a realm of power." (1 Corinthians 4:20, VOICE).
Jesus said, "I've given you true authority. You can smash vipers and scorpions under your feet. You can walk all over the power of the enemy. You can't be harmed." (Luke 10:19, VOICE).

'U Power Up: You are gaining the immediate advantage to box out your seemingly out-matched opponent by increasing power in your body, mind, and soul, having the strength, stamina, and speed to overcome the fear of defeat and REBOUND to victory.
- Nicola McFadden, Rebound Faith: Chayah

AFFIRMATIONS & DECLARATIONS
"But now, listen carefully, [because of your innocence] I am freeing you today from the chains which are on your hands. If you would prefer to come with me to Babylon, come, and I will look after you [carefully]; but if you would prefer not to come with me to Babylon, then do not do so. Look, all the land is before you; go wherever it seems good and right (convenient) for you to go." (Jer 40:4-5, AMP)

- I prayed through it! I grew through it! I moved through it!
- I improved because of it! I break through it! I got over it! I am blessed in it!

"For the law of the Spirit of life flowing through the anointing of Jesus has liberated us from the "law" of sin and death."
—Romans 8:2, TPT

PRAYER
Heavenly Father, Thank You for Your never-ending love for me and Your blessings, gladness, loving-kindness, faithfulness, empowerment, and goodness. Thank You for guiding me, correcting my destination, setting me free from every chain, and seeing me through times of uncertainty. Thank You for lifting me, leading me through the valley of darkness, lighting my path, and setting me on high. Thank You for Scriptures that reassure and remind me of Your promises, purpose, plan, protection, prosperity, power, and provision. Thank You for removing my shackles, fears, frustrations, and worries, the *could-haves*, *almost-made-it*, and *what-ifs*, and for reminding me that my help comes from You. Would You please assist me in being a good steward, kingdom-minded, living abundantly, and sowing wisely? Today, I walk and live in true freedom, victory, power, authority, grace, and glory. In Jesus' name, I pray, Amen.

MY DOPE *faith journal*

Date S | M | T | W | T | F | S

Morning: I feel my emotion! My one-word check-in: ....

DECLARATION

Consider today's verse. I implore the Holy Spirit to reveal His wisdom and truth to me and I declare it over my life.

OBSERVATION

What does the message mean? Lord, help me see it.

PRAYER

What is my prayer request? Lord, I live fully in You.

EMPOWERMENT

How will Your word empower me? Lord, give me the insight to apply my faith to be more significant than my fears.

MY FEARLESS *journey*

Evening: Feel my emotion! My one-word check-up:

What is making me FEEL like this?

What lessons did I LEARNED?

What THOUGHTS did I had?

What prompted my GRATITUDE?

Who did I CONNECTED with?

What brought me JOY?

EVENING PRAYER

WATER:

FRUIT & VEG:

MY MOOD:

My treat for today is: ....

HABIT Tracker

DAY 224 - 237

Be Present

“

Do not be anxious or worried about anything, but in everything [every circumstance and situation] by prayer and petition with thanksgiving, continue to make your [specific] requests known to God. And the peace of God [that peace which reassures the heart, that peace] which transcends all understanding, [that peace which] stands guard over your hearts and your minds in Christ Jesus [is yours].

— PHILIPPIANS 4:6-7, AMP

Day 224 - Positioned: In The Right Place And At The Right Time!

"But you must not forget this one thing, dear friends: A day is like a thousand years to the Lord, and a thousand years is like a day. The Lord isn't really being slow about his promise, as some people think. No, he is being patient for your sake. He does not want anyone to be destroyed, but wants everyone to repent."
—2 Peter 3:8-9, NLT

BELOVED,
Never put a full stop or question mark where God placed a comma! God says, To be continued...
Don't compare your journey with others. You are not too late, not too old, not too slow, not lost, not too messy, not too fat/skinny, not too broken, or forgotten. God works all things together for your excellence and His glory.
"I have observed something else under the sun. The fastest runner doesn't always win the race, and the strongest warrior doesn't always win the battle. The wise sometimes go hungry, and the skillful are not necessarily wealthy. And those who are educated don't always lead successful lives. It is all decided by chance, by being in the right place at the right time." (Ecclesiastes 9:11, NLT).
You are positioned: In the right place and at the right time, wait patiently for God's favor, anointing, and appointing of God, for time and chance shall collide, and it will happen for you.
Like Joseph
Joseph had been positioned through numerous transitions to be in the right place at the right time. He was not forsaken, forgotten, nor failed; instead, He was fearless, faithful, and favored.
Like David
Saul was named king, but David, the shepherd boy, was anointed and appointed to succeed him.
Like Joshua
God singled out Joshua as successor after Moses, a divine succession plan, to lead His people to the Promised Plan. Joshua was prepared and groomed as the next-generation leader in the wilderness.
Like Ruth
Ruth, a widow and immigrant who was gleaning on the field positioned herself by obeying the tactics outlined by Naomi. She found love, shifted to the owner, and was named in the Bloodline of Jesus.
Like Woman with the Issue of the Blood
She suffered for 12 years, then one stolen life transformational touch of the hem of Jesus' garment healed her instantaneously.
So abide and intertwine with Christ; His intimacy and influence will position you. Jesus said, *"If you abide in Me and My voice abides in you, anything you ask will come to pass for you."* (John 15:7, VOICE).

AFFIRMATIONS & DECLARATIONS
The Lord has given me yet another mission. As God drips His content, I remain connected and get confirmation every step. I will hear a small voice saying this is how, where, and when I should walk. Like Prophet Samuel's experience in 1 Samuel 16 when God sent him on the assignment to anoint the next king, God is short on specifics and details as He commissions me on what appears to be a terrifying and insane task. Nonetheless, I am going, being scared, but keep moving forward by faith, not sight, fears, or feelings!

- I am showered with grace and the gift of righteousness and positioned for purpose.
- I can do all things through Christ who strengthens me. I walk in a way that is pleasing to the Lord.
- God showers me with blessings daily, and He richly blesses my provision.
- I am blessed when I enter and blessed when I leave.

But the Lord said to Samuel, "Do not look on his appearance or on the height of his stature, because I have rejected him; for the Lord does not see as mortals see; they look on the outward appearance, but the Lord looks on the heart."
—1 Samuel 16:7, AMP

PRAYER
Lord, thank You for giving me the faith to always trust Your timing in answering my prayers and supplications. Help me to persevere in prayer and not give up. Even when I am experiencing negative emotions, I want to trust You. I prefer to live by faith and truth rather than fear, facts, and feelings. Please keep me from taking matters into my own hands. I choose to believe You rather than the enemy's lies. Give me a better understanding of what You're doing in my life. I thank You for Your infinite wisdom and promise to answer my prayers at the right time and in the right way. In Jesus' name, I pray, Amen.

MY DOPE *faith journal*

Date S | M | T | W | T | F | S

Morning: I feel my emotion! My one-word check-in:

DECLARATION

Consider today's verse. I implore the Holy Spirit to reveal His wisdom and truth to me and I declare it over my life.

OBSERVATION

What does the message mean? Lord, help me see it.

PRAYER

What is my prayer request? Lord, I live fully in You.

EMPOWERMENT

How will Your word empower me? Lord, give me the insight to apply my faith to be more significant than my fears.

MY FEARLESS *journey*

Evening: Feel my emotion! My one-word check-up:

What is making me FEEL like this?

What lessons did I LEARNED?

What THOUGHTS did I had?

What prompted my GRATITUDE?

Who did I CONNECTED with?

What brought me JOY?

EVENING PRAYER

WATER:

FRUIT & VEG:

MY MOOD:

My treat for today is: ....

Meditation

Dedicate yourself to daily meditation for at least 5 minutes. Sit comfortably and pay attention to your natural breathing patterns. Breathe deeply, causing your tummy to expand, gently letting out as your belly contracts. Connect only with the Holy Spirit in silence, stillness, and solitude, listen to His voice, develop your self-awareness and let Him be your Solace.

During my meditation, I heard...

During my meditation, I felt...

During my meditation, I understood...

My meditation has shown me...

Day 225 - Making Moves? Seek God!

"Come to me, all you who are weary and burdened, and I will give you rest. Take my yoke upon you and learn from me, for I am gentle and humble in heart, and you will find rest for your souls. For my yoke is easy and my burden is light."
—Matthew 11:28-30, NIV

BELOVED,

Are you making moves? Seek God! Making moves is described as 'pursuing or beginning a course of action toward the accomplishment of a goal or the resolution of a challenge.' At times, You are tempted to make big decisions based on your intuition, judgment, understanding, and the views of others, rather than seeking God. You are ecstatic about the prospect of attaining your goals and moving forward, it could be an exceptional offer or multiple options presented to you, and you must choose between good, better best. Seek God's guidance and wisdom through listening to God's voice. All that glitters is not gold, even if it appears like sugar to the naked eye. There is no devil with a red cape or fork. He is disguised in your goals as gold, glitter, gals/guys, and all the grandeur of this horrible world.

It is said, *"Never discuss cheese with rats, talk bread with birds, or make moves with snakes."*

The Father says, "Don't attempt to figure things out on your own; put your faith in Me. Everywhere you walk, you should be listening for My voice. I am the one who will keep you on course. If you think you know it all, think again. Are you making moves? Seek Me! Evil is on the loose, and you need to flee! The devil is in his A-game and on your heels. The results are evident as you connect and consult with Me; your entire body will radiate health and vibrate with vitality! Give Me the finest of your possessions as a sign of respect and adoration. You can never outgive Me! Your wine vats and barns will be bursting at the seams. Do not resent My discipline, my beloved; do not pout when I correct you with My love, tell you, No, not yet, wait for I have better in store for that's not my promise nor will. because I correct you because I love My child; all of this is motivated by the joy of a Me, your Heavenly Father. (Proverbs 3:5-12).

Consecrate all you do to Me, from your vision, strategy, goals, thoughts, and action. Your plans will prosper and be established if you listen to My will and guidance. *[Insert your name],* you are My anointed one, whose right hand I will strengthen you, My chosen child, My servant, so great rulers will be paralyzed with terror. I will unlock the gates of your stronghold will be opened, and they will never be closed again."

The Father says,

"And I will lead the blind in a way that they do not know; in paths that they have not known, I will guide them. I will turn the darkness before them into light, the rough places into level ground. These are the things I do, and I do not forsake them." (Isaiah 42:16, ESV).

- I will go before you, *[insert your name],* and level the mountains.
- I will go ahead of you and make the crooked places straight
- I will break into pieces the gates of brass and cut in sunder the bars of iron
- I will smash down gates of bronze and cut through bars of iron
- I will give you treasures hidden in the darkness—secret riches.
- I will do this so you may know I am the LORD, the God who calls you by name. (Isa 45:1-3)

So, beloved, if you're making moves? Seek the Lord! Take your questions to your Creator and Redeemer God, and seek His approval, anointing, appointment, and advancement.

AFFIRMATIONS & DECLARATIONS

In 1 Chronicles 14:14-15, The Philistines returned to the valley to loot. David prayed. God replied, "This time, assault from the balsam grove instead of head-on. When you hear footsteps among the balsams, assault; God will be two steps ahead, slaying Philistines." Lord, I enquire of You before making moves; may You go ahead of me, reveal the strategy, and strike and destroy my enemies in Jesus' name.

- In all I think, speak, do and plan, I surrender totally and completely to You, Lord.
- I am trusting Your direction, provision, protection, and restoration.
- I am making mighty moves into God's mission, mandate, and ministry.

"Those who tempt the lovers of God with an evil scheme will fall into their own traps. But the innocent who resists temptation will experience reward."
—Proverbs 28:10, TPT

PRAYER

LORD, I believe and accept Your Word that has been spoken to me. I am confident that I can witness and attest to Your manifestation, fulfillment, and performance in my life and all of my problems. Lord, with all I have committed to You, I desire Your presence, will, power, protection, provision, promotion, and that Your Word is done. Lord, I thank You. You give me financial breakthroughs, deliverance, salvation, healing miracles, wellness, and shalom, Your child. In Jesus' mighty name, I pray for open doors, divine protection, eternal joy, supernatural blessings, miraculous healings, overwhelming triumph, abundant provision, overflowing success, unusual favor, freedom, influential promotions, and prosperity. Amen!

MY DOPE *faith journal*

Date S | M | T | W | T | F | S

Morning: I feel my emotion! My one-word check-in: ....

DECLARATION

Consider today's verse. I implore the Holy Spirit to reveal His wisdom and truth to me and I declare it over my life.

OBSERVATION

What does the message mean? Lord, help me see it.

PRAYER

What is my prayer request? Lord, I live fully in You.

EMPOWERMENT

How will Your word empower me? Lord, give me the insight to apply my faith to be more significant than my fears.

MY FEARLESS *journey*

Evening: Feel my emotion! My one-word check-up:

What is making me FEEL like this?

What lessons did I LEARNED?

What THOUGHTS did I had?

What prompted my GRATITUDE?

Who did I CONNECTED with?

What brought me JOY?

EVENING PRAYER

WATER:

FRUIT & VEG:

MY MOOD:

My treat for today is: ....

10 Steps To Be Present

Take Note of Your Environment

Be Thankful for What You Have

Take a Social Media Break

Get some regular exercise, a prayer walk,
a praise break, or solitude with God

Deep breathing exercises should be practiced.

Associate with people who make you happy.

Quit multitasking and concentrate on one task at a time.

Accept Things for What They Are

Be Conscious of Everything You Do

Meditate on God's Word for Mindfulness

Day 226 - The Blood Still Works!

"In Him, we have redemption through His blood, the forgiveness of sins, in accordance with the riches of God's grace."
—Ephesians 1:7, NIV

BELOVED,
In Exodus, the showdown between Moses and Pharaoh can be argued as Almighty God of Israel vs. Pharoah and the Egyptian god. So when Moses and Aaron demand the freedom of the Israelites, each Pharaoh's rejection and denial to let God's people go allows the Almighty God to display His sovereignty and dominance. Each plague threatens Pharaoh's authority and administration. God gradually undermines Pharaoh's strength with plagues until he releases the Israelites. *"For I will pass through the land of Egypt that night, and I will strike all the firstborn in the land of Egypt, both man and beast; and on all the gods of Egypt I will execute judgments: I am the Lord. The blood shall be a sign for you, on the houses where you are. And when I see the blood, I will pass over you, and no plague will befall you to destroy you when I strike the land of Egypt. Then they shall take some of the blood and put it on the two doorposts and the lintel of the houses in which they eat it."* (Ex 12:7,12-13, ESV). The ultimate showdown, 'The 10th Plague,' premiered as Pharaoh's firstborn died, and God protected His children, household, and family that were marked with the blood, so the angel of death and destruction passed over.
"At midnight, the Lord struck down all the firstborn in the land of Egypt, from the firstborn of Pharaoh who sat on his throne to the firstborn of the captive who was in the dungeon, and all the firstborn of the livestock." (Exodus 12:29). Glory! The Blood of Jesus still works. It never lost its power. Apply it generously; use it lavishly! You overcame by the Blood of the Lamb and by the word of our testimony.*"You might be under attack but are also under the Blood!"*

- — You are cleansed continually from all sins by the Blood of Jesus.
- — You are healed from every curse of sickness, disease, and mental disorder by His Blood Stripes.
- — The Blood of Jesus redeems you.
- — You are reconciled to your Heavenly Father because of the Blood of Jesus.
- — You are purified and pardoned from every sin by the Blood of Jesus.
- — You have an eternally secured Salvation because of the Blood of Jesus.
- — You are loosened from your sins, shame, struggles, and setbacks by the Blood of Jesus.
- — You are ransomed by the Blood of Jesus.
- — You are now made righteous by the Blood of Jesus.
- — You are redeemed by the Blood; He purchased you not with silver and gold but with the Blood.
- — You are free from every old life and dead work to worship God by the Blood of Jesus.
- — You are transformed and made holy by the Blood of Jesus.
- — You are made new by the Blood of Jesus.
- — You have courage and confidence before God because of the Blood of Jesus.
- — You are satisfied with His fullness and abundance because of the Blood of Jesus.

AFFIRMATIONS & DECLARATIONS
"Because of the sacrifice of the Messiah, his Blood poured out on the altar of the Cross. We're a free people—free of penalties and punishments chalked up by all our misdeeds. And not just barely free, either. Abundantly free! He thought of everything, provided for everything we could possibly need, letting us in on the plans he took such delight in making. He set it all out before us in Christ, a long-range plan in which everything would be brought together and summed up in him, everything in deepest heaven, everything on planet earth." *(*Ephesians 1:7-10, MSG)

- The Blood of Jesus covers, cleanses, crowns, catapults, and changes me.
- I am '*abundantly freed*,' healed, saved, redeemed, reconciled, and delivered by the Blood.
- I am confident before God and draw closer to Him because of the Blood of Jesus.

"And they overcame him by the Blood of the Lamb, and by the word of their testimony, and they loved not their lives unto the death."
—Revelation 12:11, KJV

PRAYER
Father God, thank You for Jesus' Blood, which cleanses, protects, and sustains me. I am grateful for the power, redemption, protection, and healing. You bestowed on me through the Blood of Jesus. I pray that I will remember that I have that power and will be courageous enough to invoke the "Blood of Jesus" in my time of need. Father, let the precious Blood of Jesus cover my life, body, mind, soul, home, relationships, business, career, finances, and journey. Send Your angels to watch over me. Surround me with Your presence at all times. I surrender to You all my activities today, the places I go, and the people I meet. Keep me safe from all sin and evil. I thank You, Jesus, and I praise You. Amen.

MY DOPE *faith journal*

Date S | M | T | W | T | F | S

Morning: I feel my emotion! My one-word check-in: ....

DECLARATION

Consider today's verse. I implore the Holy Spirit to reveal His wisdom and truth to me and I declare it over my life.

OBSERVATION

What does the message mean? Lord, help me see it.

PRAYER

What is my prayer request? Lord, I live fully in You.

EMPOWERMENT

How will Your word empower me? Lord, give me the insight to apply my faith to be more significant than my fears.

MY FEARLESS *journey*

Evening: Feel my emotion! My one-word check-up:

What is making me FEEL like this?

What lessons did I LEARNED?

What THOUGHTS did I had?

What prompted my GRATITUDE?

Who did I CONNECTED with?

What brought me JOY?

EVENING PRAYER

WATER:

FRUIT & VEG:

MY MOOD:

My treat for today is: ....

The Effects of Social Media on You

Social media might make you feel uneasy and alone.

You may experience cyberbullying or trolls.

Online time is more frequent than time with loved ones and friends.

Social media is something you use to avoid feeling horrible.

Your sense of inadequacy may worsen.

You can become confused while working.

Day 227 - Yes, A Breakthrough is About to HIT Your House!

"And God is able to make all grace abound to you, so that having all sufficiency in all things at all times, you may abound in every good work."
—2 Corinthians 9:8, ESV

BELOVED,
'Yes, a breakthrough is about to **HIT** your house!' When a revelation or invention has a significant impact, it is referred to as a "*breakthrough*." Get ready to be HIT with divine **h**appiness, **i**nsight, and **t**ransformation for supernatural financial deliverance and miraculous healing.
Happiness: True happiness, inner power, tranquility, and hope are all found in God. He is also the source of healing and abundance. Your house will be hit with financial independence and healing miracles created by him, bringing joy to you and your family. *"What bliss we experience when these blessings fall! The people who love and serve our God will be happy indeed!"* (Psalms 144:15, TPT).
Insight: God's Holy Spirit will reveal you mind-blowing financial insights and incredible miracles. The Holy Spirit knows everything about God; Who else can read a man's mind? Only your inner character is praiseworthy. Only God's Spirit knows your thoughts. You don't have the rebellious and shattered worldly spirit; you have God's Spirit, enabling you to experience and grasp God's benefits. You talk of the Spirit rather than human knowledge because You with the Spirit have access to the spiritual wisdom of God for breakthroughs: innovation, investments, and inventions." *But as the Scriptures say, No eye has ever seen, and no ear has ever heard, and it has never occurred to the human heart All the things God prepared for those who love Him."* (1 Cor 2:9-13, VOICE).
Transformation: There is no transformation with a renewed mindset. Change requires a fresh perspective. Don't adhere to the world's standard; reinvent your thoughts. Then you'll know God's good, pleasant, and perfect will. God will make you a new creation and lead you to financial freedom, abundance, wellness, wholeness, and completeness.*"Now all of us, with our faces unveiled, reflect the glory of the Lord as if we are mirrors; and so we are being transformed, metamorphosed, into His same image from one radiance of glory to another, just as the Spirit of the Lord accomplishes it." (2 Corinthians 3:18 VOICE)*
Now that you've prayed, the Father tells you to lift your head and listen, for there's a sound like abundant rain. (King 18:41). When the land is thirsty and dry, "I will pour water over it, and streams over it," says the Lord. "I will bless your offspring, and I will pour my Spirit over them." (Isa 44:3).
"Let it rain, O Lord. We are ready for the overflow. Have your way, Lord. Manifest your Power. Please show us your glory!
2 Kings 4:1-7 tells the story of the financial breakthrough that HIT the widow's house. Today, God is asking you, Tell me, what do you have in the household? What do you have in your house that appears to be tiny, your little faith, little strength, little lunch, or even only a small jar of oil? Put it on God's HIT list!
This day of Exodus for you; You're coming out. Your deliverance has arrived! Whatever your situation is, God is capable of rescuing and restoring you. He will lead you out, over, through, or around it, provide for you despite it, promote you as a result, and prepare you for it with His plenty and power.

AFFIRMATIONS & DECLARATIONS
God gives me the ability, wisdom, strength, purpose, ideas, insight, direction, and strategy to work, create wealth, and build His kingdom. The One who gives the vision, He gives the provision. If I start thinking to myself, "I did all this. And all by myself. I'm rich. It's all mine!"—well, think again. Remember that God, your God, gave you the strength to produce all this wealth to confirm the covenant that he promised to your ancestors—as it is today. (Deuteronomy 8:17-18, MSG)

- I am wealthy, healthy, and wise; I stand on the word of God; I take God at His word.

"Give generously, and generous gifts will be given back to you, shaken down to make room for more. Abundant gifts will pour out upon you with such an overflowing measure that it will run over the top! Your measurement of generosity becomes the measurement of your return."
—Luke 6:37-38, TPT

PRAYER
Father God, I thank You for being the resurrection and life; death has no power over You. The power You used to defeat death now resides within me. Use Your supernatural abilities to bring a breakthrough in my life and home. Lord, may I know Your all-conquering and all-sufficiency power today. Please hear my request and HIT me up with your divine nature. You have loved, redeemed, healed, and cleansed me of my sins and struggles by Your Blood. Your grace, glory, wisdom, hope, joy, peace, righteousness, the newness of life, health, wealth, wellness, wholeness, prosperity, and power are mine. In Jesus' name, I pray, Amen.

MY DOPE *faith journal*

Date S | M | T | W | T | F | S

Morning: I feel my emotion! My one-word check-in: ....

DECLARATION

Consider today's verse. I implore the Holy Spirit to reveal His wisdom and truth to me and I declare it over my life.

OBSERVATION

What does the message mean? Lord, help me see it.

PRAYER

What is my prayer request? Lord, I live fully in You.

EMPOWERMENT

How will Your word empower me? Lord, give me the insight to apply my faith to be more significant than my fears.

MY FEARLESS *journey*

Evening: Feel my emotion! My one-word check-up:

What is making me FEEL like this?

What lessons did I LEARNED?

What THOUGHTS did I had?

What prompted my GRATITUDE?

Who did I CONNECTED with?

What brought me JOY?

EVENING PRAYER

WATER:

FRUIT & VEG:

MY MOOD:

My treat for today is:..

How to Breathe

Close your eyes and choose a comfortable position.

One hand should be on your tummy, the other on your chest.

Take a couple of deep breaths.

Does your stomach rise and fall with each breath and exhalation? This is how we breathe naturally.

If your belly remains stationary as your chest rises and falls with each breath, try breathing by letting your stomach rise and fall just when you live in and out.

Take deep breaths, focusing solely on moving your belly.

Imagine expanding a balloon in your tummy as you inhale through your nose.

When exhaling, blow out through your mouth as if you were blowing through a straw.

Day 228 - Reward For Your Faithfulness.

"Blessed is the one who perseveres under trial because, having stood the test, that person will receive the crown of life that the Lord has promised to those who love him."
—James 1:12, NIV

BELOVED,
Your fearless trust in God will be rewarded. Be persistent, and don't give up. Faith in God and conquering fear are two things you may do to strengthen your relationship with Him. For your righteousness, faith, patience, and trust in the Lord's faithfulness, you are rewarded by God. Keep your head up, and don't give up. You can't stop trying. God has plans that no one else can see, hear, or imagine to reward your faithfulness. It's like a light bulb went on in your head! Your prayers will be answered better than you thought by God. Your patience, hope, and hard work have all been rewarded. Your faith and trust in Him even if you can't see His hand at work.

Despite the discomfort, you clung to Him and allowed Him to demonstrate His faithfulness, promise, and the point and purpose of the painful process. IT IS WORTH THE WAIT AND WORTHY OF YOUR EFFORT!

Even if the waiting season is complicated and you try to control it and mistrust God's trustworthiness, your anxiety, worry, anger, fear, and feeling of frustration are forgiven when you repent and seek Him. According to His word, God has the Master plan and can handle any scenario to accomplish His objective and prophesy. God will use your blunders to bring about His marvels and miracles, purpose and promise, prosperity and power. He can even change water into wine, ashes into beauty, and diabolical plots into divine plans when you connect with Him to activate His power and anchor your faith in His faithfulness.

Genesis tells us of a mind-blowing promise and reward for Abraham and Sarah. Sarah couldn't believe God had promised to give her and Abraham a child. As far as she was concerned, she and her husband were too elderly to have a kid, and she had already reached the end of her childbearing years. Abraham had faith; although Sarah began to ridicule, fear, and doubt, it is evident in the manifestation report in Genesis 21:1-7 that God can accomplish anything. The elderly couple welcomed a boy called Isaac, meaning laughter. This story serves as a reminder that God's promises never expire, and there is no limit to God. At the appointed time, He answers. Romans 4:19-22, VOICE says, *"His faith did not fail, although he was well aware that his impotent body, after nearly 100 years, was as good as dead and that Sarah's womb, too, was dead. In spite of all this, his faith in God's promise did not falter. In fact, his faith grew as he gave glory to God because he was supremely confident that God could deliver on His promise. This is why, you see, God saw his faith and counted him as righteous; this is how he became right with God."* Like Abraham and Sarah, God will reward your little faith and reveal His tremendous faithfulness.

AFFIRMATIONS & DECLARATIONS
"Meanwhile, the moment we get tired in the waiting, God's Spirit is right alongside helping us along. If we don't know how or what to pray, it doesn't matter. He does our praying in and for us, making prayer out of our wordless sighs, our aching groans. He knows us far better than we know ourselves, knows our pregnant condition, and keeps us present before God. That's why we can be so sure that every detail in our lives of love for God is worked into something good." (Romans 8:26-28, MSG).

- I am not worried; I am waiting and worshipping. I am not backing down; I am believing.
- I am not suffering; I am surrendering and shifting. I am not fretting; God is forging my path.
- I am not falling apart; I am aligned and shall achieve the vision and my goals.
- I am not just surviving; I am created for a divine purpose, reviving, living, and thriving.
- I am not stuck; I am unstoppable and untouchable as nothing is impossible for my God.

Galatians 6:9, APMC: *"And let us not lose heart and grow weary and faint in acting nobly and doing right, for in due time and at the appointed season we shall reap, if we do not loosen and relax our courage and faint."*

PRAYER
Heavenly Father, I love You fervently and devotedly, O Lord, my Strength. The Lord is my Rock, Fortress, and the One rescues me. He is my God, my Rock of Safety, Shelter, and Source of power whom I trust and take refuge, my Shield, and the Horn of my Salvation, my High Tower—my Stronghold. I call upon the Lord, who is worthy to be praised; And I am saved from my enemies. I earnestly and diligently seek You, LORD. The Lord dealt with me according to my righteousness, moral character, and spiritual integrity; according to the cleanness of my hands, He has rewarded me. Lord, let Your oil of uncommon favor, grace, joy, blessings, success, prosperity, peace, healing, promotion, breakthroughs, deliverance, and Your Glory saturates me. Reward me for my faithfulness as I wait in You and for You. Please show me your glory, goodness, grace, and greatness as I go and grow through the process in Jesus' name. I pray, Amen!

MY DOPE *faith journal*

Date S | M | T | W | T | F | S

Morning: I feel my emotion! My one-word check-in: ....

DECLARATION

Consider today's verse. I implore the Holy Spirit to reveal His wisdom and truth to me and I declare it over my life.

OBSERVATION

What does the message mean? Lord, help me see it.

PRAYER

What is my prayer request? Lord, I live fully in You.

EMPOWERMENT

How will Your word empower me? Lord, give me the insight to apply my faith to be more significant than my fears.

MY FEARLESS *journey*

Evening: Feel my emotion! My one-word check-up:

What is making me FEEL like this?

What lessons did I LEARNED?

What THOUGHTS did I had?

What prompted my GRATITUDE?

Who did I CONNECTED with?

What brought me JOY?

EVENING PRAYER

WATER:

FRUIT & VEG:

MY MOOD:

My treat for today is:..

The Power of Breathing

Using your breath to control your emotions may be highly beneficial. Try out some of the breathing exercises listed below.

7/11 BREATHING

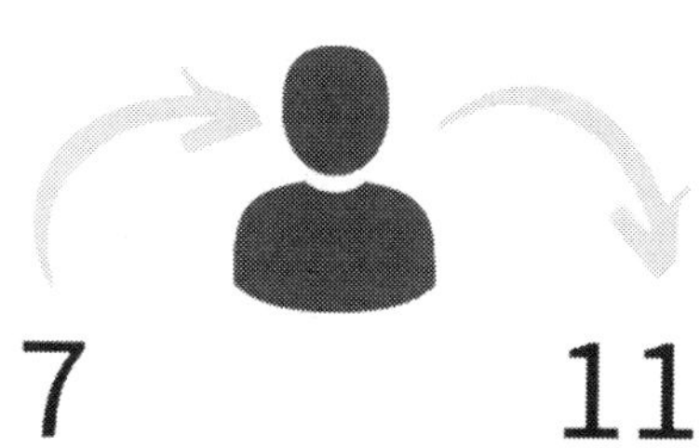

Inhale for 7 counts, then exhale for 11 counts. The lengthier exhale triggers a parasympathetic reaction, calming and relaxing your muscles.

FINGER BREATHING

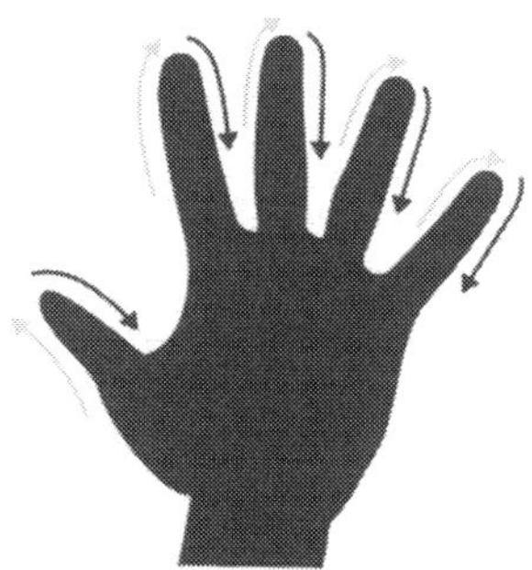

Trace around your outstretched hand's thumb and fingers. Inhale from the base of your thumb to the tip; exhale from the tip of your thumb to the bottom on the other side—rep around the entire hand.

BELLY BREATHING

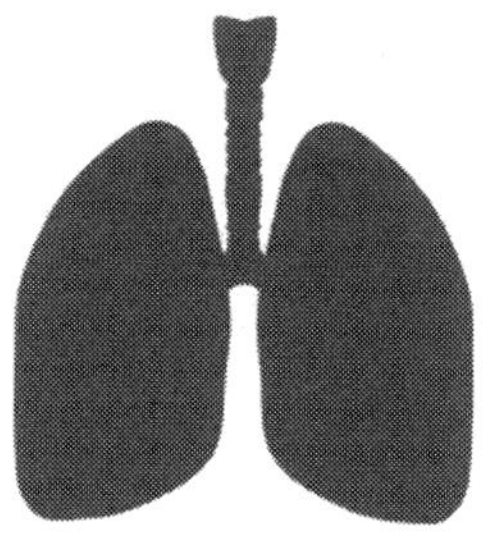

The belly rises on inhalation and falls on exhalation. This enables for more efficient usage of oxygen when it enters the lower portions of the lungs. Feel the movement with your hand on your tummy.

SQUARE BREATHING

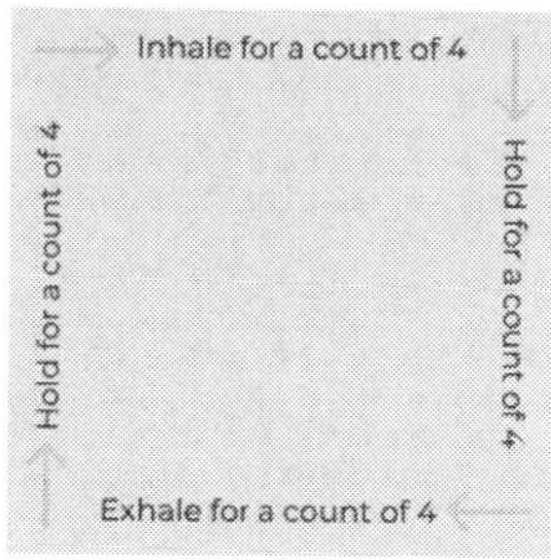

Consider walking around a square. Inhale for four counts from one corner to the next; hold your breath for four counts to the bottom; exhale for four counts to the next corner, and hold your breath for four counts to the last corner. Now do it again.

Day 229 - I Am Coming Out; God is My Way-Maker!

"See, I am doing a new thing! Now it springs up; do you not perceive it? I am making a way in the wilderness and streams in the wasteland."
—Isaiah 43:19, NIV

BELOVED,
You are coming out, climbing higher, becoming more, fulfilling my purpose, achieving my destiny, and living my best life! Keep it moving, despite what's chasing you and causing you to fear. God's miracle is to bless when you come in and go out. His blessing, victory, open door, grace, and glory of His promises are activated when you keep moving forward. Promise-Keeper, Light-in-the-Darkness, and Way-Maker God, He shall make way for your deliverance, restoration, breakthrough, and miraculous escape for you.
His name is Wonderful, Counsellor, The mighty God, The everlasting Father, The Prince of Peace. (Isa 9:6). Jesus was born, crucified, and died to free you from this mindset, mess, and misery.
In the story in John 5: One day, Jesus went through the sheep gate to Bethesda, a pool where many sick and disabled people lay, blind, lame, paralyzed, diseased, depressed, and wasted, waiting for the water to move. Jesus leads His followers to one of the most depressing locales they've ever encountered. Jesus came to love and serve these beautiful people, provide newness to life, the promise of hope for a brighter future, wellness, wholeness, a second chance, redemption, victory, fulness of joy, peace, and abundance in the face of the devil's malevolent aim. Jesus healed a man who had been ill for 38 years on this day. Jesus asked the paralyzed man who was *singled out* for his miracle, "Do you want your healing?" The disabled man answered, stating his limitation and human dependency, "I wait for the waves to stir, but I can't walk. Someone must bring me into the pool to be cured. I'm always beaten to the water's edge without a hand." Jesus told the man, "Get up! Stand up! Take up your mat, which you had bound for years, and carry it. You are coming out! Walk with your sickbed." When Jesus said these words, healing energy coursed through the man, and he stood and walked for the first time in 38 years. Running; HALLELUJAH!
This day had been set aside, predetermined, and appointed for this man to be cured, made healthy, whole, well, and liberated. He was free of the humiliation, trepidation, intimidation, depression, disability, and limitation he had felt his entire life. He no longer sat on his mat and longed for a chance; the man who couldn't walk now ran carrying the sickbed that had him bound and joined his community in jubilation. Today, embrace the testimony as a prophecy for you. Don't be like the religious people who bombard with doubts seeking explanation with disbelief of God's grace. Revival can't be articulated; Jesus must be believed, received, experienced, and encountered. Today, you're coming out; God is Your Way-Maker!

AFFIRMATIONS & DECLARATIONS
I will no longer stay in that situation; God has ordained and predestined my deliverance and a new beginning at the appointed time. "*This is God's Word on the subject: 'As soon as Babylon's seventy years are up and not a day before, I'll show up and take care of you as I promised and bring you back home. I know what I'm doing. I have it all planned out—plans to take care of you, not abandon you, plans to give you the future you hope for.'*" (Jer 29:10-11, MSG). God is my Chain-Breaker; I am a *glory-carrier* of His miracle!

- I am coming out! All my dreams are coming true, and I am living a life of significance due to this!
- I am filled with joy, prosperity, and peace! I have miraculously experienced and encountered my Way-Maker! I am delivered, blessed, healed, helped, happy, whole, and complete. I am enough!

"For thus says the Lord, When seventy years are completed for Babylon, I will visit you and keep My good promise to you, causing you to return to this place.
For I know the thoughts and plans that I have for you, says the Lord, thoughts, and plans for welfare and peace and not for evil, to give you hope in your final outcome."
—Jeremiah 29:10-11, AMPC.

PRAYER
Father in Heaven, You promised that I would be delivered from the territory of tyranny and suffering to the land of my promised inheritance, a land of abundance, a place flowing with milk and honey and plenty and peace. No matter how long the road takes, You are my refuge and strength, my God in whom I put my confidence. Because of this, I am convinced that no weapon thrown at me will succeed. Nothing terrible will happen to me, my children, or my family, and no plague will enter our homes, bodies, thoughts, hearts, souls, projects, objectives, profession, or destiny. The life of my dreams is becoming a reality, and I couldn't be happier! What I'm fleeing from or terrified of doesn't stop me from pursuing a life of abundance. You'll entrust Your angels with the responsibility of watching over me and keeping me safe, picking me up and carrying me so I don't step on me, and establishing a path for me to follow. In Jesus' name, I pray, Your will be done on Earth as it is in Heaven. Amen.

MY DOPE *faith journal*

Date S | M | T | W | T | F | S

Morning: I feel my emotion! My one-word check-in:

DECLARATION

Consider today's verse. I implore the Holy Spirit to reveal His wisdom and truth to me and I declare it over my life.

OBSERVATION

What does the message mean? Lord, help me see it.

PRAYER

What is my prayer request? Lord, I live fully in You.

EMPOWERMENT

How will Your word empower me? Lord, give me the insight to apply my faith to be more significant than my fears.

MY FEARLESS *journey*

Evening: Feel my emotion! My one-word check-up:

What is making me FEEL like this?

What lessons did I LEARNED?

What THOUGHTS did I had?

What prompted my GRATITUDE?

Who did I CONNECTED with?

What brought me JOY?

EVENING PRAYER

WATER:

FRUIT & VEG:

MY MOOD:

My treat for today is: ....

Box Breathing

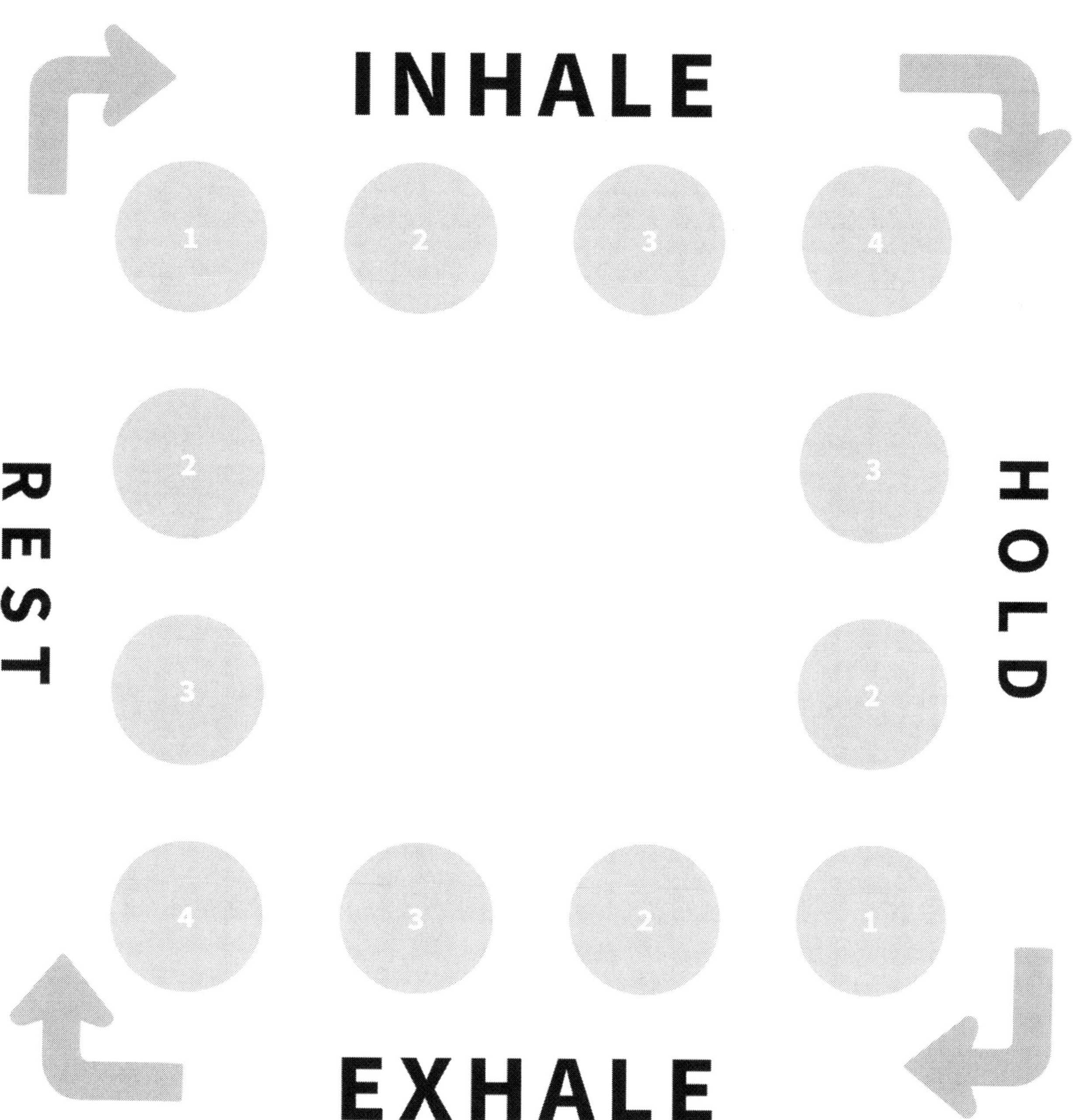

Day 230 - God Will Provide & Satisfy Every Need!

"Give, and you will receive. Your gift will return to you in full—pressed down, shaken together to make room for more, running over, and poured into your lap. The amount you give will determine the amount you get back."
—Luke 6:38, NLT

BELOVED,

Relax, breathe in and breathe out! Inhale, hold, exhale, and rest! Whatever the facts, what you saw with your eyes, and the news you heard with your hearing, the experts, media reporters, political leaders, influential people, hypocrites, and haters were claiming. Your doctors or lawyers may have told you that there is no hope for a positive outcome in terms of your case's diagnosis; the reports and trends and statistics and history and tradition and nationality and family background and generation, and your mistake, budget, and bank account balance and the apparent impossible transformation concluded by many say fear. God has the last word according to faith, however. Be steadfast! You have much to look forward to than you can imagine or think. What if I told you God had planned and prepared much more for you? Would you believe it? You would be correct if you are convinced. Philippians 4:19, VOICE says, *"I am convinced that my God will fully satisfy every need you have, for I have seen the abundant riches of glory revealed to me through the Anointed One, Jesus Christ!"*

You can be sure that God will take care of everything you need. His generosity exceeds yours in the glory that pours from Jesus.

The Story is told in John 2:1-11: Jesus Shows up at a Wedding with a Turnaround Miracle.

"But she turned to the servants. ***Mary:*** *Do whatever my Son tells you."* (John 2:5, VOICE)

Mary, His mother, also a humbled guest, approaches her Son, Jesus, at a wedding and informs Him that the wine has run out. Her Son, who appears concerned but unfazed, declares His determination to do nothing about it because His time has not yet come. "Jesus: Dear woman, is it our problem they miscalculated when buying wine and inviting guests? My time has not arrived." (John 2:4, VOICE). His mother, however, believed in her Son's supernatural abilities, confident in Who He and His divine nature. Mary told the servants, "Whatever Jesus tells you, do it!"

Jesus responded to this act of faith, obedience, confidence, and courage to fearlessly trust Him by performing His first miracle, surprisingly turning water into the best vintage wine ever. Your personal and professional life, career planning, goal setting, social gathering, family, children and relationships, leadership, and parenthood are some areas where you must invite Jesus into your life. With His help, you can transform your life from the mundane to spectacular and ordinary to legendary. God will make you in a new wineskin and pour fresh fine wine in and out of you; even the great connoisseur will attest that this is the best wine I've ever tasted. Jesus specializes in transformation; it's time for your metamorphosis to the best life ever. Listen, obey, and trust God to get the job done. There is no way to describe what an incredible life you will lead and live. God will provide and satisfy every need!

AFFIRMATIONS & DECLARATIONS

For I love the Lord, my God, He is my source of light, strength, and shelter; the Lord bestows favor and glory on Me as I seek and serve Him. He keeps nothing back from me who follow the path of righteousness. In light of this, it is clear that my God is brighter than dawn despite my darkness! He lavishes His grace and splendor on me, encircling me with favor and loving-kindness like a shield. Because I follow His way with honesty and integrity, I will never be without everything I need. He is my everything and gives me everything; With Christ, I am limitless and shall have no lack! (Psalm 84:11).

- I am drowning my fears in God's perfect love.
- I am not a mistake; I am a masterpiece.
- I am not a failure nor a victim; I am victorious and living a life of satisfaction and significance.

"So above all, constantly chase after the realm of God's kingdom and the righteousness that proceeds from him. Then all these less important things will be given to you abundantly."
—Matthew 6:33, TPT

PRAYER

Heavenly Father, You, fill my mouth with Your goodness. I am in awe of Your awesomeness to Me. I worship and exalt You. I lift You, and I sing praises to You. You are worthy and faithful. I trust You. I love You, Lord. I thank You for calming my fears, anxiety, and worries. I am ready to live my best life. I believe You will provide and satisfy my every need by Your grace and all for Your glory in Jesus' name. I pray, Amen.

MY DOPE *faith journal*

Date S | M | T | W | T | F | S

Morning: I feel my emotion! My one-word check-in: ....

DECLARATION

Consider today's verse. I implore the Holy Spirit to reveal His wisdom and truth to me and I declare it over my life.

OBSERVATION

What does the message mean? Lord, help me see it.

PRAYER

What is my prayer request? Lord, I live fully in You.

EMPOWERMENT

How will Your word empower me? Lord, give me the insight to apply my faith to be more significant than my fears.

MY FEARLESS *journey*

Evening: Feel my emotion! My one-word check-up:

What is making me FEEL like this?

What lessons did I LEARNED?

What THOUGHTS did I had?

What prompted my GRATITUDE?

Who did I CONNECTED with?

What brought me JOY?

EVENING PRAYER

WATER:

FRUIT & VEG:

MY MOOD:

My treat for today is: ....

Finger Breathing

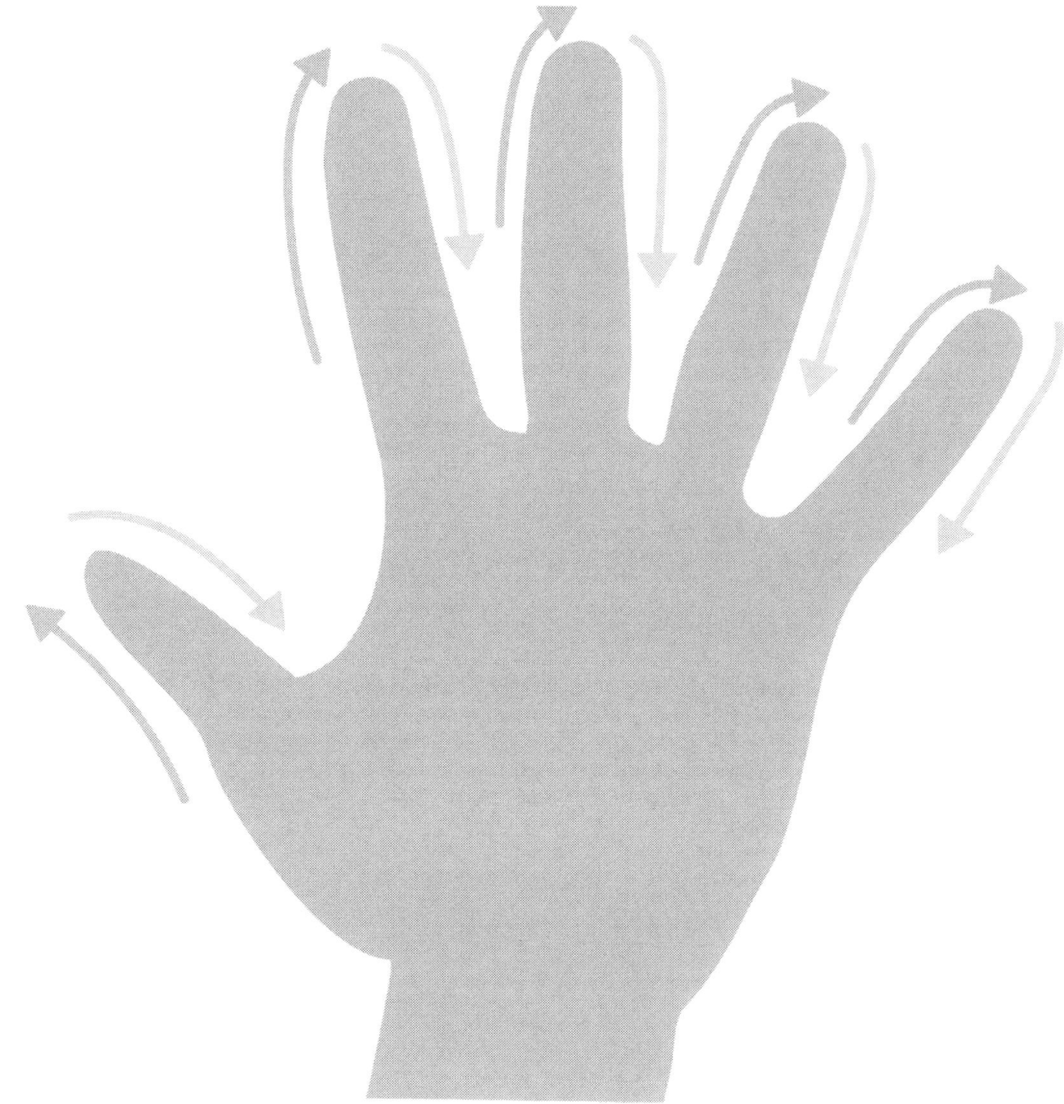

Trace around your extended hand's fingers and thumb. Inhale from your thumb's base to its tip, then exhale from your thumb's tip back to its base on the other side. Repeat around the hand.

Day 231 - You Must Trust God & Take Him at His Word!

"But blessed is the one who trusts in the Lord, whose confidence is in him. They will be like a tree planted by the water that sends out its roots by the stream. It does not fear when heat comes; its leaves are always green. It has no worries in a year of drought and never fails to bear fruit."
—Jeremiah 17:7-8, NIV

BELOVED,
The best advice amidst these unrelenting changes and unprecedented challenges is to Trust God! Trust in the Lord with all your heart. Take God at His word. Do not lean on your understanding.
"Never affirm your fears; they are afraid of your strengths! (Nicola Mcfadden, Rebound Faith: Chayah!)
"Trust God!" These two words seem simple and yet so hard to do.
It may feel like Good Friday, but Easter Sunday is coming. (John 20:1-30)
The Great Crucifixion happened, and Jesus' dead body was placed in the tomb. Many who witnessed this event fled to the city, they had seen many crucifixions before, but this one touched them because it was close to them. As they looked at the aftermath of the violation, the pain, the shame of the crucifixion, and greeted the empty, did anyone ever consider the possibility that the words uttered by Jesus have manifested that the empty tomb was a symbol of hope?
*"**Jesus:** 'Dear woman, why are you crying? Who are you looking for?' She still had no idea who it was before her. Thinking He was the gardener, she muttered:*
***Mary Magdalene:** Sir, if you are the one who carried Him away, then tell me where He is, and I will retrieve Him.*
***Jesus:** Mary!"* (John 20:15-16, VOICE)
In your darkness, have you forgotten the promises of God? Is God in your midst, but you fail to recognize Him? Are you so overwhelmed with grief, pain, sorrow, fear, anger, and hopelessness that you dismissed Jesus who is with You, the One, who promised, I will never leave nor forsake you? Today, He calls you by name, *[insert your name]*.
Mary Magdalene exclaimed, 'Rabboni, my Teacher!' Jesus said, 'Mary, you can't hold Me. I must soar above this earth to be with My Father, who is also your Father; My God. Go and tell My brothers.' Mary Magdalene obediently went to Jesus' followers. Mary Magdalene said, 'I saw the Lord, and He said...' On Resurrection Sunday evening, the followers hid behind closed doors because of fear. Jesus arrived in the room. *"Jesus said, 'May each one of you be at peace.'"* While speaking, He showed His hands and side wounds. As they realized they were witnessing the Lord, the disciples celebrated. *"Jesus said, 'I give you the gift of peace. In the same way, the Father sent Me, I am now sending you.'"* (John 20:15-19).
Jesus affirmed and prophesized in John 11:25, *"I am The Resurrection and the Life!"*
Believers believe in the resurrection power in John 20. You must trust God and take Him at His word!

AFFIRMATIONS & DECLARATIONS
"*I delight myself in the Lord, and He will give me the desires and petitions of my heart. I commit my way to the Lord. I trust in Him also, and He will do it. Make God the utmost delight and pleasure of your life, and He will provide for you what you desire the most. Give God the right to direct your life, and as you trust him along the way, you'll find, He pulled it off perfectly!"* (Psalm 37:4-5, TPT).

- Though He slays me, yet will I trust Him!
- God, I rest in You and upon Your promises. I lean on You to lead, help, and heal me.
- I am waiting for You. I am at peace; I have the gift of peace. I believe in God and His word.

*"Open up before God, keep nothing back; he'll do whatever needs to be done:
He'll validate your life in the clear light of day and stamp you with approval at high noon."*
—Psalm 37:4-6, MSG.

PRAYER
Heavenly Father, as I enter into a new day, I pray for Your wisdom, strength, courage, and confidence over me that I will trust You to work it out, to break through it, to provide for me, to protect it, and to protect me, to heal me, help me and to restore me in Jesus' mighty name, I pray, Amen.

MY DOPE *faith journal*

Date S | M | T | W | T | F | S

Morning: I feel my emotion! My one-word check-in: ....

DECLARATION

Consider today's verse. I implore the Holy Spirit to reveal His wisdom and truth to me and I declare it over my life.

OBSERVATION

What does the message mean? Lord, help me see it.

PRAYER

What is my prayer request? Lord, I live fully in You.

EMPOWERMENT

How will Your word empower me? Lord, give me the insight to apply my faith to be more significant than my fears.

MY FEARLESS *journey*

Evening: Feel my emotion! My one-word check-up:

What is making me FEEL like this?

What lessons did I LEARNED?

What THOUGHTS did I had?

What prompted my GRATITUDE?

Who did I CONNECTED with?

What brought me JOY?

EVENING PRAYER

WATER:

FRUIT & VEG:

MY MOOD:

My treat for today is: ....

Lazy 8 Breathing

Think of an 8 turned on its side.
As you inhale, begin in the center and trace along the right side of the number 8. Exhale as you trace the left portion of the 8 once you've reached the middle.

Day 232 - God Shall Remember & You Shall Rebound!

"I am with you and will watch over you wherever you go, and I will bring you back to this land. I will not leave you until I have done what I have promised you."
—Genesis 28:15, NIV

BELOVED,
You may have forgotten you prayed, but God remembers.

- God remembered Noah.
- God remembered Abraham.
- God remembered Rachel.
- God remembered David.
- God remembered Hannah.
- God remembered Joseph.
- God shall remember you, and you shall rebound.

Psalm 105 tells us that God is a Covenant-Fulfillment God and a Promise-keeping God.
Let us tell the world what He's done! Tell people about the beautiful, marvelous, victorious, and mighty things He has accomplished for us. Share your stories and testimonies of His miracles, Today; you take pride in the authority, power, and anointing of His holy name, Jesus, The Liberating King!
Be joyful, you Lord's servants! For joy and strength, you must rely on the Lord. Our God is the Lord. He is the absolute Ruler and Controller of the whole universe. You are His beloved child!
God is a Promise-Keeper. He will never forget what He has promised. God loves, provides for, leads, and protects His people. He recalls His promises, realizes His plan, recognizes His children, rewards them, and reinforces His purpose. God remembers you, relentlessly rescues, and recklessly loves you. He meets you right where you are in this life journey to reclaim, rebuild, and rebound you with His magnificent attributes and mighty actions. Despite the *violation* and *venting*, you leave this *valley* with a clarified *vision* and an unstoppable *vow*. (5 V of Rebound Faith: Chayah).

AFFIRMATIONS & DECLARATIONS
I may think God has forgotten, but He is equipping me for my best life, new trajectory, and elevation.
"God chose those whom the world considers foolish to shame those who think they are wise, and God chose the puny and powerless to shame the high and mighty. He chose the lowly, the laughable in the world's eyes —nobodies—so that He would shame the somebodies. For He chose what is regarded as insignificant in order to supersede what is regarded as prominent, so that there would be no place for prideful boasting in God's presence." (1 Cor 1:27-29. MSG)

- I am not afraid, nor am not I discouraged, because God is with me.
- God is my light of salvation, strength, shield, supplier, and safe place.
- The Lord guides and directs my steps.
- God has an eternal love for me.

"He keeps His covenant promises forever and remembers the word He spoke to a thousand generations."
—Psalm 105:8, VOICE

PRAYER
Heavenly Father, Lord, thank You for Your word that reminds me that You would never forget me, nor forsake me, and always forgive me. Lord, today You shall remember me and answer my prayer. Lord, You are the Covenant-Fulfillment, Promise-Keeping, Creator, and Redeemer God. I am Your beloved child, obedient servant, and loyal lover, and You will never leave nor refuse to help me. Thank You, Lord, for preparing me through the waiting period and blessing me far beyond what I asked, hoped, imagined, or dreamed. Lord, You have tremendous and magnificent breakthroughs, healing miracles, uncommon blessing, restoration, deliverance, and promises of a meaningful life for me. You have ordained, predestined, and positioned for me. I am prepared inside out for Your promotion – my head (my mindset), my heart (my character), my habits (my conduct), my hands (my deeds), my home (my life and living), and my career (my livelihood). Your mind-blowing miracle, promise, promotion, protection, provision, peace, prosperity, and supernatural blessings have my name on it and are delivered to me right now, all the fulfillment of Your divine plan manifested at the appointed time in Jesus' name, I pray, Amen.

MY DOPE *faith journal*

Date S | M | T | W | T | F | S

Morning: I feel my emotion! My one-word check-in:

DECLARATION

Consider today's verse. I implore the Holy Spirit to reveal His wisdom and truth to me and I declare it over my life.

OBSERVATION

What does the message mean? Lord, help me see it.

PRAYER

What is my prayer request? Lord, I live fully in You.

EMPOWERMENT

How will Your word empower me? Lord, give me the insight to apply my faith to be more significant than my fears.

MY FEARLESS *journey*

Evening: Feel my emotion! My one-word check-up:

What is making me FEEL like this?

What lessons did I LEARNED?

What THOUGHTS did I had?

What prompted my GRATITUDE?

Who did I CONNECTED with?

What brought me JOY?

EVENING PRAYER

WATER:

FRUIT & VEG:

MY MOOD:

My treat for today is:..

Grounding Method

LOOK
Find 5 objects in your immediate surroundings and list them aloud.

5

LOOK

FEEL
Pick 4 things you can sense in your body and list them aloud while maintaining body awareness.

4

FEEL

LISTEN
3 noises should be heard when listening. Out loud, pronounce the three sounds.

3

LISTEN

SMELL
Name two smells you can identify. Describe the scent aloud.

2

SMELL

TASTE
One item you can taste, please. Declare this aloud.

1

TASTE

Day 233 - Do Not Fear, I Am With You Always!

"Say to those who have an anxious heart, 'Be strong; fear not! Behold, your God will come with vengeance, with the recompense of God. He will come and save you."
—Isaiah 35:4, ESV

BELOVED,

I know everything around you is shouting FEAR but listen and obey that soft, still whisper of your heart that says *Face Everything And Rebound!* So face, feel and fight the fear but move forward in faith!
Rick Warren once said, *"Fear is a self-imposed prison that will keep you from becoming what God intends for you to be. You must move against it with the weapons of faith and love."*
Background information in Isaiah 41 reveals God's promises and plan for helping Israel despite their adversaries' diabolical plots. On the other hand, Israel must learn to trust God without fear, for God has elevated Cyrus to power and leadership as a winning strategy and excellent purpose for God's people. Today, God is working for you, bringing the right people together at the perfect time and place. He sends a timely word for you; despite it all, the Father says,
"Do not yield to fear, for I am always near. Never turn your gaze from me, for I am your faithful God. I will infuse you with my strength and help you in every situation. I will hold you firmly with my victorious right hand." (Isaiah 41:10, TPT)
The picture described in Isaiah 41 is eerily reminiscent of today's world, full of global issues; the fear is *so real* you can almost touch it. As you embrace changes and challenges, address your personal, professional, spiritual, physical, mental, emotional, financial, and social difficulties. As a covenant-fulfilling God, God's plan of supernatural intervention is not an accident or a result of your good intentions, aims, or ambitions. Believers and the church need a revival for reconciliation to God due to our disobedience and rebelliousness toward our role and responsibilities in the covenant relationship with our Heavenly Father, His righteousness, and the Kingdom of God. But God! With repentance, you can only look to Him for regeneration, redemption, restoration, and rejuvenation; He is your only hope. However, today, He brings good news and great joy that, among the numerous reasons to be scared, anxious, angry, and worried, there is a whisper of hope that you can only hear when you are still and quiet in His presence that says, "Don't be afraid. I will assist you. Do not fear; I am with you always!"

AFFIRMATIONS & DECLARATIONS

"I am constantly present among You," God declares. I, the Lord your God, am among you as a Warrior who rescues. I will be ecstatic over you. You shall be silent in My affection, not mentioning but canceling your previous crimes and not holding you captive. I will rejoice over you with joyful tidings."

- I will not fear.
- My God is with me always.
- I rebuke the Spirit of fear.
- I have the Spirit of power, love, self-discipline, self-control, and a sound mind.
- I am loved.
- I know I am and to whom I belong. I am His.
- I know my identity. I am royalty, a child of God.
- I am happy.

Jerusalem will be told: "Don't be afraid. Dear Zion, don't despair. Your God is present among you, a strong Warrior there to save you. Happy to have you back, he'll calm you with his love and delight you with his songs."
—Zephaniah 3:16-17, MSG

PRAYER

Father in Heaven, I admire and respect You for who You are. Please calm the roaring noise of the confusion, calamity, and chaos in my head to hear You whisper and promise that You are here with me to help me, and I need not be afraid. My healthy fear is directed just at You, Almighty God, Creator, Controller, and Redeemer of the entire universe. I free myself of every toxic fear with my courageous trust, steadfast love, and dunamis power. As a result, I live in awe of You and surrender to You. Help me overcome the frightening spirit that attempts to destroy the life, purpose, mission, gift, destiny, and legacy you have called me to live fully. In the name of Jesus, I pray, amen.

MY DOPE *faith journal*

Date S | M | T | W | T | F | S

Morning: I feel my emotion! My one-word check-in: ....

DECLARATION

Consider today's verse. I implore the Holy Spirit to reveal His wisdom and truth to me and I declare it over my life.

OBSERVATION

What does the message mean? Lord, help me see it.

PRAYER

What is my prayer request? Lord, I live fully in You.

EMPOWERMENT

How will Your word empower me? Lord, give me the insight to apply my faith to be more significant than my fears.

MY FEARLESS *journey*

Evening: Feel my emotion! My one-word check-up:

What is making me FEEL like this?

What lessons did I LEARNED?

What THOUGHTS did I had?

What prompted my GRATITUDE?

Who did I CONNECTED with?

What brought me JOY?

EVENING PRAYER

WATER:

FRUIT & VEG:

MY MOOD:

My treat for today is:...

Bingo for Mindfulness

Keep a diary to record your ideas.	Take a stroll in nature.	Accept your ideas	Get some rest.	Solitude with God
Practice guided Bible study.	Take some time to think about your day.	Show gratitude	Practice voluntary work	Read a long form devotion or sermon
Create something	Eat mindfully	FREE	Take a vacation from technology.	Do volunteer work
Give social media a rest.	Discover a new breathing method	List a few reassurances.	Give yourself a commendation.	Engage in what you love.
Utilize all of your senses.	Play soothing music	Shower or take a bath with awareness	Decide on daily goals.	Actively listen

Day 234 - Rescued From Stress; Rested & Blessed!

"Do not be anxious about anything, but in every situation, by prayer and petition, with thanksgiving, present your requests to God. And the peace of God, which transcends all understanding, will guard your hearts and your minds in Christ Jesus."
—Philippians 4:6-7, NIV

BELOVED,

You are being rescued from stress to be rested and blessed! The secular world has a 'day' specialized for everything. Well, declare today a Holy Spirit holiday, a vacation from stress, fear, and worry. Rearrange your priorities and re-prioritize God. Mark your calendar with the words "BOOKED FOR CHRIST." Today is a Spa day with Christ. Go in solitude with God as your Solace. You are taking a day off from the troubles, trials, tribulations, and temptations and seeking a day of triumph and an oasis of hope, despite it all —a time of peace and pleasure to be present in His presence. A day of divine rest in His rhythm to reset, rescue, rejuvenate, relax, reenergize, and restore your well-being.

The Father says, "Take a time-out from stress, burnt-out, busy yet stuck life, feeling overwhelmed, scattered, worried, depression, anxiety, fear, troubles, lack, between a rock and a hard place. Come on in to spend time with Me! Let Me sing joyful love songs of deliverance over you. I created you. I will care for you, cover, comfort, cleanse, crown, and carry you. I commit as your Caregiver and Guardian-keeper for a lifetime. Welcome to your new life, new trajectory, new dimension, new creation, and a new beginning: The refreshment of your soul brings newness, blessedness, and belovedness!"

Jesus says, Come to Me!

Matt 11:28-30, AMP says, *"Come to Me, all who are weary and heavily burdened [by religious rituals that provide no peace], and I will give you rest [refreshing your souls with salvation]. Take My yoke upon you and learn from Me [following Me as My disciple], for I am gentle and humble in heart, and you will find rest (renewal, blessed quiet) for your souls. For My yoke is easy [to bear], and My burden is light."*

There are many possibilities and advantages to self-care, and Jesus' light yoke exchanged for your heavy burdens and burnt-out life, and there was an encouragement and divine invitation to do so.

AFFIRMATIONS & DECLARATIONS

I won't worry, stress, fear, or be anxious about problems; instead, I pray about everything. You long to hear my prayers, so I pray about my wants and be grateful for what has come. I know without a doubt that the peace of God, a peace that is beyond my human comprehension, will guard my heart and mind in Jesus, the Risen King, Liberated King and Anointed One.

- I am in the secret hiding place of my Savior's arms.
- 'I am too blessed to be stressed.'
- I'm giving you my life so that you may accomplish something more significant and better.
- I am fearless, for God has not given me a spirit of fear but a measure of faith and a spirit of power, love, self-control, and a sound mind.

"Don't be pulled in different directions or worried about a thing. Be saturated in prayer throughout each day, offering your faith-filled requests before God with overflowing gratitude. Tell him every detail of your life, 7 then God's wonderful peace that transcends human understanding, will guard your heart and mind through Jesus Christ."
— Philippians 4:6-7, TPT

PRAYER

Heavenly Father, Thank You for making it such that there is nowhere I can go that You are not there. Thank You for holding me together, grasping my hands, and aligning my life to Your will, even when everything around me appears to be coming apart. Lord, please forgive me for allowing stress to take control of my life rather than You. I've let pressure dictate my mood, feelings, strength, joy, peace, attitudes, and behaviors. I'm sorry for everything. Please, Lord, give me peace of mind and calm my anxious heart. There is much unrest in my spirit. I can't find my feet, so I keep stumbling and worrying. Then I'll discover my purpose and walk the path You've laid out for me with strength and clarity of mind.

A new day begins with an emerging sun against the darkness of night, just as it does every morning. Would you please assist me in seeing the brightness of Your presence even in the deepest darkness? I release every MERIT to you: 'Money, Expertise, Referrals, Interest and Time.' Today, I signed up for Your subscription of intimacy and friendship to be forever in your company. I accept Your invitation to come for a Holy Spirit holiday and spend time with You for a divine reset, refreshing, renewal, and rebirth. In the name of Jesus, I pray, Amen.

MY DOPE *faith journal*

Date S | M | T | W | T | F | S

Morning: I feel my emotion! My one-word check-in:

DECLARATION

Consider today's verse. I implore the Holy Spirit to reveal His wisdom and truth to me and I declare it over my life.

OBSERVATION

What does the message mean? Lord, help me see it.

PRAYER

What is my prayer request? Lord, I live fully in You.

EMPOWERMENT

How will Your word empower me? Lord, give me the insight to apply my faith to be more significant than my fears.

MY FEARLESS *journey*

Evening: Feel my emotion! My one-word check-up:

What is making me FEEL like this?

What lessons did I LEARNED?

What THOUGHTS did I had?

What prompted my GRATITUDE?

Who did I CONNECTED with?

What brought me JOY?

EVENING PRAYER

WATER:

FRUIT & VEG:

MY MOOD:

My treat for today is: ....

Being Present

Giving your focus and awareness to the present is a crucial component of mindfulness. Your emotional and physical health will gain much from it, and your happiness will also increase. Try to engage in a mindful activity each day this week and pay attention to your present-moment presence.

	MINDFUL ACTIVITY	HOW IT MADE YOU FEEL
MONDAY		
TUESDAY		
WEDNESDAY		
THURSDAY		
FRIDAY		
SATURDAY		
SUNDAY		

Day 235 - What Does God Say?

"Let your eyes look directly ahead And let your gaze be fixed straight in front of you. Watch the path of your feet And all your ways will be established. Do not turn to the right nor to the left; Turn your foot from evil."
—Proverbs 4:25-27, NAS

BELOVED,
Don't make what your eyes see; make you doubt or forget what God said. For you live by faith, believing, and not by sight, seeing. God confirms in His word over and over the importance of faith, believing, hoping, and trusting in Him. We must not let what our eyes see make us forget what God said. God encourages you to keep your hope alive by affixing your ideas and thoughts to Him, and He offers scriptural truth of hope in God rather than what your eyes perceive.

The Father says, *"I am giving you a promise now while the seed is still in the barn. You have not yet harvested your grain, and your grapevines, fig-trees, pomegranates, and olive trees have not yet produced their crops. But from this day onward, I will bless you."* (Haggai 2:19).

Don't let what you see cause you to question or forget what God says.
Don't attempt to figure things out with human logic. In the name of Jesus, you should announce that no matter where you are, your adversaries must flee at twilight, and newly awaited spoils will meet you at your destination. Believe it whether you're sick, lame, depressed, struggling, or enjoying life's mountaintop view because all things are possible, miraculous, and victorious with God! A supernatural rebound! God says it is time for a revival—spiritual rebirth, superabundant restoration, and strategic renewal! Don't make what your eyes see; make you doubt or forget what God said.

AFFIRMATIONS & DECLARATIONS
I must walk by faith, not sight. The word of God reminds me repeatedly that 'the righteous will live by faith.' God reassures me to keep my hope alive, my mind and thoughts in Him.
Haggai 2:19, 2 Corinthians 5:7, Romans 8:24, 2 Corinthians 4:18, and Hebrews 11:1, provide biblical truth of hope in God not what my eyes see.

- My past doesn't define me.
- My identity is in You, Lord!
- I am created in Your image and likeness.
- I am your handiwork and masterpiece.
- I am beautiful.
- I am brave and blessed.

"For we have been saved in this hope and for this future. But hope does not involve what we already have or see. For who goes around hoping for what he already has?"
—Romans 8:24, TPT.

PRAYER
Heavenly Father, Almighty God, I confess and repent that, at times, I walk by sight, fear, and feelings rather than faith. I allow toxic fear to rule rather than trusting in You. Lord, forgive me. Today, I renew my vow to walk by faith, believing, trusting, and hoping in You to rebound me from every valley. I thank You, Lord, for God reminded me repeatedly that as a believer, I must live by faith, not because of me but because of Your faithfulness. Thank You for the Blood of Jesus that washes my sin and covers my mess, so I am spotless, blameless, priceless, fearless, and limitless, and call me righteous. Your word says when I believe, You credit my belief as righteousness. Lord, I believe You; please help my unbelief. I believe that You will help me, and You have given me a measure of faith. You will amaze me at the magnificence of Your glory that is ignited even with my little faith. I muscle up my rebound, and I proclaim my rebound, by Your grace and all for Your glory in Jesus' mighty name; I pray, Amen.

MY DOPE *faith journal*

Date S | M | T | W | T | F | S

Morning: I feel my emotion! My one-word check-in: ....

DECLARATION

Consider today's verse. I implore the Holy Spirit to reveal His wisdom and truth to me and I declare it over my life.

OBSERVATION

What does the message mean? Lord, help me see it.

PRAYER

What is my prayer request? Lord, I live fully in You.

EMPOWERMENT

How will Your word empower me? Lord, give me the insight to apply my faith to be more significant than my fears.

MY FEARLESS *journey*

Evening: Feel my emotion! My one-word check-up:

What is making me FEEL like this?

What lessons did I LEARNED?

What THOUGHTS did I had?

What prompted my GRATITUDE?

Who did I CONNECTED with?

What brought me JOY?

EVENING PRAYER

WATER:

FRUIT & VEG:

MY MOOD:

My treat for today is: ....

The Pomodoro Technique

Source: Francesco Cirillo

Decide on the task you need to do

This can be any task that you need to get done and something that will require your full attention.

Set timer to 25 minutes

Commit to spending 25 minutes on this task with no interruptions or distractions.

Work on task until timer rings

Spend the next 25 minutes immersed in the task.

Make a check on paper

This check shows you've successfully completed one session.

Take a 5 minute break

You can do anything here that's not related to the task: have a drink, stretch, take a short walk.

After 4 check marks take a 30 minute break

Now you can take a longer break. During this time your brain will assimilate the new information and be ready for your next session.

Day 236 - "You Are Going To Make It, Trust Me!" Says God.

"When you pass through the waters, I will be with you; and when you pass through the rivers, they will not sweep over you. When you walk through the fire, you will not be burned; the flames will not set you ablaze."
—Isaiah 43:2, NIV

BELOVED,
Has this season's strong waves and winds made you feel like we've been 'shipwrecked in a storm?' Unrelenting changes and extraordinary difficulties have left us battered, beaten down, broken, bewildered, perplexed, and bitter. Despite the ferocious storm, God promises you'll make it!

"I'M WITH YOU. I GOT YOU. YOU'RE GOING TO MAKE IT, TRUST ME. JUST STAND FIRM AND ALLOW ME TO FIGHT THIS STORM." **- GOD**

Act 27 draws an analogy of life journey and the story of Paul's trip by sea to Rome and his experience with a ferocious storm.

— Starting to Sail (The journey)
Luke accompanied Paul to Rome with Aristarchus, a Thessalonian Macedonian brother. They decided to sail toward Italy. Julius, an officer in the emperor's secret army, was assigned to protect Paul and other captives on the journey. They sailed near Crete. Then came the storm. The "Northeaster" blew across the island. This wind swept the ship away. They gave up attempting to sail against the wind and let the storm have its way with them.

— Struggling in a Storm.
When life's storms hit and rage, you need a strong tower, a safe place, an anchor, a Rock, an impenetrable, immovable, unchangeable God. Jesus, the One who commands the winds and waves to be quiet, invites you to come for shield, refuge, protection, and rescue. You ask Him to divinely intervene in your life to provide for your safety, security, protection, and comfort. He assures you that you will arrive safely on the other side. (Mark 4:35-41). Despite the fear of destruction and despair, the loss, and the impact of the storm, you will strengthen and secure, and safely make it to the other side with the faithfulness of God, the authority of the name Jesus, the Blood coverage, the power of Holy Spirit and the Fire that ignites you with inner strength and confident peace and courageous joy. But the big elephant in the room is: Will you put your faith in Him? Will you trust that God, He is your loving but powerful Protector and faithful Provider, the Creator, Controller of the Universe, Redeemer of God, to defend you against the terrain of the storm? God gives you His word, today's message, and a messenger – A promise of hope!"

— Surviving the Shipwreck!
However, the ship collided with a sandbank! Paul's ship was shipwrecked, but by the grace of God, they made it safely with a fresh anointing for the new era.
You will stay steady, even though the storm comes and the winds blow and the roar of the waters. Seasons vary, and storms brew, yet God remains steadfast and unfailing in his promises. His word is unchanging, and his past, present, and reputation, as well as the consistency of his word, demonstrate that God can do nothing but fail. You can trust him since He declared. "You are going to make it. Trust me!" says God.

AFFIRMATIONS & DECLARATIONS
My God responds that I will make it no matter what I am facing or have faced. You will carry me, care for me, comfort me, cover, and keep me. You will restore my peace, joy, happiness, health, abundance, security, and prosperity.

- I will make it through this storm. I will wait and worship You even in the middle of the storm.
- I am not alone; forever, I will lift my soul into Your presence, Lord.
- My God goes before me before I get there. He is already there, already made way for me.
- I am showered with grace and the gift of righteousness.

Mark 4:35-41(b), VOICE: ***Disciples (to one another):*** *'Who is this Jesus? How can it be that He has power over even the wind and the waves?'"*

PRAYER
Heavenly Father, I thank You for the life that You have given to me. Thank You for guiding me and helping me feel safe, contented, and comfortable even when facing life's storms and struggles. Every day I feel like I'm going to fall off the cliff as I *'climb and maintain'* from the valley to the mountaintop, but You never fail to save me. As I sail on this life journey, I ask you for a second wind, a fresh anointing for the journey of life to endure and be kept in perfect peace, joy, love, and righteousness. The journey seems complicated, but the truth is that the promised victorious end and favorable outcome are always just around the corner, and You have continued to lead me through every storm over the years. Thank You for always being there for me and allowing me to go and grow in my fearless faith in You. In Jesus' name, I pray, Amen.

MY DOPE *faith journal*

Date S | M | T | W | T | F | S

Morning: I feel my emotion! My one-word check-in: ....

DECLARATION

Consider today's verse. I implore the Holy Spirit to reveal His wisdom and truth to me and I declare it over my life.

OBSERVATION

What does the message mean? Lord, help me see it.

PRAYER

What is my prayer request? Lord, I live fully in You.

EMPOWERMENT

How will Your word empower me? Lord, give me the insight to apply my faith to be more significant than my fears.

MY FEARLESS *journey*

Evening: Feel my emotion! My one-word check-up:

What is making me FEEL like this?

What lessons did I LEARNED?

What THOUGHTS did I had?

What prompted my GRATITUDE?

Who did I CONNECTED with?

What brought me JOY?

EVENING PRAYER

WATER:

FRUIT & VEG:

MY MOOD:

My treat for today is:..

The Pomodoro Technique

Source: Francesco Cirillo

TASK ONE

☐

☐

☐

TARGET

25 25 BREAK 25 25 BREAK
25 25 25 25

TASK TWO

☐

☐

☐

TARGET

25 25 BREAK 25 25 BREAK
25 25 25 25

TASK THREE

☐

☐

☐

TARGET

25 25 BREAK 25 25 BREAK
25 25 25 25

Day 237 - God Has A Plan!

"Your eyes saw my unformed substance; in your book were written, every one of them, the days that were formed for me, when as yet there was none of them."
—Psalm 139:16, ESV

BELOVED,
But when you think it's too late, God has a plan! Fear leads you to foolish thoughts, perverse ways, and self-centered goals and is a setup to fail without the faith to believe in God's divine plan's guidance, manifestation, and alignment.
Jeremiah 29:11 is a well-known passage discussed numerous times in the 365 Live Fearlessly devotionals.
"For I know the plans I have for you," says the Eternal, "plans for peace, not evil, to give you a future and hope—never forget that." (Jeremiah 29:11, VOICE).
Somehow, it seems as if this scripture has become so commonplace that it is no longer believed.
1. For I know the plans I have for you.
God says He has a plan for you. He is the one who created you, His masterpiece. He is in charge of the whole procedure for your product, program, project, processes, functionality, personality, and features, including conception, research and development, innovation, rebirth, branding, design, implementation, go-market strategy, renovation, promotion, renewal, transformation, and legacy.
Consider this in the secular world: Apple owns the manufacturing rights, trademark, blueprint, and the whole end-to-end process of all their products, including brands, warranty, guarantees, authorized dealers for repairs, reconditioned, and new releases. If we can grasp the parallel in the secular world, why can't we understand it in the spiritual realm? God is your Creator, and you are His creation. You are God's property. You belong to God. You are His child! He has a great plan, divine purpose, and promise for you.
2. Plans for peace, not evil, to give you a future and hope.
His divine plan is for peace, not evil; for a future, not just a past; for hope, not despair! He created and designed you and saw you in the secret place of your mother's womb and said you are fearfully and wonderfully made. He is the Author of your story, the Architect of your life, the Perfector of your faith, the Redeemer of your soul, the Promise-Keeper say, I, Jesus, come to bring fullness, newness, and eternal life.
3. Never forget that.
No matter what happens, always remember this promise, strategy, and roadmap as the secret sauce of your life journey. But when you think it's too late, God has a plan!

AFFIRMATIONS & DECLARATIONS
I affirm and declare that I will be joy-filled and hope-filled and joyful and hopeful as I meditate on the plan and thoughts God had for my life. When my adversary thought God had forgotten, and it was too late, God sent His Son. The Redeemer, The Chain-Breaker, Resurrection, and the Life, The Light of the Work, The Lord of the Breakthrough, Burden-Bearer, Deliverer, Way-maker, Promise-Keeper, Miracle-worker!

- I believe that there is more to life than this! I believe God has a great plan and future for my life!
- I am chosen by God, my Creator. I confess that Jesus Christ is the savior of my life.
- I am His favorite child; I know my royalty identity in Christ; God loves me.
- I am wonderfully made, and God gives me the best!

"But when that era came to an end and the time of fulfillment had come, God sent his Son, born of a woman, born under the written law. Yet all of this was so that he would redeem and set free all those held hostage to the written law so that we would receive our freedom and a full legal adoption as his children."
—Galatians 4:4-5, TPT.

PRAYER
Heavenly Father, I am grateful every day for life and Your direction. I know that it is my goal to do Your will in my life, and I have been asking for guidance on discerning Your divine purpose in my life. I am a God's child, and my identity is You, Lord, with a secure inheritance and heritage. Thank You, Lord, for a solid plan over my life from Creation to Eternity, from birth to Salvation, from rebirth to legacy. Would You kindly assist me in accepting Your forgiveness, having self-compassion and forgiving myself, and promptly forgiving others regardless of the pain or severity of the violation? Please help me be filled with peace, joy, inner strength, and righteousness to assist the weak, exhibit the same patience You model to me, constantly return good for evil, and seek after what is good, beautiful, admirable, and acceptable in Your sight. I admit that even when I believe it's too late and I don't understand the purpose of the pain of the process, You have a winning strategy and unfailing plan. In Jesus' name, I pray. Amen.

MY DOPE *faith journal*

Date S | M | T | W | T | F | S

Morning: I feel my emotion! My one-word check-in: ....

DECLARATION

Consider today's verse. I implore the Holy Spirit to reveal His wisdom and truth to me and I declare it over my life.

OBSERVATION

What does the message mean? Lord, help me see it.

PRAYER

What is my prayer request? Lord, I live fully in You.

EMPOWERMENT

How will Your word empower me? Lord, give me the insight to apply my faith to be more significant than my fears.

MY FEARLESS *journey*

Evening: Feel my emotion! My one-word check-up:

What is making me FEEL like this?

What lessons did I LEARNED?

What THOUGHTS did I had?

What prompted my GRATITUDE?

Who did I CONNECTED with?

What brought me JOY?

EVENING PRAYER

WATER:

FRUIT & VEG:

MY MOOD:

My treat for today is: ....

The Pomodoro Planner

Source: Francesco Cirillo

TASK DESCRIPTION	25	5	25	5	25	5	25	30

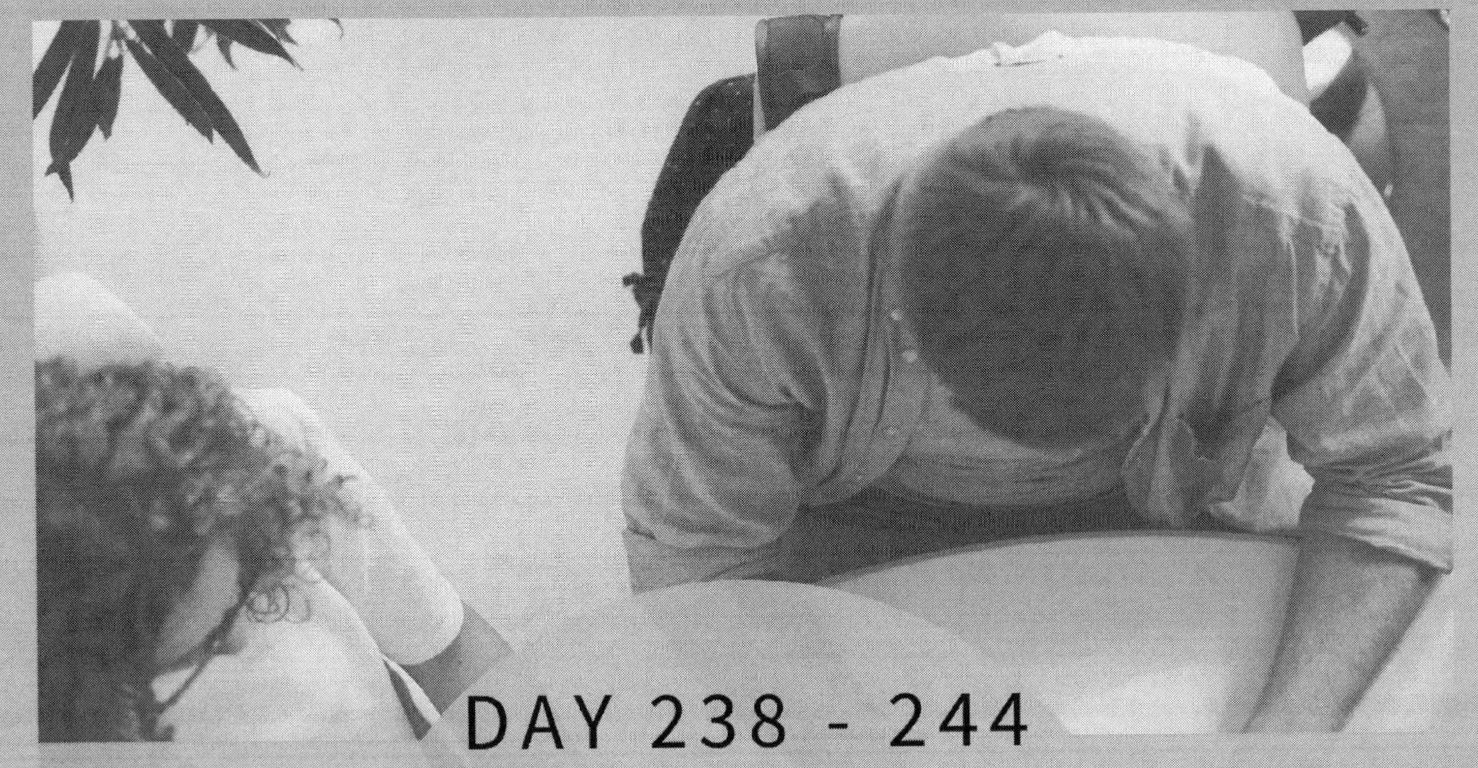

DAY 238 - 244

Learn New Skills

"Seest thou a man diligent in his business? he shall stand before kings; he shall not stand before mean men."

— PROVERBS 22:29, KJV

Day 238 - Nothing Can Stop God's Plan For Me!

"The LORD will fulfill his purpose for me; your steadfast love, O LORD, endures forever. Do not forsake the work of your hands."
— Psalm 138:8, ESV

BELOVED,
Proclaim: "Nothing is that powerful to stop God's plan for me!" No matter how 'messy' the past is, never think it's too 'mucky' for God's cleansing grace, restoration power, and glorious purpose for your life. He has the master plan for you, His masterpiece. The Father says, *"I, the Lord All-Powerful, have made these plans. No one can stop me now!"* (Isa 14:27, CEV). My dear, your enemies, you, and your past are not that powerful to stop My divine plan for you. Nothing can disqualify My plan and purpose for you. Believe! Let go. Seek Me as your priority. Trust Me and believe what I say, think, and write about you, because what and who, I, the Lord of hosts, have chosen and planned, who can undo it? My hand is extended to bless, help, heal, and deliver you, and who can turn it back? Despite it all, I will shift you from devastation and depression to deliverance and restoration. Regardless of the current state of affairs, I will restore what I have decided and planned, and who can annul it.
In Zephaniah 3, Jerusalem is described as feminine, and God is depicted as weeping for the city's plight, current condition, and inhabitants. Instead of serving, coaching, and teaching the people the truth and purity word of God, the shepherds that have been called to lead God's people were self-centered and egoistic. The land, leaders, followers, attitudes, habits, behaviors, leadership, culture, the church, and society have turned away from God and headed for doom and gloom. The prophet Zephaniah talks about how bad things have gotten then, and regrettably, he also describes the current state of affairs in the world and your life, living, and livelihood. But God!
The Father says I'm in your midst; nothing I do is wrong. Every morning I deliver mercy and judgment and show the way to live. Though I'm always there, it's remarkable that lawbreakers aren't embarrassed by their activities. My devoted, wait for Me. I'll purify the nations' speech so you may hear My truth. Then everyone can pray and serve Me as one people. My scattered disciples will return with clean offerings. On that day, you won't be humiliated by your past rebellion. I'll delete the prideful and arrogant as promised. My sacred mountain won't accept arrogance and conceit. But I'll rescue the suffering and needy individuals who believe in My reputation. If you're faithful, don't lie or fool each other. You'll eat properly and sleep soundly like protected sheep, for nothing will scare you. Hurray! Sing, King's kid! Let's yell! Happy and joyful, God's children! My judgments against you are canceled, and I destroyed your adversaries. Today, don't be scared; hold your head and hands high. I am among you and will save you. I will praise, celebrate, and rejoice over you like a new spouse.

AFFIRMATIONS & DECLARATIONS
I am moving forward – crawl, walk, run, or leap. I get started and keep going.
"He tells us everything over and over— one line at a time, one line at a time, a little here, and a little there!"
—Isaiah 28:10, NLT.
Faith says, no matter how messy my past is, my future is spotless, blameless, and limitless,

- I choose faith over fear; I choose to believe; I have a brighter and more empowered future.
- I am keeping my eyes on God; He is the Lifter of my head; I am holding my head high.

PRAYER
Heavenly Father, help me recover what I've lost. In the name of Jesus, I beg that all the dread, stress, concern, and anxiety that has built up in me and around me due to earlier losses, fear of losing, setbacks, and poor breaks be ended as I am sealed and covered in Jesus' Blood! Please, Lord, keep my heart and mind on You. Even if I feel there no hope is left because of: an incorrect course of action; almost there, then life happens; a career transition, redundancy, a pink slip to the door, being overlooked for a promotion, or rejected again; a business crash or initiative failed, efforts, resources, and time were all for naught; a crashed stock market, rising prices, increased unemployment, and slowed economy; political, social, and economic stumbling blocks. With Christ, I am more than a conqueror; no turbulence or misery can stop Your blessing; even if everyone abandons me, You are still with me; even if I am in my worst condition, I am entirely Yours. You will recognize me, remember me, reward me, never forsake me or forget me, and Your promise will come true. I prioritize our relationship, so I may turn to You as my Father and Friend, Rock of Safety, Refuge, and help in need! I announce peace, righteousness, new life, and pleasure. Nothing can stop Jesus' plan for me. Amen!

MY DOPE *faith journal*

Date S | M | T | W | T | F | S

Morning: I feel my emotion! My one-word check-in:

DECLARATION

Consider today's verse. I implore the Holy Spirit to reveal His wisdom and truth to me and I declare it over my life.

OBSERVATION

What does the message mean? Lord, help me see it.

PRAYER

What is my prayer request? Lord, I live fully in You.

EMPOWERMENT

How will Your word empower me? Lord, give me the insight to apply my faith to be more significant than my fears.

MY FEARLESS *journey*

Evening: Feel my emotion! My one-word check-up:

What is making me FEEL like this?

What lessons did I LEARNED?

What THOUGHTS did I had?

What prompted my GRATITUDE?

Who did I CONNECTED with?

What brought me JOY?

EVENING PRAYER

WATER:

FRUIT & VEG:

MY MOOD:

My treat for today is:...

How We Learn

developed from work by William Glasser

This pyramid shows the way that information is more efficiently retained when learning something new.

WHAT WE READ	10%
WHAT WE HEAR	20%
WHAT WE SEE	30%
WHAT WE SEE AND HEAR	50%
WHAT WE DISCUSS WITH OTHERS	70%
WHAT WE EXPERIENCE PERSONALLY	80%
WHAT WE TEACH OTHERS	95%

Day 239 - Don't Look Back!

"Brothers and sisters, I do not consider myself yet to have taken hold of it. But one thing I do: Forgetting what is behind and straining toward what is ahead, I press on toward the goal to win the prize for which God has called me heavenward in Christ Jesus."
—Philippians 3:13-14, NIV

BELOVED,
Don't look back! Don't stop. Keep pressing forward! Don't be distracted by the lies of the enemy. The devil wants you to descend into depression, discouragement, and disappointment. Stop looking around and press forward. Ensure that every door you exit through is closed and sealed in the Blood of Jesus.
Ask God to be your rearguard protector and order you to depart; you will not have to flee for your life in a hurry. The LORD will lead you, and the Almighty God will defend you from behind and cover your back.
"Go in confidence and grace—no rushing, no frantic escape. There's no need to be anxious—the Eternal One goes before and behind you. The God of Israel paves the way with assurance and strength. He watches your back." (Isaiah 52:12, VOICE)
In Jesus' name, I declare that everything that leads you back to what God has rescued you and broken the chain to free from is permanently damaged, and you are eternally loved, liberated, and restored. God is leading you and creating something new in, for, and through you. You only need to keep your eyes on God.
The story of Sodom and Gomorrah in Genesis 19 tells of two sinful cities and vile living. God was about to destroy the cities and everyone who lived there because of their horrible actions [18:20]. Abraham begs for the lives of many faithful ones who may be there, particularly his nephew, Lot, and his family. God offered to spare Lot and his household from the destruction, pain, and punishment of living there if they fled quickly and kept going. God's messenger said, 'Lot, get up and remove your wife and daughters. Otherwise, the city will eat you.' But Lot delayed, so two heavenly messengers snatched him, his wife, and his two daughters. They took Lot's family outside the city because the Lord showed mercy. As they led them to safety, one messenger said: 'Run! Escape! In the plain, don't look back or halt. Everyone will perish if you don't flee.' But Lot's wife **looked back** at the worldly treasures, fame, fortune, luxury, and sinful pleasures of the old life that she would be losing rather than looking forward to the future vision and the newness of life that God is leading her. She looked back and became a pillar of salt. [19:12-29].

AFFIRMATIONS & DECLARATIONS
"But I pour my trust into You, Eternal One. I'm glad to say, "You are my God!" I give the moments of my life over to You, Eternal One. Rescue me from those who hate me and hound me with their threats. Look toward me, and let Your face shine down upon Your servant. Because of Your gracious love, save me!"
(Psalm 31:14-16, VOICE.

- I stop looking back.
- I stop lamenting who left and what I have lost.
- I start praising for what remains, who has me, who is with me, and what He will do with me.

Psalm 90:17, AMP — *"And let the [gracious] favor of the Lord our God be on us; Confirm for us the work of our hands— Yes, confirm the work of our hands."*

PRAYER
Heavenly Father, I come before You humbly and thank You. In Jesus' name, I speak prophetically over my life, my day, and this future. Just as the sun never sets and the rivers never dry up, God will double the growth of my life, health, wealth, wellness, wisdom, career, business, and relationships. Fear, lack, and crisis are not in my categories, in the name of Jesus. In Jesus' name, God will guide me out of my past and into my victorious future. God will remove me from my cave, where I am hiding from my enemies, to be recognized and anoint me as a king, just as He did David. God, You have blessed me with a unique and special anointing for the new era, new beginning, and new testimony. I pray to be a channel, pillar, and steward for God's blessing. Lord, prepare me to be a servant leader and anoint me to be Jesus' heart, hands, head, feet, and habits. Lord, enable me to love, lead, and learn as Jesus did. I am still, Lord!
As I worship, I block out the devil's falsehoods and the voices of men, experts, facts, statistics, reports, feelings, and fears. I become silent and tuned in to actively listen, and I hear the Lord's whisper. My God sends me a game-changing word, a Rhema work, a living, active, and helpful message to propel me ahead. God's word, spoken to me, moves me on a new path, altering the course of my destiny, a billion-dollar concept, bestselling book, creative business strategy, global expansion, and anointed ministry and calling. The devil is a deceiver, and he is defeated. In Jesus' name, I won't look back! I won't stop. I keep pressing forward; I pray, Amen.

MY DOPE *faith journal*

Date S | M | T | W | T | F | S

Morning: I feel my emotion! My one-word check-in: ....

DECLARATION

Consider today's verse. I implore the Holy Spirit to reveal His wisdom and truth to me and I declare it over my life.

OBSERVATION

What does the message mean? Lord, help me see it.

PRAYER

What is my prayer request? Lord, I live fully in You.

EMPOWERMENT

How will Your word empower me? Lord, give me the insight to apply my faith to be more significant than my fears.

MY FEARLESS *journey*

Evening: Feel my emotion! My one-word check-up:

What is making me FEEL like this?

What lessons did I LEARNED?

What THOUGHTS did I had?

What prompted my GRATITUDE?

Who did I CONNECTED with?

What brought me JOY?

EVENING PRAYER

WATER:

FRUIT & VEG:

MY MOOD:

My treat for today is: ....

Multiple Intelligences and Learning Styles

from Gardner

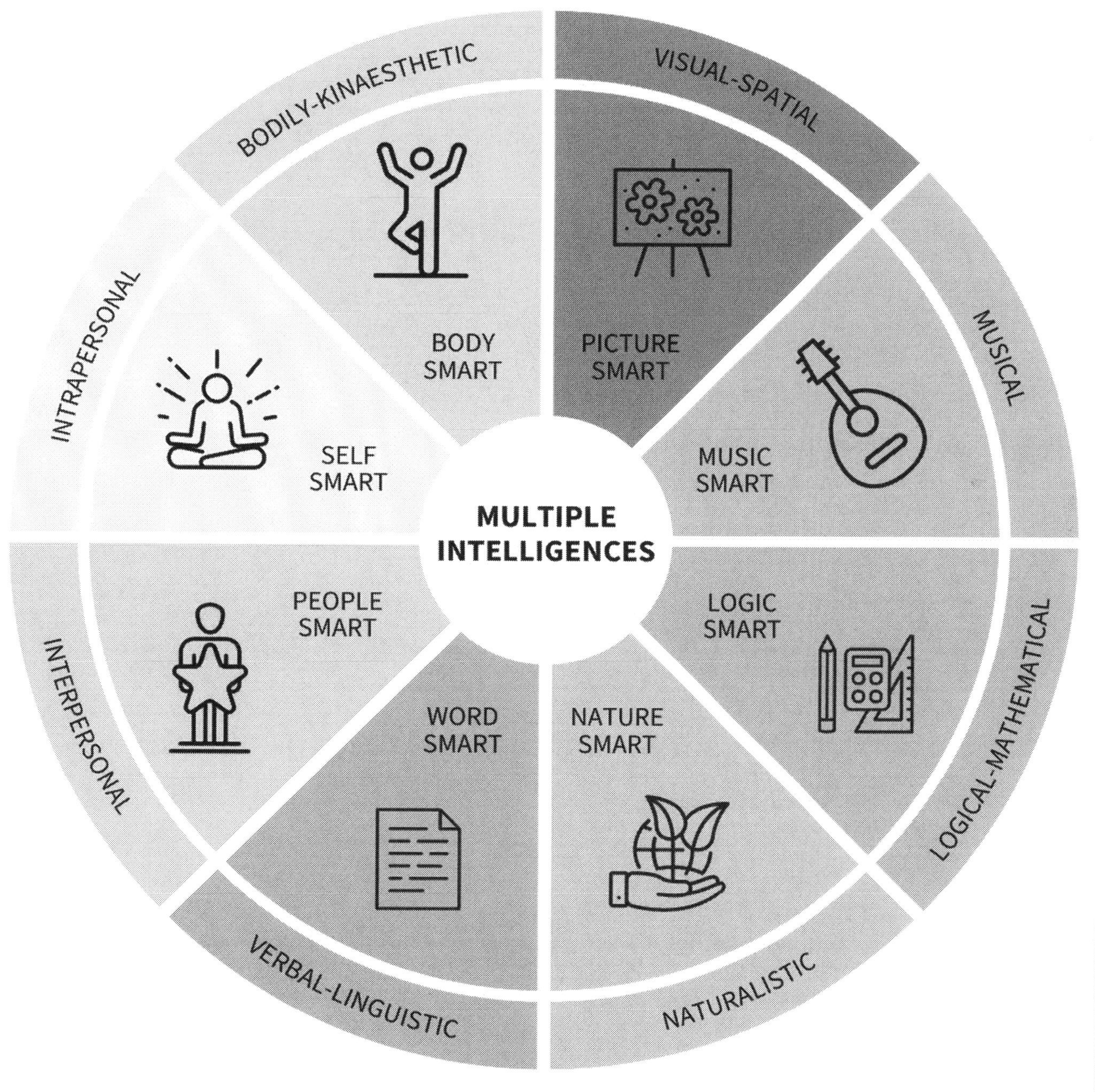

Day 240 - Lord, I Would Never Have Made It Without You!

"Who stood up for me against the wicked? Who took my side against evil workers? If God hadn't been there for me, I never would have made it. The minute I said, "I'm slipping, I'm falling," your love, God, took hold and held me fast. When I was upset and beside myself, you calmed me down and cheered me up."
—Psalm 94:17-19, MSG

BELOVED,
God's grace saved you! Despite all the hardships you've endured, you're still standing today because of your faith.
The only way you could have made it this far is because of Jesus, Lord. You're more assertive, intelligent, resilient, and all-around better now! It would not have been possible without the Lord. Every experience is a victory for you! You've come to show the world that you've been victorious! You have triumphed in battle! You have surpassed all expectations!
Let Psalm 94:17-19 be your testimony: 'Unless the Lord intervened, I would have fallen into the world of death and stillness. "My foot is slipping!" was the first thing I said. The only thing that kept me going, so I never gave up, O Lord, was your unwavering love. When I'm feeling worried, fearful, angry, anxious, and overwhelmed, Your presence gives me a lift.'
God has protected you and will continue to do so amid this global calamity on all levels of change: on a personal, professional, societal, and even individual level. You are grateful for the time He has spent with you every step of the way, He is with you and for all, He has already done, is doing, and going to for you. In the name of Jesus, you thank and worship Heavenly Father. He is capable of anything, and the devil is powerless to stop you from achieving your dreams. You've only heard about God, but now you can actually and tangibly see His glory. Let the Lord examine you and reveal what hinders your breakthrough, blessings, and deliverance He has in store for you. You should humbly confess your sins, return to Him through the Blood of Jesus, and ask for His grace, mercy, forgiveness, second chance, a new beginning, liberation, wisdom, victory, joy, peace, and righteousness.

AFFIRMATIONS & DECLARATIONS
Now praise God, who can keep you from slipping away and will bring you into his glorious presence without a single flaw: LORD, I WOULD NEVER HAVE MADE IT WITHOUT YOU!
"*Now to the One who can keep you upright and plant you firmly in His presence—clean, unmarked, and joyful in the light of His glory— to the One and only God, our Savior, through Jesus the Anointed our Lord, be glory and greatness and might and authority; just as it has been since before He created time, may it continue now and into eternity. Amen.*" (Jude 1:24-25, VOICE.)

- God keeps me.
- I am keeping my eyes on Him.
- My God has kept me, and He will be keeping me.

"And now to Him who can keep you on your feet, standing tall in his bright presence, fresh and celebrating—to our One God, our only Savior, through Jesus Christ, our Master, be glory, majesty, strength, and rule before all time, and now, and to the end of all time. Yes."
—Jude 1:24-25, MSG.

PRAYER
Heavenly Father, God Almighty, I thank You! Lord, I praise You! I know that You can do everything and that no purpose of Yours can be withheld from me. I have heard of You by the ear, But now my eyes have seen You, encounter and experienced the demonstration of your grace, power, goodness, and glory. Therefore I hate myself for the wrong choices, doubts, disobedience, waywardness, and selfishness, and I repent in dust and ashes. Lord, search me and reveal if anything is blocking my breakthrough, blessings, and deliverance. I repent, regret, return to You, and seek Your forgiveness and mercy upon me. Holy Spirit, help me to receive your forgiveness, forgive myself of guilt and shame, let go, forgive others their offenses and give room for You to avenge on my behalf. Lord, I pray for everyone who has done me wrong. I choose to forgive others and pray that You will also forgive their folly and bless them. May the Grace of God be with them and me; in Jesus' name, I pray, Amen.

MY DOPE *faith journal*

Date S | M | T | W | T | F | S

Morning: I feel my emotion! My one-word check-in: ....

DECLARATION

Consider today's verse. I implore the Holy Spirit to reveal His wisdom and truth to me and I declare it over my life.

OBSERVATION

What does the message mean? Lord, help me see it.

PRAYER

What is my prayer request? Lord, I live fully in You.

EMPOWERMENT

How will Your word empower me? Lord, give me the insight to apply my faith to be more significant than my fears.

MY FEARLESS *journey*

Evening: Feel my emotion! My one-word check-up:

What is making me FEEL like this?

What lessons did I LEARNED?

What THOUGHTS did I had?

What prompted my GRATITUDE?

Who did I CONNECTED with?

What brought me JOY?

EVENING PRAYER

WATER:

FRUIT & VEG:

MY MOOD:

My treat for today is: ....

VAK Learning Styles

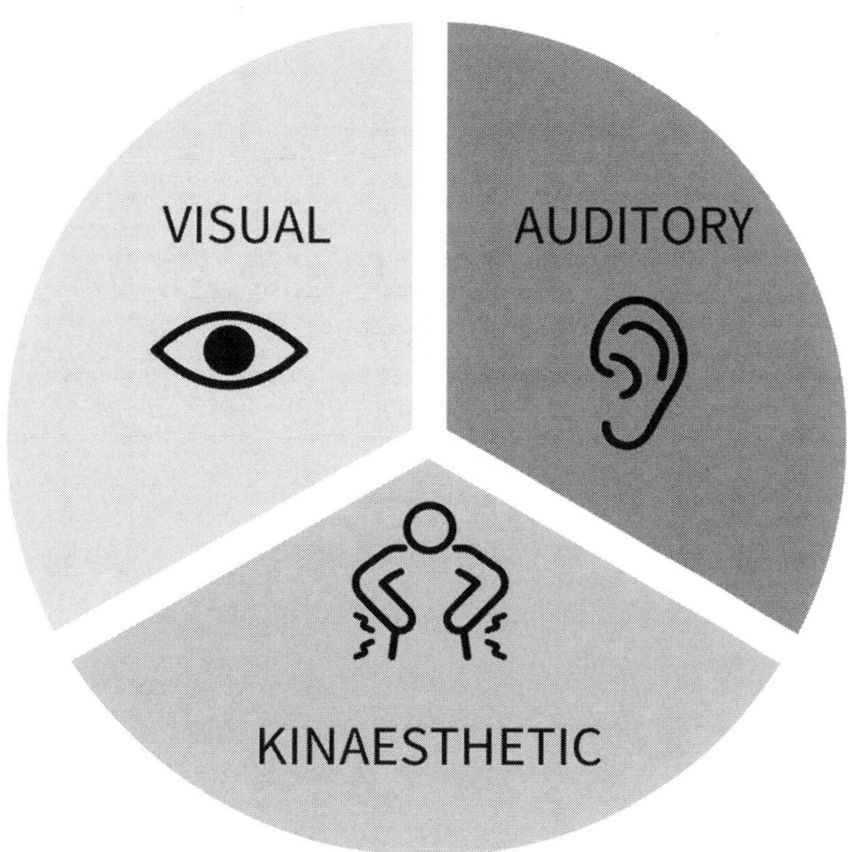

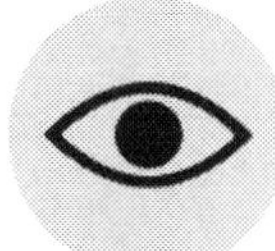

VISUAL LEARNERS

Use visual aids to educate yourself, such as photographs, displays, maps, graphs, diagrams, and infographics.

AUDITORY LEARNERS

Learn via listening and hearing the spoken word, podcasts, sounds, noises, verbal instructions, conversation, music, pitch, and rhythm.

KINAESTHETIC LEARNERS

Learn via physical experience through sports, the performing arts, dancing, role-playing, feeling, doing, movement, and hands-on learning.

Day 241 - Annoyingly Positive Vibes: With God, I got this!

"And do not be conformed to this world, but be transformed by the renewing of your mind, so that you may prove what the will of God is, that which is good and acceptable and perfect."
—Romans 12:2, NAS

BELOVED,
Be confident in your abilities and know God has a life plan for you. Acknowledge and follow Him with awe-inspiring respect. Don't back down because you don't think you're not up to the challenge because you think you're unqualified or unprepared. You are a change agent, a shaker, and a mover! God doesn't call the well-prepared, know-it-all, and qualified. God gives those who are called the necessary tools and training. Believe in yourself, and trust God as He placed you there for a reason. Do not back down because you believe you are inexperienced for the position, ill-prepared, or unfit for the adventure. Your positivity: spirit, energy, or vibe should be in sync with Philippians 4:13, which states, "I can do all things through Christ who strengthens me."
Positivity is 'the habit of being or having a proclivity to be positive or optimistic in outlook.'
You may have a positive vibe when you trust God and believe in yourself. **I got this! God got me!**
"I can do all things [which He has called me to do] through Him who strengthens and empowers me [to fulfill His purpose—I am self-sufficient in Christ's sufficiency; I am ready for anything and equal to anything through Him who infuses me with inner strength and confident peace.]." - Philippians 4:13, AMP
In Philippians 4:13, the scripture talks of the faithfulness and fearlessness that God has given you.
It speaks against the fear-based self-talk, disempowering ideas, and self-doubt paralyzing you.
Through the Anointed One, Jesus Christ, who is my power, sufficiency, and strength, I can be satisfied, strengthened, sufficient, happy, calm, courageous, confident, and contented in any scenario. He is enough to last me beyond a lifetime; therefore, I am enough!
Many times, you have the faith to think God got this. Still, you have poor self-worth, self-doubt, self-condemnation, self-sabotaging ideas, limiting belief, impostor syndrome, and other negative factors that make you fearful. Still, you must convince yourself that God got you, and thus you got it!
According to God, faith without work is dead.
You must persuade yourself that you can do it so you can go through the door He has opened for you.
Indeed, there is a miracle in the place with your name on it, and you will not be rattled for a moment because the Lord is in this location, and you must allow Him room to display His grandeur and glory.

AFFIRMATIONS & DECLARATIONS
Though I doubt at times, I maintain a refreshingly positive and unwavering optimism about my prayer that God, the fount of all hope, will saturate my life with pleasure and serenity in my faith. This optimism has been bestowed on me by the Holy Spirit.

- I got this!
- God got me!
- Lord, you are my rearguard.
- Lord, keep an eye on what's going on behind my back!
- Reverse every curse and negative utterance into a blessing and positive outcome.

"Now may God, the inspiration and fountain of hope, fill you to overflowing with uncontainable joy and perfect peace as you trust in him. And may the power of the Holy Spirit continually surround your life with his super-abundance until you radiate with hope!"
—Romans 15:13

PRAYER
O Divine Heavenly Father, I truly appreciate Your kindness, even when I don't deserve it. I am thankful to have someone who stays loyal and loves me even when circumstances are challenging. Would You please help me keep going when I feel like I have nothing left? Would You please grab my hand when I start to slip and help me through the darkness? You are the one I believe I and rely. Lord, please love me unconditionally when I need it. Never let my broken heart breaks my faith to believe in You and myself. Erase the hurt and make me whole again. Would You please remind me that You are the one who has absolute control over every area of my life? I am cheerful because I believe in Your supernatural blessings on the way to find me, Lord Jesus. In Your name, I pray, AMEN!

MY DOPE *faith journal*

Date S | M | T | W | T | F | S

Morning: I feel my emotion! My one-word check-in: ....

DECLARATION

Consider today's verse. I implore the Holy Spirit to reveal His wisdom and truth to me and I declare it over my life.

OBSERVATION

What does the message mean? Lord, help me see it.

PRAYER

What is my prayer request? Lord, I live fully in You.

EMPOWERMENT

How will Your word empower me? Lord, give me the insight to apply my faith to be more significant than my fears.

MY FEARLESS *journey*

Evening: Feel my emotion! My one-word check-up:

What is making me FEEL like this?

What lessons did I LEARNED?

What THOUGHTS did I had?

What prompted my GRATITUDE?

Who did I CONNECTED with?

What brought me JOY?

EVENING PRAYER

WATER:

FRUIT & VEG:

MY MOOD:

My treat for today is: ....

Learning Planner

PROJECT DESCRIPTION

TOOLS AND RESOURCES

START DATE:

END DATE:

BUDGET:

MILESTONES

BREAK IT DOWN

☐
☐
☐
☐
☐

☐
☐
☐
☐
☐

☐
☐
☐
☐
☐

TIMELINE

Day 242 - The Shift Happens; Happiness Is In His Presence.

"Therefore my heart is glad and my tongue rejoices; my body also will rest secure, because you will not abandon me to the realm of the dead, nor will you let your faithful one see decay. You make known to me the path of life; you will fill me with joy in your presence, with eternal pleasures at your right hand."
—Psalm 16:9-11, NIV

BELOVED,
It would be best if you renounced bondage, slavery, and imprisonment. You must progress! You receive His faithfulness, boldness, courage, strength, extraordinary favor, grace, mercy, anointing, and moving power. God's tremendous hand empowers and transforms you. God offers the lonely the gift of families; the captives give freedom, joy, and wealth. The LORD sets prisoners free. Jesus' Blood broke your chains. You are free of shame, tears, and fears! You'll laugh again, for all this sadness is shifting—the LORD guides and positions you to accomplish your role and destiny. Everything works for your good and His glory. God will take you to a living well of fresh flowing water amid your wilderness. In Jesus' name, you must command hindrances and impediments to give way.

Hold on to Jesus with your tired hands and feeble feet - '*Let the weakling say I am a warrior!*' The Lord has called you, and you must respond to it. He extends a helping hand to you. Feel His warmth, His affection, and the reassurance of His holiness. The shifting is happening; Jesus offers you a light and easy yoke in exchange for your heavy loads, gladness instead of sadness, faith instead of fear! *"There are two primary forces in this world, fear, and faith. Fear can move you to destructiveness or sickness or failure. Only in rare instances will it motivate you to accomplish. But faith is a greater force. Faith can drive itself into your consciousness and set you free from fear forever."* **—Norman Vincent Peale.**

A Powerful exercise to personalize your relationship with God: Make a "Fearless Psalm" of your own. Beloved, write your own Psalms, be honest with God, tell Him where hurts and enter into His presence to receive His comfort. Worship Him for who He is—Prophesy of His promises made for us.

Today, the shift happens, and your happiness is in His presence. You've been transformed, reformed, reclaimed, rebuilt, reborn, redeemed, resurrected, and restored. May you receive a mighty miracle in your life, body, mind, soul, finances, household, children's life, and in this community, Chayah Club!

AFFIRMATIONS & DECLARATIONS
God is inviting me to come, and I am accepting the call with the anticipation of a tremendous move of God. I announce that this is a miraculous healing move, a deliverance move, a supernatural blessing move, a restoration move, a refreshment of my soul, heart, mind, body, life, children, home, family, this community - Chayah Club, and all your faithful ones.

- I am healed. I am happy. I am healthy.
- I am redeemed.
- I am celebrating my turnaround. My shifting is happening.

"Are you weary, carrying a heavy burden? Come to me. I will refresh your life, for I am your oasis. Simply join your life with mine. Learn my ways, and you'll discover that I'm gentle, humble, easy to please. You will find refreshment and rest in me. For all that I require of you will be pleasant and easy to bear."
—Matthew 11:28-30, TPT

PRAYER
Heavenly Father, make Your WORD apparent in me and my life. Change my life. Rewrite my story for my victory and Your glory! In the name of Jesus, O Lord: Turn my circumstance around.

Make my name memorable, my mission meaningful, and my life marvelous and magnificent. Make my children beneficial to God's Kingdom. Make my house a haven of ultimate peace and decency, brimming with joy, love, prosperity, and your Presence. In the name of Jesus, I declare a complete 180-degree turnaround in my finances, business, leadership, life, projects, goals, mission, ministry, educational aspirations, dreams, today, and destiny. In the name of Jesus, I proclaim a miraculous breakthrough with limitless progress! I'm progressing and becoming better! In the name of Jesus, I demand every stronghold connected with every trial and tribulation to release me. In the name of Jesus, I decree that I am a danger to the adversary, not a victim. Satan is terrified of God's revealed supernatural might in me. In Jesus' name, I pray for supernatural deliverance, restoration, and change. AMEN! Hallelujah. Thank you, Jesus; all praise to GOD!

MY DOPE *faith journal*

Date S | M | T | W | T | F | S

Morning: I feel my emotion! My one-word check-in: ....

DECLARATION

Consider today's verse. I implore the Holy Spirit to reveal His wisdom and truth to me and I declare it over my life.

OBSERVATION

What does the message mean? Lord, help me see it.

PRAYER

What is my prayer request? Lord, I live fully in You.

EMPOWERMENT

How will Your word empower me? Lord, give me the insight to apply my faith to be more significant than my fears.

MY FEARLESS *journey*

Evening: Feel my emotion! My one-word check-up:

What is making me FEEL like this?

What lessons did I LEARNED?

What THOUGHTS did I had?

What prompted my GRATITUDE?

Who did I CONNECTED with?

What brought me JOY?

EVENING PRAYER

WATER:

FRUIT & VEG:

MY MOOD:

My treat for today is:...

Learning Review

WHAT WENT WELL TODAY

ACHIEVEMENTS

- [ ]
- [ ]
- [ ]

THOUGHTS AND FEELINGS

HOW I'LL IMPROVE TOMORROW

Day 243 - He Did It Before, And Will Do It Again!

"And he did rescue us from mortal danger, and he will rescue us again. We have placed our confidence in him, and he will continue to rescue us."
—2 Corinthians 1:10, NLT

BELOVED,
God will do it again! God will make way for you. He did it before, and He will do it again.
"The stories your ancestors told you about God's actions, historical reputation, undefeatable track record from long ago—about how God saved the day—have come to your ears. The nations were driven out of this land with God's great hand, but God planted you here. God planned that you and your children would enjoy the benefits of His covenant promise. Your adversaries are unable to get a foothold in the battle with swords. Their physical prowess did not secure the win. Because God cared for you, His strength—His right hand, His strong arm, and His revelation light of His presence—led to your victory.
O Lord God, You are the King of the Universe! Thank You for everything! God decreed success for you, your home, your family, and everyone else who has anything to do with me. With the mention of His name, you can stomp out the resistance. When it comes to winning, you don't put your faith in your carnal flesh, weapons, or power but the name of the Lord. This chapter is not the end of the story; if it is not well, it's not over. God saves you. The Lord put your adversaries in their place. You shall sing your praises for as long as you live!" (Psalm 44:1-8)
You shall receive this testimony as a prophecy and say, do it again, O Lord.
"Then I fell down at his feet to worship him, but he said to me, "You must not do that! I am a fellow servant with you and your brothers who hold to the testimony of Jesus. Worship God." For the testimony of Jesus is the spirit of prophecy." (Revelation 19:10, ESV).
In Jesus' name, decree and pray that what my arm cannot do in life, the favor and the power of the Lord GOD Almighty will accomplish for me. In Jesus' mighty name, GOD will send you a jaw-dropping surprise, a mind-blowing miracle, and dreamlike benefits. Amen.
John F. Kennedy once said, *"Be strong and of good courage; be not afraid, neither be thou dismayed."*
David kills Goliath – in David's fearless perspective, the battle is already won. (1 Samuel 17:32-37).
David observed how afraid Goliath's threats caused God's people. David peeled back the curtain to reflect on earlier combats and experiences with God, stating that the same unchanging God will offer even greater deliverance this time. David gained courage by remembering past victories, God's constant character, and the truth, possibility, and chance for God to accomplish it again. He'll do it again.

AFFIRMATIONS & DECLARATIONS
I declare that I serve The Unchangeable God!
Lord, You see my adversary attacking me and hear my summons. You are my fortified fortress. I invoke the name of Jesus. Jesus the Anointed One is the same yesterday, today, and forever. Your name is a strong tower; the righteous seek and find protection, security, peace, and comfort in Your name. I have everything I need to thrive.

- I HAVE A HOPEFUL FUTURE. FEAR DOES NOT KEEP ME CAPTIVE.
- I HAVE PEACE THAT EXCEEDS ALL UNDERSTANDING. EVERY DAY, I WILL PUT ON GOD'S FULL ARMOR.

"God himself will hear me! God-Enthroned through everlasting ages, the God of unchanging faithfulness— he will put them in their place, all those who refuse to love and revere him! Pause in his presence"
—Psalm 55:16, TPT.

PRAYER
I confess, Father God, that You, Lord, are the God of Comfort. The same God has returned, and the same God is here right now! God, You did it before and will do it again, the Unfailing God! Father, You've repeatedly blessed me and helped me overcome difficult situations. As a result, I am confident that You will do it again! Today, fear and worry have no hold on me, and I put my complete confidence in Your faithfulness to save me from all my difficulties. So, instead of worrying, I will worship you; instead of panic, I will praise You and thank You in advance for everything You have done in my life.
Thank You, Lord, for being at work in my life. "Thank You!" I thank God for bringing me from Breakdown to Breakthrough. O Lord, I confess and pray each verse of Psalm 44, and I invoke the unchanging God. Help me to have faith in You to deliver me in any scenario. That same God has returned, and that same God is here right now! I'll find a way because God will provide a way for me. He's already done it, and He'll do it again. Amen! In Jesus' name, Amen!

MY DOPE *faith journal*

Date S | M | T | W | T | F | S

Morning: I feel my emotion! My one-word check-in: ....

DECLARATION

Consider today's verse. I implore the Holy Spirit to reveal His wisdom and truth to me and I declare it over my life.

OBSERVATION

What does the message mean? Lord, help me see it.

PRAYER

What is my prayer request? Lord, I live fully in You.

EMPOWERMENT

How will Your word empower me? Lord, give me the insight to apply my faith to be more significant than my fears.

MY FEARLESS *journey*

Evening: Feel my emotion! My one-word check-up:

What is making me FEEL like this?

What lessons did I LEARNED?

What THOUGHTS did I had?

What prompted my GRATITUDE?

Who did I CONNECTED with?

What brought me JOY?

EVENING PRAYER

WATER:

FRUIT & VEG:

MY MOOD:

My treat for today is:..

THIS WEEK'S TASK

Learning New Skills

Learning something new has been shown to boost levels of happiness. Therefore, this week choose some new skills to learn and track your progress in the table below.

	NEW SKILL	WHAT IT WAS LIKE LEARNING THIS
MONDAY		
TUESDAY		
WEDNESDAY		
THURSDAY		
FRIDAY		
SATURDAY		
SUNDAY		

Day 244 - Keep Alert; God Will Heal!

"Nevertheless, keep watching! I will restore this city and heal the wounds of My people. I will lavish them with peace and stability.
Jeremiah 33:6, VOICE

BELOVED,
Nevertheless, Keep watch; God will restore and heal! The world is in dread, pain, and mayhem. Globa, individual, business, leadership, technological, and life paradigm shifts paralyze life, living, and livelihood! You face disruptive innovation and technology, social discontent, increased joblessness and career unhappiness, widespread resignation, an economic crisis, mental, emotional, and financial storms, global health concerns, a rise in death and loss of loved ones, suicidal rates, addictions, substance abuse, depression, anxiety, other mental disorders, novel and dangerous viruses, deadly plagues, pestilences, chronic disease, sickness, and infirmities. Personal issues may also arise. Natural disasters too, earthquakes, storms, tornadoes, wildfires, flooding, and landslides also occur. So you must cry out to God and dig deeper in Him!

"Then they cried to the Lord in their trouble, and he saved them from their distress. He sent out his word and healed them; he rescued them from the grave. Let them give thanks to the Lord for his unfailing love and wonderful deeds for mankind."—Psalm 107:19-21, NIV.

It seems as if the world has been flipped upside down. But, in the middle of all this madness, God offers a promise of hope for restoration and healing in the land and lives in Jeremiah 33:6:

God says, **"Nevertheless, despite it all, keep watching! I will restore it. I will heal you."**

In Jeremiah 33, the city is under siege, and the enemy is gaining ground. Many people's hope seemed dashed as loss seemed assured. Jeremiah faced his predicament as he remained in captivity, chained with guards in the king's hands amid the crisis in the land. Nevertheless, Jeremiah attracted many people. God sent His prophet a message. Jeremiah saw God's people's destiny, despite their suffering. the clarity of this vision goes beyond the current problems to the Controller of the Universe, God's eventual restoration of His people and land. "Call to Me, and I will answer," God told Jeremiah, and telling you, I'll tell you about significant accomplishments that surpass all you've known. (Jer 33:3).

Whether it's a worldwide disaster, a personal storm, a health issue, or the death of a loved one, the Lord can heal and restore it all. He transforms your grief into joy, despair into praise, and ashes into beauty, as He leads you through the darkest valleys and shadows of death. **God offers comfort and consolation.** "I have seen how they act, but I will still bind them up and make them well again. I will show them the way, comfort and console them. I will create in them a desire to praise. "Peace, peace, to those far away. All will be well, wherever you are." And I will heal them." (Isaiah 57:18-19, VOICE).

AFFIRMATIONS & DECLARATIONS
"Behold, [in the restored Jerusalem] I will bring to it health and healing, and I will heal them; and I will reveal to them an abundance of peace (prosperity, security, stability) and truth." (Jeremiah 33:6, AMP).

- I am coming out of captivity, chains, and storms! I am healed. I am restored.
- MY TIME OF SUFFERING IS OVER! I am not worried. I am standing on the promises of God.
- He will restore me. He will heal me. He will bring health and healing to this city.

Psalm 103:2-3, VOICE: *"O my soul, come, praise the Eternal; sing a song from a grateful heart; sing and never forget all the good He has done. Despite all your many offenses, He forgives and releases you. More than any doctor, He heals your diseases."*

PRAYER
Heavenly Father, I love You, Abba. Thank You for demonstrating Your love for me in Christ Jesus. No one is more loving than those who lay down their lives for their friends. Oh, Lord, You sacrificed Yourself and took all my burdens and iniquities! I've crucified myself with Christ, and as a result, my old life of chaos has ceased; I'm a new creation, healed and restored. I belong to You, Lord; You care about me because of the pain You endured for me, redeemed, and healed me in all areas of my life in Jesus' name. Starting today, I shall live as if I am healed and restored in peace, prosperity, kindness, security, safety, stability, wellness, and wholeness that the LORD provides me. My life, journey, story, destiny, and legacy will be better according to the predictions and hopes of the Lord. In His word today, health, restoration, and financial freedom are mine. Money will become my slave and flows from the fount of wealth from Christ's riches. My life testifies to God's blessings of goodness, loving-kindness, and uncommon favor and reflects His supreme glory's magnificent opulence and excellence. In Jesus mighty and matchless, I pray, AMEN!

MY DOPE *faith journal*

Date S | M | T | W | T | F | S

Morning: I feel my emotion! My one-word check-in:

DECLARATION

Consider today's verse. I implore the Holy Spirit to reveal His wisdom and truth to me and I declare it over my life.

OBSERVATION

What does the message mean? Lord, help me see it.

PRAYER

What is my prayer request? Lord, I live fully in You.

EMPOWERMENT

How will Your word empower me? Lord, give me the insight to apply my faith to be more significant than my fears.

MY FEARLESS *journey*

Evening: Feel my emotion! My one-word check-up:

What is making me FEEL like this?

What lessons did I LEARNED?

What THOUGHTS did I had?

What prompted my GRATITUDE?

Who did I CONNECTED with?

What brought me JOY?

EVENING PRAYER

WATER:

FRUIT & VEG:

MY MOOD:

My treat for today is:..

DAY 245 - 251

Sleep

“

Your mind will be clear,
free from fear;
when you lie down to
rest, you will be
refreshed by sweet
sleep.

— PROVERBS 3:24, VOICE

Day 245 - Confidence and Courage For The Conqueror!

"Be strong and courageous, because you will lead these people to inherit the land I swore to their ancestors to give them."
—Joshua 1:6, NIV

BELOVED,

Even though you may feel as if you're stuck between two boulders, God has your back! Ruth and Noami were dealing with adversity, struggle, and loss in the Bible book of Ruth. Even though Noami was a believer, she was overcome by her fear. Ruth was an aspiring Christian who hoped to one day know God and experience His wonders, grace, mercy, and love. While grieving her husband's death, she cared for her depressed mother-in-law while also caring for herself. Though she was still afraid, Ruth's rekindled faith was more important.

It would help if you were change-resilient and change-ready to adapt and accept new beginnings and the unknown future with open arms. You, like Ruth, should be fueled by your shame and nourished by irritation to grow your faith in Jesus Christ. In God, Ruth had confidence. He showed her how much he cared for her. Ruth was unfazed by the hiccup. It was just a ruse to get her back in the game.

Ruth challenged God's faithfulness. A testament to God's commitment is her confidence, trust, belief, and hope in God's ability to guide her through her destiny, restore her life, and care for and while God cures Naomi.

Self-reflection: Is God a good God? Faithful? True? Do you believe in God's promises, plans, purposes, and thoughts? Is your faith in God's unconditional love strong? What do you think about God's ability to work all things together for good and His glory? How confident are you that he can handle the next phase of your life?

Dale Carnegie once said, *"Inaction breeds doubt and fear. Action breeds confidence and courage. If you want to conquer fear, do not sit home and think about it. Go out and get busy."*

Ruth is an excellent example of how to be confident and fearless. Even though you have no idea what's going to happen or how, when, or where it's going to happen, you place your faith and trust in God and take the risk to put your faith into action against all doubt and fear.

With Christ, the conqueror has confidence and courage; believe and do it, even if afraid!

AFFIRMATIONS & DECLARATIONS

I lead while I bleed. I am a legend, building and leaving a legacy of faith and glory greater than currency."
We [earnestly] urge you, believers, admonish those who are out of line [the undisciplined, the unruly, the disorderly], encourage the timid [who lack spiritual courage], help the [spiritually] weak, be very patient with everyone [always controlling your temper]." (1 Thessalonians 5:14 AMP.)

- I am victorious in all of my battles.
- My actions are always fruitful, and my harvest is plenty because I have God in my life as the Great Gardener. He prunes, plows, cultivates, nurtures, and waters my seed for exponetntial growth.
- I believe in God's goodness because I know He loves me. I am a winner!

"We appeal to you, dear brothers and sisters, to instruct those who are not in their place of battle. Be skilled at gently encouraging those who feel themselves inadequate. Be faithful to stand your ground. Help the weak to stand again. Be quick to demonstrate patience with everyone."
—1 Thessalonians 5:14 TPT.

PRAYER

God Almighty, I appreciate Your sharing Naomi's story and her triumph against despair. I frequently view the book of Ruth as a dreamy love story through Ruth's eyes. I appreciate Your viewpoint on Naomi's depression, the source, the symptoms, and the Sovereignty of Your action. I ask Your power to reignite my resurrected trust in Your word regarding my circumstances, the strength to continue ahead, and the bravery to help others. I repent of my self-indulgence, poor self-worth, and self-hurt.

Would You please assist me in embodying the character mentioned in 1 Thess 5:14, which is to encourage myself and others while being patient and kind with everyone, including myself? *"Brothers and sisters, we strongly advise you to scold the rebels who devote their lives to wreaking havoc, encourage the downcast, help the sick and weak, and be patient with all of them."* (1 The 5:14, VOICE). Please help me never to give up and to keep going. Thank You, Lord, for Your love for me and confidence in believing my triumph is sure and secure; I pray in Jesus' name; I pray, AMEN.

MY DOPE *faith journal*

Date S | M | T | W | T | F | S

Morning: I feel my emotion! My one-word check-in: ____________

DECLARATION

Consider today's verse. I implore the Holy Spirit to reveal His wisdom and truth to me and I declare it over my life.

OBSERVATION

What does the message mean? Lord, help me see it.

PRAYER

What is my prayer request? Lord, I live fully in You.

EMPOWERMENT

How will Your word empower me? Lord, give me the insight to apply my faith to be more significant than my fears.

MY FEARLESS *journey*

Evening: Feel my emotion! My one-word check-up:

What is making me FEEL like this?

What lessons did I LEARNED?

What THOUGHTS did I had?

What prompted my GRATITUDE?

Who did I CONNECTED with?

What brought me JOY?

EVENING PRAYER

WATER:

FRUIT & VEG:

MY MOOD:

My treat for today is:...

Improving Sleep

To sleep better you might need to make some changes to your behaviour and daily habits. Use this table to identify areas that you will change to help you become a better sleeper.

Focus area	How I will change this to improve my sleep
Bedroom	
Bedding	
Temperature	
Diet	
Daily exercise	
Alcohol consumption	
Medication/drugs	
Noise	
Bedtime routine	
Thoughts	

Day 246 - I'm Waiting, Not Worried. I'm Worshiping.

"In that day you will say: "Give praise to the Lord, proclaim his name; make known among the nations what he has done, and proclaim that his name is exalted."

—Isaiah 12: 4 , NIV

BELOVED,

Be brave while waiting for the LORD. Be patient, worship, and don't fret. You can anticipate His happy rescue. You won't worry if you worship Him. Those who wait for the Lord won't be humiliated but truthfully feed you His word, to declare: "I'll wait for the Lord...I'll hope in him!" (Isa 8:17). Many people are awaiting the arrival of the Lord's promises. Are you waiting? You've earned it, you're in good company, and the wait has been well-spent. The wait for Joseph lasted 13 years. When his envious brothers' evil plot against him forced Joseph to be sold as a slave at 17, they sold him. It is mentioned (Genesis 37:2). When he was 30, Pharaoh summoned 30-year-old Joseph from prison to the palace, where he immediately installed him as Prime Minister. (Gen. 41:46). It took Abraham 25 years to receive his promised blessings. Genesis 12 tells how God met with Abram and Sarai and promised to bless them as part of a covenant. Abraham was 75 years old when he first received the promise. It is mentioned (Genesis 12:1–6). Abram had just celebrated his 100th birthday at the time he had Isaac. At the time of her death, Sarah was 90 years old. As a result, Abraham and Sarah patiently awaited the fulfillment of God's promise for 25 years. It is mentioned (Genesis 21:5-8). The wait for Moses was 40 years. As we see in Exodus 2, Moses consciously decided to take charge of his future. As the emancipator, he had to kick things off by killing an enslaver. Moses' activities led him to Midian, a desert country, where he spent the next forty years of his life. (Exodus 2:1-15). Thirty years were required for Jesus's ministry to start. When He was thirty, Jesus, the son of Joseph and Mary and the son of Adam and God, began His earthly ministry according to Luke 3:23 (Mary's side of the family) and Matt 1:16 (Joseph's side of the family).

Waiting is a valuable practice. It's a metamorphosis from the inside out to refine your faith. Rather than punishment, this exercise is self-preparation. Patience is honed as you wait on God, for He is the mastermind and has the Master plan behind all that happens, is purposed, and promised in your life.

AFFIRMATIONS & DECLARATIONS

Lord, I've waited and trusted in You for so long. Because I am still learning to be patient, these waiting are being used to improve my skills, values, and virtues. Even when I can't find You, please teach me how to wait on You and yet trust Your heart and worship You. As evidence of my testimony and Your prophecy, I bore witness to Your goodness towards me today. "Be brave in patiently waiting on God, even though it appears to be delayed and God seems absent. As for me, I will wait for the Eternal, even though He feels absent, even though He has hidden His face from the family of Jacob. I will put all hope in Him." (Isaiah 8:17, VOICE).

I waited patiently, confident that You would provide for my needs. At long last, You knelt to hear my screams, see my tears, and the deep longing of my soul. Squatting, You pulled me from the lonely pit I'd fallen into and the mucky mess I'd landed. Now, I'm in a safe and secure position, and You're helping me ascend the route You've chosen for me. There is a new song for a new day in my heart whenever I think about how You come through for me! My tongue is exuberant praise until everyone hears how You have freed me. My life will be filled with Your marvels and miracles, and many people will fall in love with You!

- I am always patient because I am secure, steadfast, and strong in Christ.
- I am a marvelous creation because nothing can separate me from Christ's love.
- I've been chosen, and God has accepted me. I won't faint, fear, fall, or fail during the wait!

"Gather up the testimony, preserve the teaching for my followers, While I wait for God, as long as he remains in hiding, I wait and hope for him. I stand my ground and hope. I and the children God gave me as signs to Israel, Warning signs and hope signs from God-of-the-Angel-Armies, who makes his home in Mount Zion."

—Isaiah 8:16-18, MSG

PRAYER

Heavenly Father, Thank You because You taught me how to wait on You in prayer, praise, peace, perseverance, and patience so that I would adequately understand what it means to wait on You. Help me be still, hear Your voice through Your word, and stay in You. Keep me from fear and worrying, and instead allow me to learn more about You. Bring me closer to You and keep me from anxious, arrogant, and agonized thoughts; rather, teach me the humility of heart, knowing that Your desire for me all that I do justice, love mercy, live wisely, and walk humbly before You. I pray that as I learn to wait on You and dig deeper into Your Word of truth, I will bring glory to Your name. In Jesus' mighty name, I pray, Amen.

MY DOPE *faith journal*

Date S | M | T | W | T | F | S

Morning: I feel my emotion! My one-word check-in:

DECLARATION

Consider today's verse. I implore the Holy Spirit to reveal His wisdom and truth to me and I declare it over my life.

OBSERVATION

What does the message mean? Lord, help me see it.

PRAYER

What is my prayer request? Lord, I live fully in You.

EMPOWERMENT

How will Your word empower me? Lord, give me the insight to apply my faith to be more significant than my fears.

MY FEARLESS *journey*

Evening: Feel my emotion! My one-word check-up:

What is making me FEEL like this?

What lessons did I LEARNED?

What THOUGHTS did I had?

What prompted my GRATITUDE?

Who did I CONNECTED with?

What brought me JOY?

EVENING PRAYER

WATER:

FRUIT & VEG:

MY MOOD:

My treat for today is: ....

Improving Sleep

To sleep better you might need to make some changes to your behaviour and daily habits. Use this table to identify areas that you will change to help you become a better sleeper.

	MON	TUE	WED	THU	FRI	SAT	SUN
Time I went to bed							
Time I turned out light							
Time it took to fall asleep							
Number of times I woke in the night							
Number of times I got up in the night							
Number of times I went to the toilet							
Time I woke up							
Time I got up							
Total time I slept							
Total time I was awake in the night							
Units of alcohol							
Sleeping pill							
Quality of sleep - marks out of 10							
How rested I feel - marks out of 10							

Day 247 - Let God Finish The Work He Started In You!

"For we are God's masterpiece. He has created us anew in Christ Jesus, so we can do the good things he planned for us long ago."
—Ephesians 2:10, NLT

BELOVED,
Let God finish the work He started in you. He is not done yet. He is at work right now. He is preparing you for His promises and your purpose. An analogy to waiting on God can be like waiting in a restaurant. The waiter (the Intercessor) takes your order (faith-filled request) to the chef (Heavenly Father). Do you sit still and actively wait, relying on the chef to take the time to make your order as you patiently wait? If you allow the process in the secular realm, why don't you patiently wait and trust the process in the spiritual realm? Why don't we trust the All-knowing, All-loving, Only-wise God that He will finish what He started, that God is at work, that God will never forget our prayer requests, His plan, and His promises, and that He has the right ingredients to get it done perfectly and on time?
The crucifixion, empty tomb, Blood of Jesus, His name, His Holy Spirit, and your faith, along with all of your *good-bad-ugly* events, are striving to get you cured, whole, well, and complete: fixed, finished, and thriving! So, bolster up your confidence, knowing that He who began this glorious work in you will faithfully finish it until the revelation of our Lord Jesus Christ! He'll consider you flawless, fearless, faultless, and faithful on that day. (Philippians 1:6). It implies you can worship the Lord our God during the wait, journey, and wilderness to the Promised Lan. You're His creation. He accepts and adores you. God finishes everything He starts; He never leaves anything undone. He's the Mighty Finisher, Creator, Architect, Author, Perfector, Founder, Finisher, Liberator, Redeemer, Divine Strategist, Master Potter, and Creator God. By the way, didn't Jesus' last remarks suggest that all was over? Anyone's final words are noteworthy, but Jesus' final words certainly have a crucial relevance. Jesus exclaimed, "It is finished!" just before taking his last breath. These three words are a testimony and a prophecy for your life and everything you are going through, every step of the way, your history, your mistakes, your messed-up past, and your optimistic future. Be not afraid; the conquest has been completed, the wages fully paid, the war has been won, the triumph has been secured, the work is finalized, and your recompense is assured; a warranty has been given for the masterpiece I made you be. I, the Master, have the master plan and strategy, as well as the goals, objectives, and description of your desired future condition. I know the entire narrative, and if you continue to follow me, Christ Jesus, as your personal Lord and Savior, all of this chaos is a message.

AFFIRMATIONS & DECLARATIONS
I announce and pray for my beloved companions; we are now God's children, but He has not yet revealed to us what we will be like when Christ returns. But we know we'll be like Him because we'll see Him for who He truly is.

- I reject the world's idea of success and accept God's plan for your life's significance, meaning, and purpose. Jesus came to offer me life in its fullness, wholeness, completeness, and wellness.
- I am accomplished because I listen to God, obey His plan, accept His finished work on the cross, and trust Him to carry me through as I do my best. I thank you for the Lord's blessings on vision and goals.
- I can excel because I avoid the path of destruction and follow the Lord's direction.

"Beloved, we are God's children right now; however, it is not yet apparent what we will become. But we do know that when it is finally made visible, we will be just like him, for we will see him as he truly is."
—1 John 3:2, TPT

PRAYER
Heavenly Father, Oh, Lord, every promise You've ever made to me has been kept! I applaud and thank You that since Your love for me is constant and joy eternal, I praise and pray to You, Lord, please complete every wonderful thing You've started in me! Lord, please help me not to manipulate the result because I am tired, concerned, and weary while waiting and while You work on making me ready, polishing me up, and putting the finishing touches on me. Lord, please forgive me for whatever Sarah's traits (self-doubt) I have, such as how she helped God out with His promise of a son. Instead, nurture Mary's character, obedient and trustworthy even when the task appears impossible or difficult. Lord, I can trust You with the result because You know how the narrative will conclude. In the name of Jesus, I focus on the goal rather than the discomfort of the process. After all, Lord, You are the author and architect, and You have already written the book, and faith tells us that it will end in victory. Amen. In the name of Jesus, Amen.

MY DOPE *faith journal*

Date S | M | T | W | T | F | S

Morning: I feel my emotion! My one-word check-in: ....

DECLARATION

Consider today's verse. I implore the Holy Spirit to reveal His wisdom and truth to me and I declare it over my life.

OBSERVATION

What does the message mean? Lord, help me see it.

PRAYER

What is my prayer request? Lord, I live fully in You.

EMPOWERMENT

How will Your word empower me? Lord, give me the insight to apply my faith to be more significant than my fears.

MY FEARLESS *journey*

Evening: Feel my emotion! My one-word check-up:

What is making me FEEL like this?

What lessons did I LEARNED?

What THOUGHTS did I had?

What prompted my GRATITUDE?

Who did I CONNECTED with?

What brought me JOY?

EVENING PRAYER

My treat for today is: ....

Sleep Thoughts Tracker

Use this tracker to write down your sensations and ideas around sleep. When you recognize a negative thought, work to replace it with one that is more reasonable, beneficial, and truthful.

Negative thought about sleep	How this thought makes me feel	A more positive way to think about this	How I feel when I think this way

Day 248 - You Will Laugh, Love, Learn, Live, Be A Light, & Leap For Joy!

"I pray that God, the source of hope, will fill you with joy and peace because you trust in him. Then you will overflow with confident hope through the power of the Holy Spirit."
—Romans 15: 13

BELOVED,
When your negative self-talk, disempowering thoughts, and self-doubt consume you, it causes you to feel depressed, despair, discouraged, and hopeless, overwhelming you with fear. It zaps your joy and steals your happiness and hope in a Faithful father. Lamentation 3:17 says, "My soul has been cast far away from peace; I have forgotten happiness."

Today, God has given a message to confuse your enemies and disrupt your concerns, fears, anxieties, mental illnesses, and emotional turbulence that are wreaking havoc in your life, living, and livelihood. God says you will laugh, love, learn, live, be a light, and leap forward.

Your first laugh... like really! What was it that made you laugh for the first time? Is it fear, uncertainty, or admiration for the Almighty God's miraculous might, whose designs no one can thwart? Is your toxic fear preventing you from trusting that nothing is too challenging or unattainable for God to handle? Is false pride preventing you from breaking gracefully, walking humbly, living truthfully, and believing without reservation?

Examine these two distinct forms of laughter at the same prophecy.

- **Abraham laughs in the faith of the purpose:** Then Abraham fell flat on his face before God and burst out laughing in a private moment of awe-inspired reverence, thinking to himself, *"Yeah, right! How can a centenarian father a child? Am I supposed to believe that Sarah, my 90-year-old wife, is going to have a baby?"* (Genesis, 17:17, Voice).
- **Sarah laughs in fear of the process:** So Sarah chuckled to herself, muttering under her breath, *"At my age-old and decrepit, as is my husband—both of us long past having any desire to engage in lovemaking?"* (Genesis 18:12, VOICE)

Your response to God's promise must be awe-inspired reverence and a bold yes and amen! You are in a motion-activated and voice-sensitive Kingdom. You must not react in fear but respond in anticipation and awe-inspired laugh at God's beautiful wonders and mighty power. You will laugh again!

AFFIRMATIONS & DECLARATIONS
I declare that I will be delighted in the Lord, joy-filled and joyful.
"You'll take delight in God, the Mighty One, and look to him joyfully, boldly. You'll pray to him, and he'll listen; he'll help you do what you've promised. You'll decide what you want, and it will happen; your life will be bathed in light. To those who feel low, you'll say, 'Chin up! Be brave!' and God will save them. Yes, even the guilty will escape; escape through God's grace in your life." (Job 22:28-30, MSG.)

- I am singing, "Goodbye, temporary happiness. Hello, permanent Joy!
- Good riddance, energy zappers.
- Good morning, energy boosters.
- God restores the years and gives me joy. The world didn't provide me with satisfaction, and the world can't take it because He who promised is faithful.

"You will pronounce something to be, and He will make it so; light will break out across all of your paths. God will humble, but you say, "Raise them up." He will save the downcast. He will even consent to deliver those who are not innocent through the purity of your then-washed-clean hands."
—Job 22:28-30, VOICE.

PRAYER
Father God, kindly help me find peace, fulfillment, satisfaction, happiness, purpose, comfort, and contentment within Your plan, despite my suffering, grumbling, doubts, and stupid laughs of fear. Thank You for allowing me to wake up each morning with You as my source of hope for all the You world has to give in terms of the daily load of benefits and rewards. Lord, it is a blessing that You are always with me, no matter how black the night or valley becomes. Despite the facts, fears, feelings, and frailty that reveal to me my current position, a timetable of waiting, and challenging situations, I know You not only go before me, but You also walk with me and live inside of me. Could You please give me more hope, peace, joy, trust, grace, love, patience, and strength? Would You please assist me in finding endless delight, Your joy as my inner strength in every moment I go through each day to improve my happiness? I've been wounded and embarrassed, and it's distressing. In Jesus' name, I declare that I will laugh, love, learn, live, be a light, and leap forward sooner than I expect, better than I dream. In the name of Jesus, I pray, Amen.

MY DOPE *faith journal*

Date S | M | T | W | T | F | S

Morning: I feel my emotion! My one-word check-in: ....

DECLARATION

Consider today's verse. I implore the Holy Spirit to reveal His wisdom and truth to me and I declare it over my life.

OBSERVATION

What does the message mean? Lord, help me see it.

PRAYER

What is my prayer request? Lord, I live fully in You.

EMPOWERMENT

How will Your word empower me? Lord, give me the insight to apply my faith to be more significant than my fears.

MY FEARLESS *journey*

Evening: Feel my emotion! My one-word check-up:

What is making me FEEL like this?

What lessons did I LEARNED?

What THOUGHTS did I had?

What prompted my GRATITUDE?

Who did I CONNECTED with?

What brought me JOY?

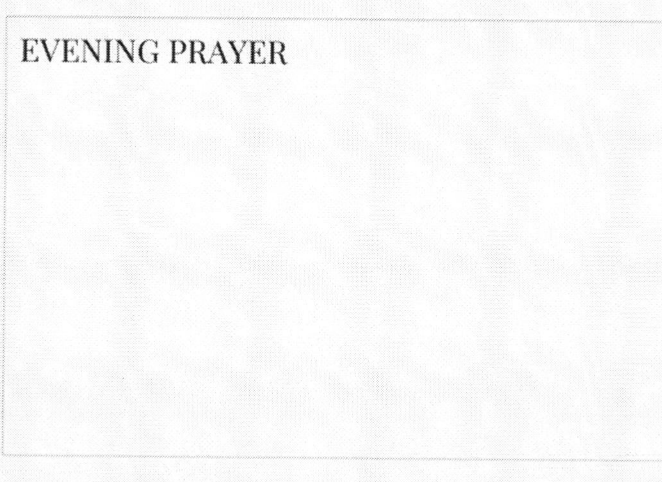

My treat for today is:

Get A Great Sleep

SCHEDULE

- Drastically reduce alcohol and caffeine
- Daytime healthy eating and regular exercise
- Daily outside time should be at least 30 minutes.
- Ascertain that your bedroom is dark.
- Avoid taking a daytime sleep.
- To relax before bed, do something enjoyable.

RELAXATION

- If you feel drowsy, go to bed.
- Only sleep and sexual activity should be done in bed.
- After 30 minutes, if you still can't go asleep, get up and do something soothing in a room with low lighting.
- To get up in the morning, set the alarm.

MINDSET

- Be open-minded when
- making changes to sleep habits
- Check expectations of sleep - are they reasonable?
- Look at lack of sleep as a problem that can be solved
- Don't engage in unhelpful behaviors to cope with a lack of sleep

THOUGHTS

- Empty your mind at the
- end of the day by journaling
- Reframe negative thoughts about sleeping into positive thoughts
- Use your Sleep Thought Tracker
- If you're lying awake, accept it
- and try not to force sleep.
- Try not to focus on the sleeping problem.

Day 249 - Be Encouraged. Nope! God Never Fails.

"Because of the LORD's great love we are not consumed, for his compassions never fail.
They are new every morning; great is your faithfulness."
—Lamentations 3:22-23, NIV

BELOVED,

Don't Be Discouraged. It's not over! There is no failure with God. God stopped it because something better was coming! God's word brings empowerment and encouragement to whatever situation you face today. May you experience His peace that surpasses all understanding. God never wastes our pain. He uses the painful process of building your character and honing your conduct to prepare for your purpose. The name of Jesus is a higher, more prominent, more significant authority above: fear, discouragement, depression, disappointment, sickness, disease, broken-hearted, exhaustion, trauma, drama, disaster, relationship trouble, financial crisis, joblessness, loneliness, isolation, humiliation, whatever the situation is.

The Name of Jesus is immense and sovereign above it!

You might feel forsaken with dreams in your heart like Joseph, Moses, or David did before God revealed His glory to them. But God! He is still at work, and He will remember you. Even if you find yourself in the pit, the palace, the prison, the wilderness, the cave, the fiery furnace, the lion's den, or the storm – Whatever God has promised, according to His word, will come to pass in your life. God never fails!

"Rise up in splendor and be radiant, for your light has dawned, and Yahweh's glory now streams from you! Look carefully! Darkness blankets the earth, and thick gloom covers the nations, but Yahweh arises upon you, and the brightness of his glory appears over you! Nations will be attracted to your radiant light and kings to the sunrise-glory of your new day. "(Isaiah 60:1-3, TPT).

In Isaiah 60:1-3, God gives His disappointed people hope for a new beginning. Many are struggling, and God's people are also impacted, yet you must wait for the manifestation of the prophetic message being persistent in prayers, fasting, and faith leaders' pledges. Other individuals may dispute God's existence: Is God alive? Is He strong? Is He's here? However, as a Believer, believe, yes, amen, obey, and wait because these are signs of your faith in God. Not everyone accepts His word, enjoys waiting, or views trusting God, believing in oneself, obedience, and giving thanks as viable faith approaches. They question God's character: Does God exist? Can He help? Does God value us? Does He care? But you, a faithful covenant partner, know God is strong and cares; you are committed to showing your children, household, and family that God cares about their spiritual, emotional, mental, financial, physical, and social welfare. If you trust, wait and follow Him, you and your children, household, family, career ministry, and your integration of vision, purpose, passion, vocation, and profession will be tremendous and fantastic again. In no time, the world will see God's incredible work in your life, and you'll become a shining exhibition of God's glorious and triumphant work in you, for you, through you, and for others. "Arise!" God demands.

AFFIRMATIONS & DECLARATIONS

Today, I arise! I am not a spectator but an active competitor in this race. I have to run graciously to win the race and to win. When I trust and run and do not become weary, tired, or fearful, I will receive the award for the ultimate gift of eternal life in heaven.

- I am not to be bored but boundless! I am blessed in my going out and coming in.
- I thank you, Lord, for the name of Jesus. I am like a light set upon a mountain. I shall not be hidden.
- My finances, my health, my household, my children, and the work of my hands are blessed.

1 Corinthians 9:24, VOICE—: *"We all know that when there's a race, all the runners bolt for the finish line, but only one will take the prize. When you run, run for the prize!"*

PRAYER

Thank you, Almighty God, for Your word, encouraging and empowering me on this new day. I understand that even the most challenging aspects of my life are instruments and ingredients. You are using me to shape me into Your likeness and image and prepare me for what You have already prepared for me. Today, I look at who I am and where I am fit for purpose. I proclaim that there is no reason for me to be disheartened since You have not given me a spirit of fear but a Spirit of love, power, sound mind, self-discipline, and self-control. I chose to listen to and follow your commands. You instructed me to be courageous and strong: Don't be disheartened; it's not the end of the world! There is no false start, no fear, no fake, no-fault, and no failure with God. "Be strong and courageous. Never be afraid or discouraged because I am your God, and I will remain with You wherever you go." (Joshua 1:9). In Jesus' tremendous name, I activate the manifestation of Your light and divine design for my purpose, prosperity, protection, promotion, provision, wealth, and peace in my life. In Jesus' mighty name, I pray, Amen.

MY DOPE *faith journal*

Date S | M | T | W | T | F | S

Morning: I feel my emotion! My one-word check-in: ....

DECLARATION
Consider today's verse. I implore the Holy Spirit to reveal His wisdom and truth to me and I declare it over my life.

OBSERVATION
What does the message mean? Lord, help me see it.

PRAYER
What is my prayer request? Lord, I live fully in You.

EMPOWERMENT
How will Your word empower me? Lord, give me the insight to apply my faith to be more significant than my fears.

MY FEARLESS *journey*

Evening: Feel my emotion! My one-word check-up:

What is making me FEEL like this?

What lessons did I LEARNED?

What THOUGHTS did I had?

What prompted my GRATITUDE?

Who did I CONNECTED with?

What brought me JOY?

EVENING PRAYER

My treat for today is:..

Sleep Cycle

Non-rapid eye movement (NREM): Phase 1, Phase 2, and Phase 3 of NREM sleep are all parts of non-rapid eye movement (NREM) sleep. REM: The lightest stage of sleep occurs when dreaming and brain activity are at their peak. Four phases of sleep take place in cycles. Several sleep cycles last night, each lasting around 90 minutes. The first four hours of the night are when most people experience profound sleep.

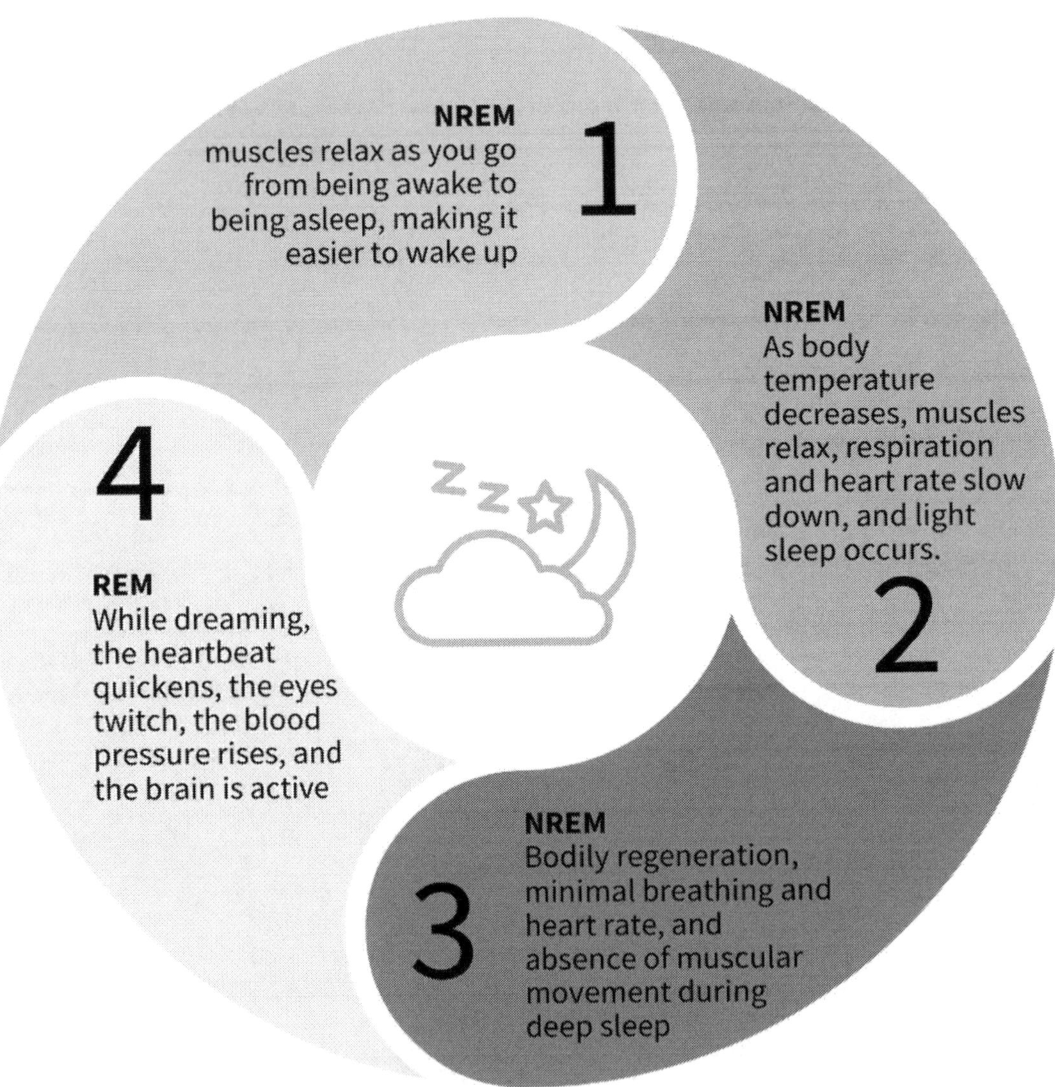

Day 250 - Do Not Be Afraid; Your Reward Will Be Grand!

After these things happened, the Lord spoke his word to Abram in a vision: "Abram, don't be afraid. I will defend you, and I will give you a great reward."
—Genesis 15:1, NCV

BELOVED,
There is nowhere in the Bible where God said to be fearful repeatedly; He said to be fearless, and the inspiration for 365 Live Fearlessly mandate. For the remaining days in this Quarter 3 and through Quarter 4, you'll begin an ascend; you'll be equipped on an expedition through the Bible, from Genesis to Revelation, camping each day on true-life circumstances where God or His messenger advised His people not to be scared and to believe in Him, His intentions, purpose, and promise. Today, you start the journey and camping on Genesis 15:1. With God, you shall Face Everything And Rebound. It will help if you overcome every fear with faith. The Father is saying to you today: "Do not fear. I am your Shield and Protector, the God who will reward you with significant abundance."

- — I will rebound as though you had never suffered the setback.
- — I will revive those dreams as though they never died.
- — I will overcome your challenge accurately and smoothly.
- — I am making you fruitful as if you were never barren.
- — I am repairing you as if nothing ever occurred.
- — I will recover as if it never happened.
- — I will make you as good as new!

God promised Abram in Genesis 15:1-6, an impotent older man with a barren wife, a generation more significant than the stars. God invited Abram to look up, let Him show him what's possible with Him, and dream large with a vision of eternal, endless, countless, limitless, immense reward, abundance, significance, destiny, and legacy. Despite being childless, Abram trusted God and His divine intervention. God deemed Abram's faith righteous. God appeared to Abram in a vision and said, *"Do not be afraid, Abram. I am always your shield and protector. Your reward for loyalty and trust will be immense."* (Genesis 15:1, VOICE). You must accept and believe God's word as your portion and promise. Regardless of your current suffering and situation, do not be afraid, be fearless and faithful to believe in God's promises. *"Because Abraham obeyed my voice and kept my charge, my commandments, my statutes, and my laws."* (Gen 26:5, NIV).

AFFIRMATIONS & DECLARATIONS
In Jesus' name, I declare that I walk by faith, not sight. According to Psalm 121:1-3, "I look up to the mountains; does my strength come from mountains?" No, my power comes from God, who created the heavens, the earth, and the mountains. He will not let me fall, and my Guardian God will not fail. Never in my wildest dreams! My God will never slumber or doze. God protects and provides for me.

- I accept your bounties of importance and abundance. My benefit goes beyond worldly prosperity.
- My life has meaning, purpose, aim, aspiration, ambition, satisfaction, fulfillment, and enrichment.
- My God favors me. His favor surrounds me like a shield. I choose to be obedient to His voice and word.

"Bless our God, O peoples! Give him a thunderous welcome! Didn't he set us on the road to life? Didn't he keep us out of the ditch? He trained us first, passed us like silver through refining fires, Brought us into hardscrabble country, pushed us to our very limit, Road-tested us inside and out, took us to hell and back; Finally, he brought us to this well-watered place."
—Psalm 66:9-12, MSG.

PRAYER
Father God, I cry out to You, LORD; do not turn a deaf ear to me, O my Rock. For if You do not speak, manifest, and intervene divinely, there will be no intervention, and I will be like others who are being destroyed. Be my secure haven, my salvation's stronghold, and my unfathomable recompense. I'll ask God, my Rock. "Why have You forgotten about me?" "I will not give up since You have promised to defend me and provide me with an ample recompense. I will watch for You, O my Strength; for You, O God, are my Fortress. My God is my shield, my protector, and the one who subdues peoples under me.
I will put my confidence in the God of my Rock: You are my armor and the horn of my salvation, my stronghold, and refuge, my Savior; He rescues and delivers me from danger, diseases, depression, and disadvantage, drought, and despair. In Jesus' name, I am prepared for my reward of significance and abundance. In Jesus' glorious name, I pray, worship, and proclaim His word for the manifestation of His mercy, compassion, grace, and favor to surround me like a shield. AMEN!

MY DOPE *faith journal*

Date S | M | T | W | T | F | S

Morning: I feel my emotion! My one-word check-in:

DECLARATION

Consider today's verse. I implore the Holy Spirit to reveal His wisdom and truth to me and I declare it over my life.

OBSERVATION

What does the message mean? Lord, help me see it.

PRAYER

What is my prayer request? Lord, I live fully in You.

EMPOWERMENT

How will Your word empower me? Lord, give me the insight to apply my faith to be more significant than my fears.

MY FEARLESS *journey*

Evening: Feel my emotion! My one-word check-up:

What is making me FEEL like this?

What lessons did I LEARNED?

What THOUGHTS did I had?

What prompted my GRATITUDE?

Who did I CONNECTED with?

What brought me JOY?

EVENING PRAYER

WATER:

FRUIT & VEG:

MY MOOD:

My treat for today is:

Sleep Tracker

MONTH:

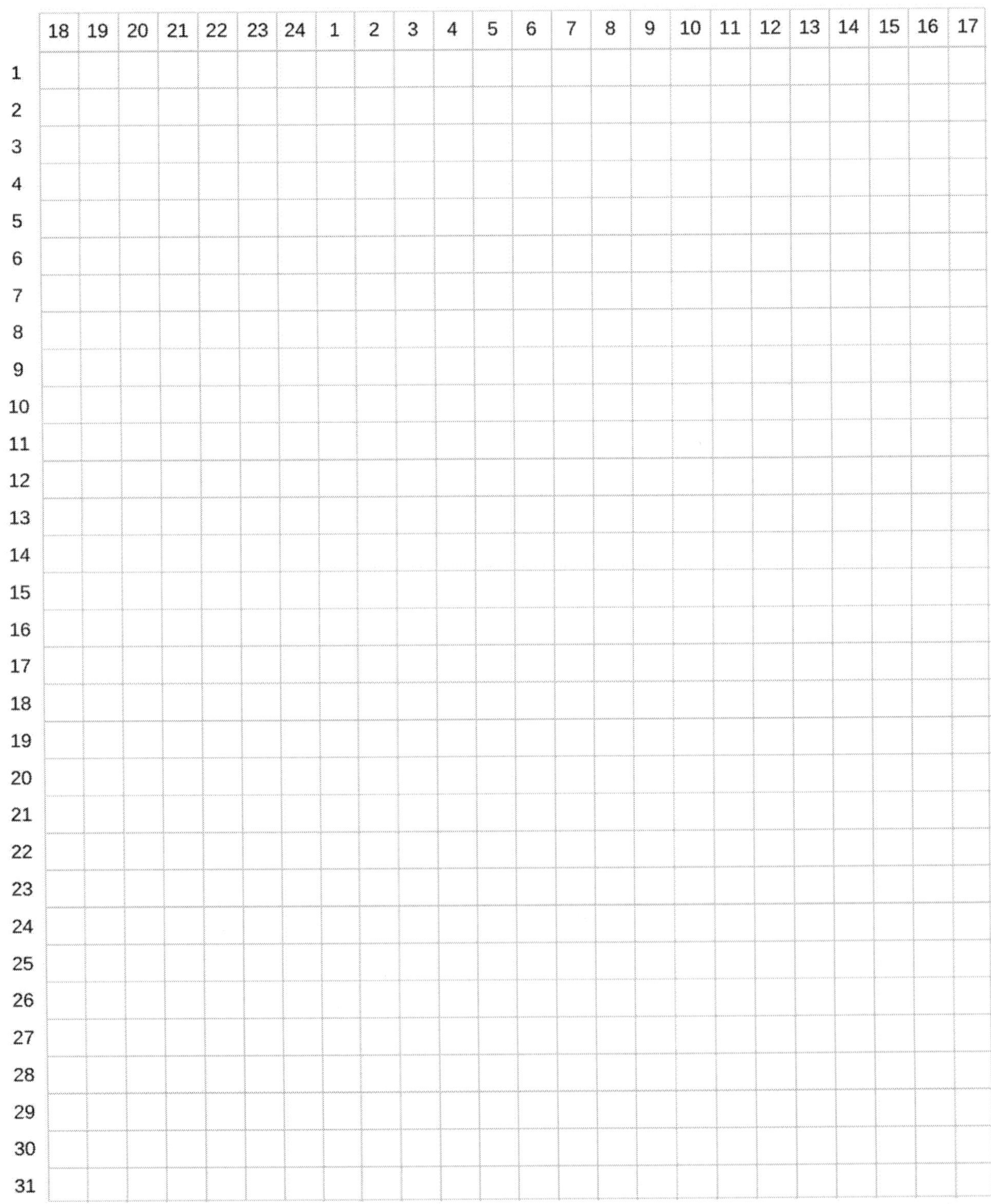

	18	19	20	21	22	23	24	1	2	3	4	5	6	7	8	9	10	11	12	13	14	15	16	17
1																								
2																								
3																								
4																								
5																								
6																								
7																								
8																								
9																								
10																								
11																								
12																								
13																								
14																								
15																								
16																								
17																								
18																								
19																								
20																								
21																								
22																								
23																								
24																								
25																								
26																								
27																								
28																								
29																								
30																								
31																								

Day 251 - God Hears. He Sees. He Knows. He Will Deliver!

God heard the boy crying, and God's angel called to Hagar from heaven. He said, "What is wrong, Hagar? Don't be afraid! God has heard the boy crying there."
—Genesis 21:17, NCV

BELOVED,
The Father says, Do not be afraid. I hear. I see. I know. I will deliver! Here is My promise to you in Isaiah 66:13: "*As a mother soothes her child, so I will comfort you. And Jerusalem will be so nice, feel so good and safe to you. When you see what I have in store, it will ease your mind and lift your heart; you will flourish like the grass!*" (VOICE).
Are you pleading for assistance and support? God is listening and eager to save, rescue, and deliver you. Even though you are afraid and feel like a failure, as you've been discarded, rejected, humiliated, ignored, and uncertain about your future, the Father says, *"I hear your cry, and I will rescue you!"*
"In my distress, I cried out to you, the delivering God, and from your temple throne, You heard my troubled cry, and my sobs went right into your heart." (Psalm 18:6, TPT).
As you continue your journey through the Bible, from Genesis to Revelation, you will pause at every point in the text where God directly urges you not to be frightened. Today's story is about Hagar, an abandoned, single, broken-hearted mother who found herself rejected and dismissed from Sarah's home, affecting her life, living, and livelihood. Now found herself without a family, jobless, no sense of belonging, absent biological father for her child, feeling like a failure, insufficiency, lack of provision, and such significant loss. But God! Despite the intricacies, complexity, ambiguity, and uncertainty, God saw her pain, heard distress call (SOS), listened to Ishmael's plea, and answered her son's cry. It also serves as a message to you, as culture, society, and complicated relationships have harmed, labeled, and written you off as a result of your mistake, experience, or what has happened to you, negatively disempowering you with the statistics, history, and tradition of what happens to others you faced your predicament. Despite the mess, mistakes, and what society says or thinks of my complicated situation, leadership, single-parenthood, motherhood/manhood/fatherhood, and fatherless children, God says your story is different. In Genesis 21:8-20, you learned of some of the consequences of Abraham and Sarah's strategy that was not in sync with God. They had manipulated, masterminded, and managed to seize control of the plot and partner with the devil to help their agenda. They rejected God's plan, timing, and promised deliverance of a son, hooking up Hagar and Abraham to give birth to Ishmael. Ishmael was the counterfeit, not the promised son; Issac was God's promise. (Galatians 4:23). Regardless, cry out to God, He hears, sees, knows, and God will deliver!

AFFIRMATIONS & DECLARATIONS
I declare that when I, Your child, call out to my Abba Father for help, He hears my plea, sees my tears, and rescues me from all my difficulties.

- I am rescued, redeemed, and delivered.
- I am not a slave to fear; I am a servant of faith; I am not forsaken nor abandoned anymore.
- I am a child of God. God has seen my pain and heard my voice. He has listened to the cry of my children and household. He will bless and deliver us.

"Yet when holy lovers of God cry out to him with all their hearts, the Lord will hear them and come to rescue them from all their troubles."
—Psalm 34:17, TPT.

PRAYER
Heavenly Father, I cry out to You with fears, anxieties, and worries, and I confess, repent, proclaim, affirm, pray, and believe Your word. I seek Your supernatural intervention, answers, aid, deliverance, mercy, and grace in Jesus' mighty name. O Lord, You hear my voice in the morning; I prepare a sacrifice for You and give you the first fruit of my morning. I repent of my many sins and ask for Your pardon. Lord, please bend Your ear to me and listen to my voice, O Almighty God; hear my heart's profound cry. Listen to my prayer for assistance, my King, my True God; I pray only to You. Every morning, I command my day, Almighty God, to listen for Your voice in the early light of the day, and I give my petition to You, and I wait for Your response. Lord, You are the One who bestows all good things on the righteous. Thank You, Lord, that You hear my cry for help, see my desperation, You respond to deliver me. You are the God who sees, hears, and blesses me. In the name of Jesus, I pray. Amen.

MY DOPE *faith journal*

Date S | M | T | W | T | F | S

Morning: I feel my emotion! My one-word check-in: ....

DECLARATION

Consider today's verse. I implore the Holy Spirit to reveal His wisdom and truth to me and I declare it over my life.

OBSERVATION

What does the message mean? Lord, help me see it.

PRAYER

What is my prayer request? Lord, I live fully in You.

EMPOWERMENT

How will Your word empower me? Lord, give me the insight to apply my faith to be more significant than my fears.

MY FEARLESS *journey*

Evening: Feel my emotion! My one-word check-up:

What is making me FEEL like this?

What lessons did I LEARNED?

What THOUGHTS did I had?

What prompted my GRATITUDE?

Who did I CONNECTED with?

What brought me JOY?

EVENING PRAYER

My treat for today is: ....

Sleep Diary

THIS WEEK FOCUS

Understanding your current sleep pattern is the first step to sleeping better. You'll use this sleep diary to improve your sleep quality and better understand your sleeping patterns. To record the amount of sleep you got the night before, fill out this diary first thing in the morning.

	MON	TUE	WED	THU	FRI	SAT	SUN
The time I went to bed							
The time I switched off the light							
length of time needed to fall asleep							
How often did I wake up during the night?							
The number of times I got up in the night.							
The number of times I went to the toilet.							
The time I woke up							
The time I got up							
The total time I slept							
The total time I was awake in the night							
Units of ethanol							
Sleeping pill							
Quality of sleep - marks out of 10							
How rested I feel - marks out of 10							

DAY 252 - 258

Nutrition

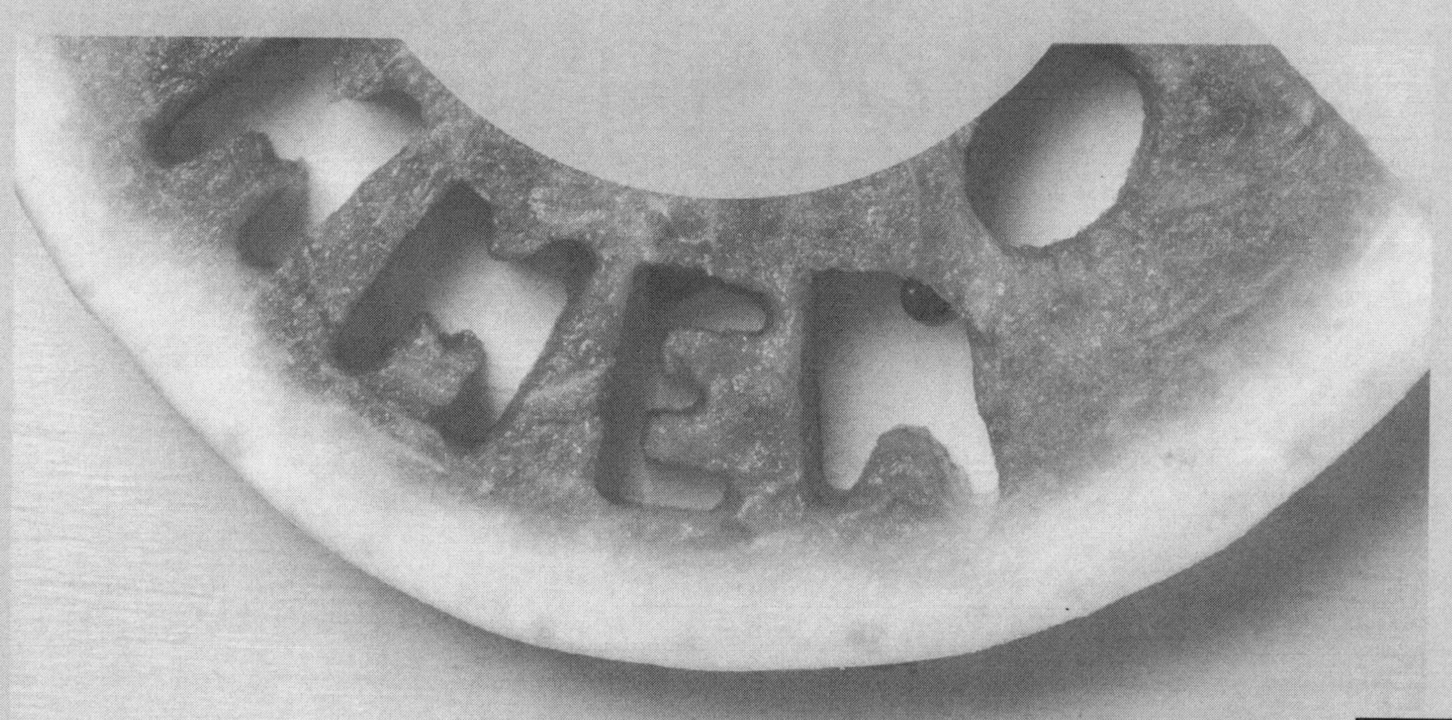

Whatever you do—
whether you eat or
drink or not—do it all to
the glory of God!

— 1 CORINTHIANS 10:31, VOICE

Day 252 - I'm With You. I'll Bless You & Your Children.

"Do not be afraid, for I am with you and will bless you. I will multiply your descendants, and they will become a great nation. I will do this because of my promise to Abraham, my servant."
— Genesis 26:24 , NLT

BELOVED,

The Father says, Don't fear a thing. I'm with you. I'll bless you and your children. Regardless of how many setbacks, traps, schemes, haters, crises, difficulties, and hardships you face this season, I, the Promise-keeping, Covenant-Fulfillment God declares, nevertheless, despite it all, do not be frightened; have faith and trust in the Lord. I will never abandon you. I am constantly by our side.

God informed you yesterday that He hears your call, sees your pain and the cry of your children, and would deliver you. He will rescue you! Today, God confirms His word to reassure you that He will bless you and your children because He is a Covenant-Fulfillment God, a Promise-Keeper, Creator, and Redeemer God. *"Don't fear a thing because I'm with you. I'll bless you and make your children flourish because of Abraham, my servant."* (Genesis 26:24, MSG).

God blessed Abraham as a father and many generations in Genesis 17:3-8. God changed Abram's name to Abraham and promised to bless his descendants. Abram worshipped God on his knees in amazement. After some time, God gave Abraham the means to fulfill the promise of becoming the father of many nations. Genesis 22:15-18, based on his faith in following God when He instructed him to sacrifice his only son, Issac. Abraham obeyed God and didn't withhold Isaac because he had confidence in Him. *"Due to Abraham's faith and faithfulness, God reaffirmed His promise to bless him and his descendants. The angel of God spoke from Heaven a second time to Abraham: "'swear—God's sure word!—because you have gone through with this, and have not refused to give me your son, your dear, dear son, I'll bless you—oh, how I'll bless you! And I'll make sure that your children flourish—like stars in the sky! like sand on the beaches! And your descendants will defeat their enemies. All nations on Earth will find themselves blessed through your descendants because you obeyed me.'"* (Genesis 22:15-18, MSG). Today, God promises to be with you and bless you and your children, despite the journey.

- "May the Lord richly bless both you and your children." (Psalms 115:14, NLT).
- May you seek and thank the Promiser-keeper more than the promise.
- May you admire and adore the Miracle Worker more than the miracle itself.
- May you love, worship, praise, and honor the Giver more than the gift and blessing.
- May the Lord bless you and yours and those who come after you with health and wealth.

AFFIRMATIONS & DECLARATIONS

The All-Powerful God blesses me, makes me fruitful, and multiplies my children so I will give and rise.

- I am blessed by God, me, and my children. My household is blessed. My hands are blessed. My heart is blessed. My head, mind, heart, hands, body, soul, habits, home, and land are blessed.
- I am a new creation. My thoughts are blessed. My projects are blessed and established by God.

"And may The Strong God bless you and give you many, many children, a congregation of peoples; and pass on the blessing of Abraham to you and your descendants so that you will get this land in which you live, this land God gave Abraham."
—Genesis 28:3-4, MSG

PRAYER

Father God, Master of all existence, supreme Lord, the Almighty who fulfills promises, I am approaching You today with prayers for a favorable outcome in my life and the presence of God's glory. Support and be mindful of my prayer requests as I seek Your mercy in my life and home. Blessed am I in the country. Blessed and protected am I from every evil arrow and sinister enemy plot. The Lord will bless me as a financial pillar, kingdom builder, and grace steward to nations; I will lend to many others, but I will not borrow. So in the name of Jesus, I will not deviate from any of the words He has given me this day, to the right or left, to seek and serve other gods. The LORD, the God of my fathers, will increase and multiply me a thousand times over and bless me, as He has promised! (Deuteronomy 1:11). The LORD blesses me with an increase and causes me and my children to flourish more and more. (Psalms 115:14). Surely, goodness, mercy, and everlasting love will accompany us throughout the days of our lives, and we will live forever in the home and presence of the Lord. (Psalm 23:6). I pray, praise, and proclaim these prophetic words in Jesus' mighty name. AMEN!

MY DOPE *faith journal*

Date S | M | T | W | T | F | S

Morning: I feel my emotion! My one-word check-in: ....

DECLARATION

Consider today's verse. I implore the Holy Spirit to reveal His wisdom and truth to me and I declare it over my life.

OBSERVATION

What does the message mean? Lord, help me see it.

PRAYER

What is my prayer request? Lord, I live fully in You.

EMPOWERMENT

How will Your word empower me? Lord, give me the insight to apply my faith to be more significant than my fears.

MY FEARLESS *journey*

Evening: Feel my emotion! My one-word check-up:

What is making me FEEL like this?

What lessons did I LEARNED?

What THOUGHTS did I had?

What prompted my GRATITUDE?

Who did I CONNECTED with?

What brought me JOY?

EVENING PRAYER

WATER:

FRUIT & VEG:

MY MOOD:

My treat for today is: ....

9 Foods To Boost Happiness

DARK CHOCOLATE
Chocolate with at least 70% cacao boosts mood as it raises endorphin levels

VITAMIN C
Found in broccoli, potatoes, oranges, kale. Boosts immune system with antioxidants

VITAMIN D
Vitamin D regulates production of serotonin. Found in mushrooms, liver and beef

SALMON
Salmon is a source of omega 3 fatty acids, which are proven to improve mood.

QUINOA
Quinoa is packed with protein and has an anti-depressant effect which boosts mood

MAGNESIUM

B6 VITAMINS
Regulate serotonin levels. Found in chicken, seafood, beef, kale, spinach, leafy greens

FOLIC ACID
Folic acid is involved in regulation of serotonin. Found in leafy greens, liver, seafood, beans

PROBIOTICS
Contain good bacteria that live in the gut. Found in kimchi, yogurt, pickled cabbage

Day 253 – You Will Give Birth To A Legacy!

"And as she was having great difficulty in childbirth, the midwife said to her 'Don't despair, for you have another son"
—Genesis 35:17, NIV

BELOVED,
Are you struggling with the birth of a vision, and you feel like giving up? Are you feeling the pain and pressure of labor? God is in the labor room with you, saying, "Do not despair; despite the pain of the process, you will give birth, and you will have another son." A son is a seed. It's your vision. Don't despair! Despite the pain, You will give birth and leave a legacy!
You've been on a quest since Day 250, traversing the Bible from Genesis to Revelation, camping on every verse where God instructed His people to be brave. As you continue this trip, you must grasp the background and Abraham's family history. Today you are going to visit Jacob and Rachel's labor room. She had an intense birthing experience, and the midwife encouraged and comforted her. Genesis 35:17 (VOICE) says, *"And when the labor pains were most intense, the midwife tried to comfort her. Rachel's Midwife: Don't be afraid. You're going to have another son."* The Father encourages and comforts you by saying, I know it hurts. I know the process is painful. But if you keep your eyes on Me, focus on the purpose, and press through the pain and pressure, you will give birth – '**PUSH**! *Pray Until Something Happens!'* Shift your self-talk! Change the narrative! Stop saying that you are stressed out. Start saying you are under divine pressure because you are giving birth to a new nation.
God never wastes your pain, but you can. *"In the same way, I will not cause pain without allowing something new to be born," says the Lord. "If I cause you the pain, I will not stop you from giving birth to your new nation," says your God.* (Isaiah 66:9, NCV).
You can never understand how God pulls everything together to display His glory. You must trust Him and seek His supernatural support when facing difficulty in life and labor pain. His presence brings you calm, comfort, and strength, telling you that, even if you don't understand how His agenda matches with the misery of the process, You can rely on His character and actions. Do not lose hope since God has the last say and guarantees that things will get better! Life is full of ups and downs, but God is constant. God's perfect plan continues to bring all things together for your good; He who promises is reliable. Your testimony is that God will utilize for good what the devil intended for evil.

AFFIRMATIONS & DECLARATIONS
God has promised me beauty for my ashes because He loves me. Delight instead of sadness. A song filled with joy, victory, and extravagance rather than sorrow. Trees of righteousness! Intense and majestic! I am distinguished for honesty, justice, and standing right with God! I will get these blessings due to my faithfulness in my faithful Father. I am an instrument of the His work, planted for His glory.

- I am pregnant with purpose. I appreciate the process despite the pain.
- I am giving birth to a legacy more remarkable than currency on earth but of victory, faith, and glory.
- I was born an individual but will be remembered as an institution.
- I shall not die but live to declare God's glory. I PUSH and shall have my rebirth and revival!

"As for those who grieve over Zion, God has sent me to give them a beautiful crown in exchange for ashes, To anoint them with gladness instead of sorrow, to wrap them in victory, joy, and praise instead of depression and sadness. People will call them magnificent, like great towering trees standing for what is right. They stand to the glory of the Eternal who planted them."
—Isaiah 61:3, VOICE.

PRAYER
Father in Heaven, I come into Your presence praising You. Thank You for who You are and what You have done for me. I thank you that I am now pregnant with a promise since You cured me of my barrenness. Thank You, Lord, for the agony indicates that my pregnancy has reached full term and that I am in labor, ready to give birth to a new nation, a legacy of faith and glory. I will no longer be in despair, Lord. Lord, I confess and repent of my sins. Lord, grant me the knowledge and wisdom to know what to seek for Your restoration and when to release You. Cleanse me thoroughly, O Lord. Help me persevere amid the agony, knowing that You are preparing me for a greater purpose. I choose to trust in myself and have unwavering faith in You. Despite the pain, I will give birth to a legacy! Lord, let Your will be done, and Your kingdom come on earth as it is in Heaven. In Jesus' mighty and matchless name, I pray. Amen.

MY DOPE *faith journal*

Date S | M | T | W | T | F | S

Morning: I feel my emotion! My one-word check-in: ....

DECLARATION

Consider today's verse. I implore the Holy Spirit to reveal His wisdom and truth to me and I declare it over my life.

OBSERVATION

What does the message mean? Lord, help me see it.

PRAYER

What is my prayer request? Lord, I live fully in You.

EMPOWERMENT

How will Your word empower me? Lord, give me the insight to apply my faith to be more significant than my fears.

MY FEARLESS *journey*

Evening: Feel my emotion! My one-word check-up:

What is making me FEEL like this?

What lessons did I LEARNED?

What THOUGHTS did I had?

What prompted my GRATITUDE?

Who did I CONNECTED with?

What brought me JOY?

EVENING PRAYER

My treat for today is:

My Favorite Mood and Soul Food

I know there is nothing better for us than to be joyful and to do good throughout our lives; 13 to eat and drink and see the good in all of our hard work is a gift from God.
Ecclesiastes 3:12-13, VOICE

What are some of my favorite foods?
Here are a few of my go-to meals in the pots below:

Day 254 - Treasure In Your Sacks!

"Be at ease, do not be afraid. Your God and the God of your father has given you treasure in your sacks..."
—Genesis 43:23, NAS

BELOVED,
What sort of treasures are in your sacks? The sacks are your heart, hands, head, habits, home, and Heaven. Is your pocket filled with earthly wealth or heavenly treasures? Do you fear losing material riches, position, prestige, fame, fortune, status, and recognition if you dedicate yourself to spiritual growth and maturity, such as the title and honor of man?

As we continue through the Bible from Genesis to Revelation, rest stops on God's words that declare, "Do not fear!" Genesis 39:42-43 provides background for today's spiritual empowerment. *The plot was a plan!* Despite his misfortune and his brothers' malicious scheme, Joseph acquired food for his family. God was with Joseph, giving him the favor with both God and man, putting him, and directing him from one setback to another were ways God brought Joseph to the right place at the right moment since time and chance happen to us all. Everything had a purpose, despite the pain.

Now there is a famine, but there is food in Egypt; Jacob told his sons about it and organized a journey to obtain food. Joseph's brothers came, but they didn't recognize him. Joseph questioned his ten brothers for three days and demanded to meet Benjamin, his half-brother. The brothers thought Joseph's treatment was their punishment and portion. Joseph developed a new plan for them to bring Benjamin to him when they returned for more food. The nine brothers recounted to Jacob what transpired in Canaan. The brothers and their father were startled when they found treasures in their sacks.

When they returned to Egypt, they were ready to plead their innocence, but the steward said, *"Everything's in order. Don't worry. Your God and the God of your father must have given you a bonus. It was paid in full."* (Genesis 43:23, MSG). Have you found your treasure in God's kingdom? Jesus paid it in full! Don't be afraid. God has recognized your effort and faith and has given you treasure in your sacks! Are you living a life of God-Worship or man-pleasure? What does success means to you? Is your aim in life successful or effective and significant? What is your motivation? Is it love and service to inspire, impact, and influence others to God, or is it man's power, pride, greed, authority, and applause?

"Some people store up treasures in their homes here on earth. This is a shortsighted practice—don't undertake it. Moths and rust will eat up any treasure you may store here. Thieves may break into your homes and steal your precious trinkets. Instead, put up your treasures in Heaven where moths do not attack, where rust does not corrode, and where thieves are barred at the door. For where your treasure is, there your heart will be also." (Matt 6:19-21, VOICE).

AFFIRMATIONS & DECLARATIONS
Today, I come to know, feel, and meet my God such that the warmth of His love fills my heart. So that I will be at peace, not anxious, unhappy, disturbed, or nervous, but at rest and focused on Christ. I want to be woven into a masterpiece of love, in touch, and in synch with everything God offers. Then my mind will be calm and at ease, focusing on Christ, God's grand mystery. All of the best treasures of wisdom, prophetic insight, revelation, truth, and knowledge are hidden within that enigma and can be found nowhere else. And the revelation, riddle, and rhythm have been revealed to me! He tells me, "I'm telling you this because I don't want anyone leading you off on some wild-goose chase, after other so-called mysteries or 'the Secret.'" (Colossians 2:2-3, MSG). I am His treasure, and He is Mine!

- I am a child of God. My sack, heart, seed, mind, life, home, and habits are filled with His treasures.
- I am blessed to be a blessing to others.

PRAYER
Heavenly Father, I honor You. I exalt Your holy name. Lord, I confess and repent of all my sins and foolishness that I have stored in my sacks rather than the obedience to Your wisdom, word, will, ways, and walk. I am shifting my perspective on life and living, aligning with Your purpose, Your values, Your vision of my future, my relationship with You, and Your divine plan. Thank You, Lord, that You are doing a new thing in me. Lord, You are capable of so many awe-inspiring, indescribable, something more amazing than I could ever ask or imagine. You have done extraordinary things through Your power at work in me; all glory be to You. Thank you for the treasures of righteousness, joy, peace, love, grace, goodness, wisdom, new life, and abundance in my sack; in Jesus' name, I pray, Amen.

MY DOPE *faith journal*

Date S | M | T | W | T | F | S

Morning: I feel my emotion! My one-word check-in: ....

DECLARATION

Consider today's verse. I implore the Holy Spirit to reveal His wisdom and truth to me and I declare it over my life.

OBSERVATION

What does the message mean? Lord, help me see it.

PRAYER

What is my prayer request? Lord, I live fully in You.

EMPOWERMENT

How will Your word empower me? Lord, give me the insight to apply my faith to be more significant than my fears.

MY FEARLESS *journey*

Evening: Feel my emotion! My one-word check-up:

What is making me FEEL like this?

What lessons did I LEARNED?

What THOUGHTS did I had?

What prompted my GRATITUDE?

Who did I CONNECTED with?

What brought me JOY?

EVENING PRAYER

My treat for today is: ....

Food Diary

NEXT 7-DAYS FOCUS

The following week will be devoted to emphasizing a nutritious, balanced diet. Foods that encourage the body to manufacture feel-good neurotransmitters like serotonin and dopamine may be found in many dishes. This week, research these items and try to include them in your diet. To keep track of your progress, keep a food journal.

	MEALS	MY FEELINGS
MONDAY	B.	
	L.	
	D.	
	S.	
TUESDAY	B.	
	L.	
	D.	
	S.	
WEDNESDAY	B.	
	L.	
	D.	
	S.	
THURSDAY	B.	
	L.	
	D.	
	S.	
FRIDAY	B.	
	L.	
	D.	
	S.	
SATURDAY	B.	
	L.	
	D.	
	S.	
SUNDAY	B.	
	L.	
	D.	
	S.	

Day 255 – Go! I Am Going to Make You into a Great Nation.

"And He said, 'I am God, the God of your father; do not be afraid to go down to Egypt, for I will make you (your descendants) a great nation there.'"
—Genesis 46:3, AMP

BELOVED,

Don't be afraid. Go! God will make you into a great nation. Abba says, Do not be scared. Refuse to be intimidated, discouraged, depressed, worried, disheartened, angry, or anxious no matter what you face or fight or the unfamiliar pathways where I lead you. I have already gone ahead and made grand plans with divine instructions and preparation, just as I have promised to you. I will go before you, and I will make way for you. I will never leave you nor forsake you. I got you. I am your rearguard. I will bless and multiply you despite all your afflictions. I will make you into a great nation. "**God:** '*I am the True God, the God of your father. Don't be afraid to go down to Egypt and leave the land I promised you, for I am going to make you into a great nation there.*'" (Gen 46:3, VOICE).

Please do not be frightened to leave your comfort zone since you are entering your change zone where growth, new creation, and creativity happen. Sometimes God leads you to a place where the deliverance strategy appears frightening, and you are uncomfortable because you need to conquer your fear and victoriously face the challenges and overcome obstacles to build change resilience over change resistance. Go! He is going to make you into a great nation. He creates and transforms your character from the inside out. Always have faith in Him because He has a beautiful plan for you.

From Genesis to Revelation, we continue the mission of faith over fear by studying God's word and noting every time He declares, *"Do Not Fear!"* Meditate on their story and His story with wisdom to apply pertinent knowledge to your life right now. God is constant and unchanging. He is the same yesterday, today, and tomorrow, and He will always be the same. Today, trust that God will bless you despite challenging circumstances and assist you in achieving His divine goal; for His benefit, guide you through strange places. Though you may not understand, you trust His wisdom and sovereignty. He uses a novel approach to match you with your outcome. Complex journeys lead to beautiful destinations. So enjoy your voyage through life! On your adventure today, you will visit Genesis 45-46.

You invited yourself to the Palace, where Joseph is Prime Minister, and his brothers have returned in search of more food. His brothers have returned, bringing Benjamin with them. Joseph had exposed himself to them and showed them great compassion; now, they are asked to travel from Canaan to Egypt with their families. Stress is both positive (eustress) and negative (distress). This decision to go to Egypt is laden with emotions: reunion and joy after years away, as well as the apprehension of the change and the newness of life. But Joseph and God reassured them that everything would be well!

AFFIRMATIONS & DECLARATIONS

As I enter into a new era, as I pivot my life, relationship, business, and career, as I rewrite my story to synch and align with God's plan, as I shift my life, livelihood, and living to become more purposeful and fulfilling, I hear the Lord saying, I'll instruct and guide you through life. I'll direct you with my eyes. Don't resist when I take you somewhere new or unfamiliar. Don't drag along; join me! (Psalm 32:8-9). Despite the journey, go! Look at how I blessed Joseph, who resided at his Egyptian master's house. When his master saw that I was with him and granted him prosperity, Joseph gained his favor, became Potiphar's attendant, and was entrusted with his property and possessions (Genesis 39:2-4). Proclaim: In Jesus' name, Lord, grant me a successful and contagious blessing. I am fearless and favored; Lord, make me in a great nation!

- I am listening to God. I am not afraid to go! I am building, but my God is making me.
- I am obeying, trusting, and taking Him at His word. I am taking the time to study the word of God.
- I am applying His truth to my life; I am going forward!

PRAYER

Heavenly Father, I honor and exalt Your name. I enter into Your presence with praise and thanksgiving. You are holy and wise, and You know all things. I seek Your mercy and grace as I draw closer to You by the Blood of Jesus. Wash me thoroughly from all my sins, disobedience, fear, and unfaithfulness. Lord, I confess and repent. Lord, I know You are calling me to *go* so I may grow. Grow through an unfamiliar path. Grow through the darkness. Help me trust that You are faithful even when I am fearful and faithless. Lord, I take You at Your word, and I believe that You are preparing me and positioning me for the promise, the predestined and ordained plan, purpose, provision, promotion, and protection that You have in store for me. I say yes to the call. I am available to *go*! O Lord, take a firm grip of me, and steady my feet, shift my crown, which moved in the call, strengthens my feet, as I move forward towards Your loving, everlasting arm, and I am confident that You will catch me, if and when I fall. I surrender everything to You, Lord. I believe. I receive. I activate Your promises in my life. In Jesus' mighty name, I pray. Amen.

MY DOPE *faith journal*

Date S | M | T | W | T | F | S

Morning: I feel my emotion! My one-word check-in: ____________

DECLARATION

Consider today's verse. I implore the Holy Spirit to reveal His wisdom and truth to me and I declare it over my life.

OBSERVATION

What does the message mean? Lord, help me see it.

PRAYER

What is my prayer request? Lord, I live fully in You.

EMPOWERMENT

How will Your word empower me? Lord, give me the insight to apply my faith to be more significant than my fears.

MY FEARLESS *journey*

Evening: Feel my emotion! My one-word check-up:

What is making me FEEL like this?

What lessons did I LEARNED?

What THOUGHTS did I had?

What prompted my GRATITUDE?

Who did I CONNECTED with?

What brought me JOY?

EVENING PRAYER

WATER:

FRUIT & VEG:

MY MOOD:

My treat for today is:...

GROCERY *list*

FRUITS AND VEGETABLES

DAIRY AND EGGS

MEAT AND FISH

FROZEN

CANNED

BEVERAGES

BREAD/PASTA/GRAINS

BAKING

SNACKS

OTHER

Day 256 – You're not broken but positioned with grace.

"But Joseph said to them, 'Don't be afraid. Am I in the place of God?'"
—Genesis 50:19, NIV

BELOVED,
It is not what it looks like; it is not what it feels like; this scene is not the whole story. Yes, the process of preparing you for your purpose and God's promise is painful, but God. He is positioning for purpose. He is preparing you for His promise. You may feel broken, but you are beautifully blessed with grace and favor, only set right and made fit-for-purpose. They intended to harm you, but God, by grace, is working all things together for good and His glory.
*"We are confident that God can orchestrate everything to work toward something good and beautiful when we love Him and accept His invitation to live according to His plan." (*Romans 8:28, VOICE). Joseph's brothers intended to harm, hurt, and hinder him, but God! Joseph testified, "*Even though you intended to harm me, God intended it only for good, and through me, He preserved the lives of countless people, as He is still doing today." (Genesis 50:20, VOICE).*
Joseph realized that the painful process had a powerful promise, a beautiful purpose, and a carefully crafted divine plan. He was not broken but strategically positioned with grace. Joseph's preparation process was from the pit to the palace, Pharoah-wife's wrongful accusation, and prison. His private anointing led to his public appointment and advancement. Despite the journey, process, violation, isolation from his family and household, harsh treatment, false allegations, setbacks, bad breaks, and the waiting season, Joseph showed kindness to His brother, even though, He was in a position of power. He showed them unmerited and undeserved grace, forgiveness, compassion, empathy, and a second chance. Life happens, and they face another change as Joseph's father, Jacob, dies. Gripped with fear, they pondered the uncertainty of their future, will they get what they deserve?
So, even though it hurts. It seems like you are hindered, helpless, and hopeless. Don't be afraid. You are not broken but positioned with grace. A glorious and thankful new day to you; you continue to trot through the Bible from Genesis to Revelation, making rest stops at every mention of God's word that reminds you to be fearless! Today, you rest, pause at Gen 50:19-21 and seek God's revelation as you look at grace through Joseph's eyes, the pain of the process, the heart, and the character of God.

AFFIRMATIONS & DECLARATIONS
"But he replied, 'My gift of undeserved grace is all you need. My power is strongest when you are weak.' So if Christ keeps giving me his power, I will gladly brag about how weak I am." (2 Cor 12:9, CEV).

- I am bent but not broken. I am beautifully blessed.
- God is positioning me by grace. His grace is sufficient for me and cleanses me from every disgrace.
- God rearranges things, people, circumstances, journeys, and outcomes to favor and honor me.
- I am healed, well, and whole. I am happy, healthy, spiritually empowered, and divinely elevated.

"So do not fear, for I am with you; do not be dismayed, for I am your God. I will strengthen you and help you; I will uphold you with my righteous right hand."
—Isaiah 41:10, NIV

PRAYER
Father God, Thank You, Heavenly Father, for Your word, assuring me that my shattered sentiments and experiences are chances for Your blessings and grace to alter me. Lord, You provide for me and strengthen me as I mourn my brokenness. I will be known as the oaks of righteousness, a planting of the LORD to display his glory. So I muster the bravery and faith of a mustard seed to say to every mountain of brokenness in my life – Be moved in Jesus' Mighty name. I am not broken but instead gloriously blessed and placed by grace. Lord, You are my Shepherd. Lord, You extend Your grace to me despite my brokenness. You use Your grace to position me for Your glory. I am at the right place at the right moment since time and chance happen to all of us. You will lead me through life, and I will follow You. I choose to forgive and let go of any resentment, rage, fear, negativity, evil thoughts, or vengeance that may be impeding my blessings and breakthroughs. After all, God, You set the table in front of me in the sight of my foes. In Jesus' name, I pray, Amen.

MY DOPE *faith journal*

Date S | M | T | W | T | F | S

Morning: I feel my emotion! My one-word check-in: ....

DECLARATION

Consider today's verse. I implore the Holy Spirit to reveal His wisdom and truth to me and I declare it over my life.

OBSERVATION

What does the message mean? Lord, help me see it.

PRAYER

What is my prayer request? Lord, I live fully in You.

EMPOWERMENT

How will Your word empower me? Lord, give me the insight to apply my faith to be more significant than my fears.

MY FEARLESS *journey*

Evening: Feel my emotion! My one-word check-up:

What is making me FEEL like this?

What lessons did I LEARNED?

What THOUGHTS did I had?

What prompted my GRATITUDE?

Who did I CONNECTED with?

What brought me JOY?

EVENING PRAYER

My treat for today is: ....

THIS WEEK FOCUS

MEAL *Planner*

MONDAY

Breakfast	Lunch	Dinner	Snacks

TUESDAY

Breakfast	Lunch	Dinner	Snacks

WEDNESDAY

Breakfast	Lunch	Dinner	Snacks

THURSDAY

Breakfast	Lunch	Dinner	Snacks

FRIDAY

Breakfast	Lunch	Dinner	Snacks

SATURDAY

Breakfast	Lunch	Dinner	Snacks

SUNDAY

Breakfast	Lunch	Dinner	Snacks

Day 257 - Fear not! You Serve a God of Second Chances.

"'So then, don't be afraid. I will provide for you and your children.'
And he reassured them and spoke kindly to them."
—Genesis 50:21, NIV

BELOVED,

Amid the daily grind, there are times when you wonder if there's more to life than this. There must be more than the rat race and the hustle culture that burns and stresses you out. There must be more in store for you to be part of something bigger, to build and leave a legacy and make this world better than it was when you found it, to work in your passion and still fulfill your purpose, and to live a meaningful life. Still, life happens! But God, you serve a God of Second Chances. Sometimes you find yourself at the wrong place and at the wrong time. You feel like you messed up so badly, your poor choices, miscalculated judgment, instant gratification, settling for less than you deserve, and foolish mistakes impacting not just you but also your children. But God, when you think you ran out of chances, steps in His grace and compassionate mercy. When you surrender to God and seek His redemption, you receive His love, assurance, and comfort. He washes your foolish mistakes, messy, and misery away with His Blood. You don't get what you deserve by His grace and mercy, your disgrace and errors. You serve a God of Second Chance, and He is saying to you, fear not; nevertheless, I will take care of you and your children.

Joseph's brothers messed up big time. They allowed jealousy and envy to overtake them, so they plotted to remove him as a threat to their family and his destiny. The world would say that they deserve karma. But Joseph extended the complete opposite to them. Even though he could lead with authority and power and exercise judgment against them, he served them with empathy and humility and showed them grace, love, kindness, forgiveness, and God's goodness.

Joseph replied, *"Don't be afraid. Do I act for God? Don't you see, you planned evil against me, but God used those same plans for my good, as you see all around you right now—life for many people. Easy now, you have nothing to fear; I'll take care of you and your children." He reassured them, speaking with them heart-to-heart."* (Genesis 50:19-21 MSG). By God's grace, Joseph's brothers received a second chance.

DO YOU NEED THE GOD OF THE SECOND, THIRD, FOURTH... MANY CHANCES... MORE GRACE AND MERCIES? As You go from Genesis to Revelation, stop where God tells you to be bold and trust Him. You seek God's revelation in Gen 50:19-21. On Day 256, you *looked through Joseph's eye*; despite it all, fear not, you're not shattered but positioned by *grace*. On Day 257, don't worry; *look through the brothers' eyes* as you experience the God of Second Chances; *grace*, not judgment or condemnation.

AFFIRMATIONS & DECLARATIONS

"No weapon that is formed against you will succeed, and every tongue that rises against you in judgment you will condemn. This [peace, righteousness, security, and triumph over opposition] is the heritage of the servants of the Lord, and this is their vindication from Me," says the Lord. (Isa 54:17, AMP)

- I am free from all trouble, shame, sin, and guilty of my past mistakes, failures, and low self-worth.
- I owe nothing for my past sins; Jesus paid my wages for my sin, death, and debts in full.
- I was lost but now found. I was a slave to sin, but now, I am a child of God.

Luke 10:1, AMP: "Listen carefully: I have given you authority [that you now possess] to tread on serpents and scorpions, and [the ability to exercise authority] over all the power of the enemy (Satan), and nothing will [in any way] harm you."

PRAYER

Almighty God, I exalt and honor Your holy name. I draw closer to You through the Blood of Jesus, Lord. I thank You that Your power is powerful enough to wash me spotless and clean. Lord, I thank You for the many second chances You have given me. Lord, Jesus, I thank You for taking my place on the cross and setting me free from my sin, shame, suffering, and struggles. I am growing. Lord, as I have experienced Your grace, favor, love, compassion, kindness, and goodness, I vow to exercise this same goodness of conduct and character to others. Lord, I can't do this alone, but I am shifting from self-centered to servant leader with You dwelling in me. Today, I forgive everyone who has done me wrong, hurt, harmed, used, humiliated, rejected, abused, or wrongfully accused me. I release grace upon every violation and offense. Despite it all, O Lord, Your grace is sufficient in my insufficiency, and I believe in the Sovereignty. By Your grace and mighty name of Jesus, You have done it, are doing it, and going to it, all for Your glory. In His name, I pray. Amen.

MY DOPE *faith journal*

Date S | M | T | W | T | F | S

Morning: I feel my emotion! My one-word check-in: ______________________

DECLARATION

Consider today's verse. I implore the Holy Spirit to reveal His wisdom and truth to me and I declare it over my life.

OBSERVATION

What does the message mean? Lord, help me see it.

PRAYER

What is my prayer request? Lord, I live fully in You.

EMPOWERMENT

How will Your word empower me? Lord, give me the insight to apply my faith to be more significant than my fears.

MY FEARLESS *journey*

Evening: Feel my emotion! My one-word check-up:

What is making me FEEL like this?

What lessons did I LEARNED?

What THOUGHTS did I had?

What prompted my GRATITUDE?

Who did I CONNECTED with?

What brought me JOY?

EVENING PRAYER

My treat for today is: ....

RECIPE *card*

RECIPE:

FROM THE KITCHEN OF:

SERVES:

PREP TIME:

COOK TIME:

TOTAL TIME:

NOTES

INGREDIENTS

METHOD

Day 258 – Stand Your Ground & Watch God!

"Moses (to the people): Don't be afraid! Stand your ground and witness how the Eternal will rescue you today. Take a good look at the Egyptians, for after today you will never see them again."

—Exodus 14:13, VOICE

BELOVED,

Don't Be Afraid! Stand your ground and watch God as you face everything and rebound! Choose faith over fear! God reminds you to live daily with confidence more significant than your fears. Ephesians 6:10–17 explains that one aspect of God's whole armor is the shield of faith to block the enemy's fiery darks and evil arrows. Ephesians 6:10 (VOICE) says, *"Don't forget to raise the shield of faith above all else, so you will be able to extinguish flaming spears hurled at you from the wicked one."*

Fear can't reign in a life ruled by faith, worship, and gratitude towards God's faithfulness!

Fear has two meanings: "Face Everything And Rebound!" and **"False Evidence Appearing Real!"**

Today, God is saying to you, Face Everything And Rebound!

Moses spoke to the people: *"Don't be afraid. Stand firm and watch God do his work of salvation for you today. Please look at the Egyptians today, for you'll never see them again. God will fight the battle for you. And you? You keep your mouths shut!"* God said to Moses: *"Why cry out to me? Speak to the Israelites. Order them to get moving. Hold your staff high and stretch your hand out over the sea: Split the sea! The Israelites will walk through the sea on dry ground."* (Exodus 14:13-15, MSG).

You continue our trip from Genesis to Revelation, pausing at the verses where God encouraged you to be brave, not scared, anxious, angry, or discouraged. Today's treasured scripture is Exodus 14:13-15. God enables you to stand firm, be still, face it, and watch Him bring you deliverance and make a way!

AFFIRMATIONS & DECLARATIONS

In every area of my life, where I have been held down, held back, or locked out by my enemies in any of these ways—spiritually, mentally, emotionally, physically, financially, or socially—in the name of Jesus Christ, I will now receive evidence of a singular and sovereign voice of God that cannot be contradicted as well as powerful proclamations that cannot be disputed. In the name of Jesus Christ, He delivers this testimony of glory to me. I GET MY HANDS ON THE VICTORY, DELIVERANCE, SPOILS, AND PLUNDER OF THE BATTLE. I declare: "But upon mount Zion shall be deliverance, and there shall be holiness, and the house of Jacob shall possess their possessions." (Obadiah 1: 17, KJV).

- Every day, I choose faith over fear! I am a holier, healthier, wealthier, and happier child of God.
- I let go of my fear and insecurity, allowing my supernatural confidence in God to shine.
- I'm growing better; I conquer and possess my possession. I take territorial rights of what is mine.
- I am a strong person who never gives up. I stand my ground and watch God in my deliverance.

"But on Mount Zion will be a place of safety. Some will escape to that holy hill, And the people of Jacob will conquer and possess those who conquered and dispossessed them."

—Obadiah 1:17, VOICE

PRAYER

Father God,

The fear is real, Heavenly Father, yet I choose to trust You. I decided to re-establish my faith in Your faithfulness. You are my God, and I will worship Him; You are my father's God, and I will exalt You in the face of every fear. Guide me in Your truth and educate me because You are the God of my salvation; I wait for You all day! Today I testify and proclaim that I waited for the LORD patiently. Be kind to me, O LORD! I am waiting for You. Every morning, be my strength, and in times of distress, be my deliverance. I've been waiting for You to arrive and shower me with grace, favor, and honor, Almighty God. Be my pillar of strength when I am not strong enough, be with me every morning as I command my day, commit all things to You, and be ready for the conversation with My God. In times of hardship, be the why, who, what, when, where, and how You save me. I am standing on Your word. Lord, I place my unwavering trust and fearless faith in You for Your supernatural intervention, my salvation, rescue, and triumph. All eyes will witness the majesty of my God in the name of Jesus. I pray and announce these prophetic words in Jesus' name. Amen.

MY DOPE *faith journal*

Date S | M | T | W | T | F | S

Morning: I feel my emotion! My one-word check-in: ....

DECLARATION

Consider today's verse. I implore the Holy Spirit to reveal His wisdom and truth to me and I declare it over my life.

OBSERVATION

What does the message mean? Lord, help me see it.

PRAYER

What is my prayer request? Lord, I live fully in You.

EMPOWERMENT

How will Your word empower me? Lord, give me the insight to apply my faith to be more significant than my fears.

MY FEARLESS *journey*

Evening: Feel my emotion! My one-word check-up:

What is making me FEEL like this?

What lessons did I LEARNED?

What THOUGHTS did I had?

What prompted my GRATITUDE?

Who did I CONNECTED with?

What brought me JOY?

EVENING PRAYER

My treat for today is: ....

RECIPE *Tasting*

RECIPE	RATING
	☆☆☆☆☆
	☆☆☆☆☆
	☆☆☆☆☆
	☆☆☆☆☆
	☆☆☆☆☆
	☆☆☆☆☆
	☆☆☆☆☆
	☆☆☆☆☆
	☆☆☆☆☆
	☆☆☆☆☆
	☆☆☆☆☆

DAY 259 - 265

Spend Time in Nature

"But ask the animals, and they will teach you, or the birds in the sky, and they will tell you;
or speak to the earth, and it will teach you, or let the fish in the sea inform you.
Which of all these does not know that the hand of the LORD has done this?
In his hand is the life of every creature and the breath of all mankind.

— JOB 12:7-10, NIV

Day 259 - Don't Panic! It is Only a Test. God is with You!

"Moses said to the people 'Do not be afraid. God has come to test you, so that the fear of God will be with you to keep you from sinning.'"
—Exodus 20:20, NIV

BELOVED,

With faith, you can overcome any fear. Don't be frightened; you'll be OK. You are being tested for your benefit by these terrifying experiences, which are God's means of instilling a wholesome fear and awe-inspired reverence of God in your heart. (ex 20:20). You need to be equipped with the right spiritual skills, divine capabilities, supernatural capacity, and competencies to perform at the next level of your assignments, anointings, and appointments. Rely on His love; Revive your attitudes; Assess your ambitions. Vow to be free of fear, able to tackle any challenge, and unstoppable as one of God's children. "New levels bring new devils. Stay unapologetically committed to your goals and let go of anyone who poisons your spirit." — Steve Maraboli. God is saying to you, "Don't be afraid. So you are praying for the breakthrough and promotion but are you prepared for the position? You want growth and recognition, but are you ready for the lessons that come with blessings? God uses various trials, troubles, tribulations, and temptations as excellent instructors, teachers, tutors, and valuable tools and tactics to test, make us ready and sharpen our faith, wisdom, understanding, and application of His word, as well as to build our courage and confidence in Him.

An excellent Servant Leader, like Jesus, serves you in humility and love, modeling the character and conduct you should emulate as His follower. I pray that the fiery test of your faith will purify you and make you' whole and complete.'

God saved His people from slavery in Egypt, where they saw His wonders, miracles, reckless love, and action to save them. The Blood covered them. He kept His word to deliver them and take them to the promised land. The law must be given and explained as the mandated standards, requirements, and guidelines regarding the expected mindset, behavior, character, relationships, and culture of God's people, which will govern the righteousness, moral standards, core values, belief system, and reverence to a Holy God for your life, living, and livelihood, as well as being accountable to God.

AFFIRMATIONS & DECLARATIONS

"I don't know about you, but I'm running hard for the finish line. I'm giving it everything I've got. No sloppy living for me! I'm staying alert and in top condition. I'm not going to get caught napping, telling everyone else all about it, and then missing out myself." (1 Corinthians 9:26-27, MSG).

- I obey God's 10 Commandments, His Word, and precepts.
- I commit to following Jesus' first and greatest commandment to love God love with all my heart, mind, soul, and life, with everything in me and everything I have, my self-love and brotherly love.
- I seek God as my priority; I love others as myself; I take God at His word. I am accountable to God.

"So I don't run aimlessly. I don't let my eyes drift off the finish line. When I box, I don't throw punches in the air. I discipline my body and make it my slave so that after all this, after I have brought the gospel to others, I will still be qualified to win the prize."
—1 Corinthians 9:26-27, The Voice.

PRAYER

Almighty God, You are the Sovereign God. I exalt You and honor Your holy name. Lord, thank You for Your word that clarifies the season of testing, calamity, affliction, adverse life events, personal circumstances, and challenging situations that I am going through and growing through at this time. O Lord, take me by the hands and navigate me through this darkness and these unfamiliar ways. Equip and empower me with new faith and fresh fire. Lord, lead me, go before me and guide me. Lord, I increase my confidence to believe, and please help my unbelief. Lord, I make a vow to live and obey Your Commandment. May my life honor You and Your name. I take my part of the covenant with You seriously. I repent of all my sins. I start a new chapter governed by Your ways, will, and timing in my life. Do it for me, Lord, help me ace this test and reveal Your glory in my restoration and victory in my story, my children, generation, and legacy in Jesus' mighty and precious name. Amen.

MY DOPE *faith journal*

Date S | M | T | W | T | F | S

Morning: I feel my emotion! My one-word check-in: ....

DECLARATION

Consider today's verse. I implore the Holy Spirit to reveal His wisdom and truth to me and I declare it over my life.

OBSERVATION

What does the message mean? Lord, help me see it.

PRAYER

What is my prayer request? Lord, I live fully in You.

EMPOWERMENT

How will Your word empower me? Lord, give me the insight to apply my faith to be more significant than my fears.

MY FEARLESS *journey*

Evening: Feel my emotion! My one-word check-up:

What is making me FEEL like this?

What lessons did I LEARNED?

What THOUGHTS did I had?

What prompted my GRATITUDE?

Who did I CONNECTED with?

What brought me JOY?

EVENING PRAYER

My treat for today is: ....

How To Keep A Nature Journal

Keep a journal and a pencil in your pocket so you may jot down any thoughts or observations that occur to you.

Make a note of the time, date, and place of your remarks and the local weather.

To fully appreciate your environment, use all of your senses.

Observations, feelings, thoughts, and ideas may all benefit from prompting.

In any weather conditions, go out and play. Dance in the rain!

When you come back to your house, do some more research.

Observe and document animals seen.

Make a to-do list and then head out to some natural areas.

Day 260 - God promises you His blessings to live for Him.

"I will grant peace in the land, and you will lie down and no one will make you afraid. I will remove wild beasts from the land and the sword will not pass through your country."
—Leviticus 26:6, NIV

BELOVED,
Don't worry; God guarantees you His benefits and blessings if you live for Him. So don't be concerned; God has a message for you today. God, who keeps His promises, says, If you walk in My decrees and keep My commandments in your daily lives, I will grant you plenty of rain in the seasons when you need it, and your land will produce abundant crops, and your trees will be filled with fruit. *"I am the Eternal One, your God, who led you out of the land of Egypt so that you would no longer be their slaves. I have shattered the yokes that broke your backs and helped you walk straight and upright."* (Leviticus 26:3-13, The Voice). Do not fear; God has assured you that He will bless your life, living, and livelihood because you serve Him, obey Him, trust Him, and wait for and live for Him.
What are the conditions for these blessings?
Every day 365/24/7, live fearlessly and faithfully! Don't Panic, pray! Never give up; persist! You will ace every faith-shattering test despite the obstacles, setbacks, blockages, afflictions, trials, problems, temptations, sufferings, and valley experiences. It's only a test. God is on your side! Obey God's commandments in your life, living, relationships, leadership, and livelihood: The Ten Commandments (Exodus 20); Jesus' First and Greatest Commandment (Matthew 22:35-40, Mark 12:28-31, Luke 10:25-28); To receive God's love and care; To love yourself (self-love, self-care); To love others as yourself (brotherly love, community care); To live by His decree – His word, His will, His timing, and His ways.

AFFIRMATIONS & DECLARATIONS
My God is unchanging. He is loyal to His promises. You don't change His mind. You are the One who gives every good and perfect gift, and no good thing will You withhold no good thing from me. You strengthen me in the wait and process, and I give You the glory and thanksgiving. You show me off as a crown of Your creation and miracle. *"Every good gift bestowed, every perfect gift received comes to us from above, courtesy of the Father of lights. He is consistent. He won't change His mind or play tricks in the shadows."* (James 1:17, VOICE)

- I am keeping my contract with God. He is a Covenant-Fulfillment God.
- I am obeying God's commandments. I am full of joy, patience, peace, and hope!
- Testing my faith produces joy, perseverance, endurance, and refined dedication; I lack nothing!
- I am waiting in great expectation and trusting God with my life, living, and livelihood.
- I live by His word and will in my daily life, career, relationships, and financial stewardship.

Every gift God freely gives us is good and perfect, streaming down from the Father of lights, who shines from the heavens with no hidden shadow or darkness and is never subject to change.
—James 1:17, TPT

PRAYER
Father God, Thank You, Almighty God, for Your promises to benefit me when I obey Your commands and decrees. Lord, I repent of my disobedience and promise to dedicate my life to bringing honor to Your name. I choose to live a life that pleases You, Lord, and even my adversaries will be at peace with me because of it. I voice my declarations in the atmosphere now. I praise God in the middle of my transformation. My God brings me to the promised land because I choose to obey Him, love Him, live for Him, and live in Him. Let the devil knows that I know what God says, who I am, and to whom I belong, and God is faithful. I give thanks to the One who has strengthened me beyond comprehension. Lord, You make all things beautiful in Your time and design. I won't hate the process; I will wait and trust the pause. My God, who can do immeasurable things, things more amazing than I could ever ask or conceive through the power of His Holy Spirit at work in me, to Him be all praise and glory, in Jesus the Anointed from this day, generationally and globally, in His name, I pray, Amen.

MY DOPE *faith journal*

Date S | M | T | W | T | F | S

Morning: I feel my emotion! My one-word check-in: ______

DECLARATION

Consider today's verse. I implore the Holy Spirit to reveal His wisdom and truth to me and I declare it over my life.

OBSERVATION

What does the message mean? Lord, help me see it.

PRAYER

What is my prayer request? Lord, I live fully in You.

EMPOWERMENT

How will Your word empower me? Lord, give me the insight to apply my faith to be more significant than my fears.

MY FEARLESS *journey*

Evening: Feel my emotion! My one-word check-up:

What is making me FEEL like this?

What lessons did I LEARNED?

What THOUGHTS did I had?

What prompted my GRATITUDE?

Who did I CONNECTED with?

What brought me JOY?

EVENING PRAYER

My treat for today is: ....

What To Include In A Nature Journal

diagrams of insects

details of a pinecone

trees through the seasons

lists of birds, mammals, insects

lists of plants

what you find under a rock

what you find in a stream

root system of a plant

leaf/bark rubbings

pressed flowers

wild feathers

different life cycles, seasons, changes

Day 261 - Don't Rebel Against God; Don't be Afraid of Them!

Do not rebel like this against the Eternal. Don't be afraid of the land's inhabitants. It is we who will devour them! They are now defenseless, and nothing can protect them from the Eternal, who is with us. You don't need to be afraid of them!
—Numbers 14:9, NIV

BELOVED,
Don't go against God. He is by your side. You don't have to be terrified of the land's adversaries since you will consume them. Their support is no longer available, but the Lord's protection is with you. It would be best if you were not terrified of them. Do not be scared when dealing with the consequences of a global pandemic and your situation; you are an overcomer. Even though you face terrible news from experts, influencers, media personalities, statistics, reports, facts, your feelings, and all the evidence the enemy uses to distract and fear you, be fearless. You must choose wisdom, faith, and love to find assurance, courage, and confidence in God. Doubt and rebel against the Father of Lies and believe the Lord's report. God has repeatedly reassured you that He is with you amidst your situation. There is not one time in His word that God says, "worry about, stress over it, have sleepless nights and restlessness about it, figure it out, fix it by yourself" Repeatedly, He assures you to trust Him. God will never leave you, and nothing is impossible with Him. So do not let self-doubt, fear, limiting beliefs, self-condemnation, discouragement, guilt, and unforgiveness cause you to vent, complain, cuss, and lament to question God's faithfulness and character. If you are unfaithful, He remains faithful. Don't let what your eyes see; doubt what God said. He is with you even in the most challenging conditions and terrible life occurrences. He is your refuge, shield, protection, security, safety, shepherd, strength, supplier, song, and Saviour.
As you proceed from Genesis to Revelation, you stop to be nourished when God tells His people not to worry, fear, or fret but to be unafraid. You're focusing on Numbers 14:9 today. Read Numbers 13 and 14 for perspective. Spies went to scout out the promised land. As directed, they surveyed the ground and found: 'It was wealthy. It runs with milk and honey; look at its fruit. The property is appealing, but the locals are tough.' This news discourages the Israelites since it's worrying concerning the natives. Caleb said, 'We should invade immediately. Definitely!' But the other scouts say, 'No. Nope. We can't beat the locals.' The negative report was discouraging, making the people doubt God's promise. Joshua and Caleb said, "Fantastic land! It's a milk and honey land, the greatest ever. Stop whining! If we all obey God's will, the Eternal will give us the land. Don't defy the Eternal. Don't fear locals. We'll defeat and devour them. They're powerless against God and us. Not to worry!'
God demands bravery from you to trust His promise and go forward, do not be afraid. He is with you!

AFFIRMATIONS & DECLARATIONS
My God says, *"I will lead blind Israel down a new path, guiding them along an unfamiliar way. I will brighten the darkness before them and smooth out the road ahead of them. Yes, I will indeed do these things; I will not forsake them."* (Isaiah 42:16, NLT)

- My setback is temporary and momentary; it won't last very long compared to the greater glory.
- I am not rebellion or resisting; I am change-resilient and change-ready for my comeback.
- I am shifting from wandering in my wilderness to worshipping, praising, conquering, and possessing my possession, territory, and promised land.

Joshua 22:19, NIV: *"If the land you possess is defiled, come over to the Lord's land, where the Lord's tabernacle stands, and share the land with us. But do not rebel against the Lord or against us by building an altar for yourselves, other than the altar of the Lord our God.*

PRAYER
Heavenly Father, Although I am not always as faithful to You, I appreciate Your faithfulness. Father, please assure me that no matter what You ask of me or the unfamiliar path I take, You are with me always, and I trust You, be strong and brave. The transition, the in-between rock and hard place, the meantime, the wilderness, valley of deepest darkness, joblessness, brokenness, sickness, barrenness, I will go and do it to honor You and not rebel but revere Your faithfulness. I don't want to be a disobedient child who doesn't live in harmony with You. I desire to be under Your protection, provision, and prominence, follow You wherever You lead, receive everything You have in store for me, and become everything You are created and make me. Renew, resurrect, reclaim, rebuild, revitalize, and restore me in You! In Jesus' name, amen!

MY DOPE *faith journal*

Date S | M | T | W | T | F | S

Morning: I feel my emotion! My one-word check-in:

DECLARATION

Consider today's verse. I implore the Holy Spirit to reveal His wisdom and truth to me and I declare it over my life.

OBSERVATION

What does the message mean? Lord, help me see it.

PRAYER

What is my prayer request? Lord, I live fully in You.

EMPOWERMENT

How will Your word empower me? Lord, give me the insight to apply my faith to be more significant than my fears.

MY FEARLESS *journey*

Evening: Feel my emotion! My one-word check-up:

What is making me FEEL like this?

What lessons did I LEARNED?

What THOUGHTS did I had?

What prompted my GRATITUDE?

Who did I CONNECTED with?

What brought me JOY?

EVENING PRAYER

WATER:

FRUIT & VEG:

MY MOOD:

My treat for today is: ....

Nature Observation

Get outside and use your senses to take in the animals and surroundings. Make a note of your observations in the table below.

I notice...
I wonder...
This reminds me of...

Day 262 – God decided you will defeat this enemy!

"The Eternal One encouraged Moses. **Eternal One:** 'Don't be afraid of him. I've already determined that you'll defeat King Og. He, his people, and all his land shall be yours. You'll treat him just as you did the Amorite king, Sihon, in Heshbon.'"
—Numbers 21:34, VOICE

BELOVED,

You only question God when you forget His former successes. Today, the Father encourages you, saying, "Don't be scared of your adversary and adversities; I've already established the end at the beginning and declared you as a champion of this battle; you will vanquish this adversary and reap the benefits of triumph. I shall treat this opponent like I treated your enemies in previous fights and give you victory, deliverance, and breakthroughs.

As you move through life, you will face obstacles, opposition, and even persecution from your adversaries. However, if you are journeying with Me, prioritizing Me, you must be strong and courageous that the conquest has been completed and that triumph is the only conclusion for every fight you have fought, faced, or faced. No opponent stands before Me and My divine plan, promises, and intentions, and this is a crucial concept that God's children must understand and use to control their lives, living, and livelihood. Nothing can stand in the way of what I have planned to flourish. You are My beloved, and I will crush every resistance and give you more than you requested, imagined, thought, prayed, or even believed and hoped. Please do not allow the adversary to use his poisonous fear techniques to get you to question My character or reject My faithfulness. Introduce your adversaries to the strength of Me, your All-Powerful Almighty Eternal God. Let your adversaries know that you are My miracle, masterpiece, and a manifestation of My grandeur, majesty, and splendor. Don't be scared or anxious. God has determined that you will conquer your adversaries.

Today, you are camping on Numbers 21:34 as you proceed from Genesis to Revelation, pausing at every mention in God's word as He encourages His people to trust Him and take Him at His word. The Israelites go through the desert. As they were within borders, they needed permission to cross others' land. Amorite King Sihon told the Edomite messenger, "You can't get through here." Meaning? Where have you been that you haven't heard of God's reckless love and steadfast ability to deliver, protect, and provide for His people? Everyone knows God's favor on His people. Despite this, the Amorite king attacked God's children after refusing them his property. Like seriously! God exposed His strength. Read Numbers 21. The Father says, "Study My word and use its wisdom truths to alter your knowledge, mindset, vision, conduct, and culture. Learn about Me as Your God and how I've shown My power, performance, and presence in the past to defend My children. Check My resume! Today, when you seek Me, I encourage you. 'Don't be frightened of your adversaries. I've already decided to hand them over to you, that you'll beat them and their wicked minions, and that triumph will be yours.'"

AFFIRMATIONS & DECLARATIONS

"Beloved, never avenge yourselves, but leave it to the wrath of God, for it is written, Vengeance is mine, I will repay, says the Lord." (Romans 12:19, ESV).

- If God is with me, who dare be against me.
- I am a God-chosen, hand-picked, and God's favorite child.
- I am the apple of my Father's eye.
- I know who I am and to whom I belong. I am victorious. I am a winner.

"Put on the whole armor of God, that you may be able to stand against the schemes of the devil."
—Ephesians 6:11, ESV

PRAYER

Father God, Thank You for Your assurance that I am safe and secure in the name of Jesus, in You, and with You. You are my Provider and Protector. You are the one that fights my war against the adversaries (physical, mental, emotional, spiritual, social, and financial) that I am now fighting. I will not be scared in Jesus' name. My God, You have decided to overcome all of my adversaries. I put my confidence in You and pray, confess, proclaim, declare, and pronounce Psalm 91 over my life. In Jesus' name, I raise my faith to believe, be assured, and trust that I am safe and secure in God. Lord, You are actively watching over Your word, making haste, and ready to perform it. Manifest Your goodness in my life, household, children, family, and all connected and concerning me. Do it, Lord, defeat every adversary and bring the victory by Your grace and all for Your glory, in Jesus' mighty name, I pray. Amen.

MY DOPE *faith journal*

Date S | M | T | W | T | F | S

Morning: I feel my emotion! My one-word check-in: ____________

DECLARATION

Consider today's verse. I implore the Holy Spirit to reveal His wisdom and truth to me and I declare it over my life.

OBSERVATION

What does the message mean? Lord, help me see it.

PRAYER

What is my prayer request? Lord, I live fully in You.

EMPOWERMENT

How will Your word empower me? Lord, give me the insight to apply my faith to be more significant than my fears.

MY FEARLESS *journey*

Evening: Feel my emotion! My one-word check-up:

What is making me FEEL like this?

What lessons did I LEARNED?

What THOUGHTS did I had?

What prompted my GRATITUDE?

Who did I CONNECTED with?

What brought me JOY?

EVENING PRAYER

My treat for today is:

Phenology Wheel

In the natural world, a phenology wheel is a monthly visual showing what's happening. In each area, draw what you perceive in the natural world at this time of year.

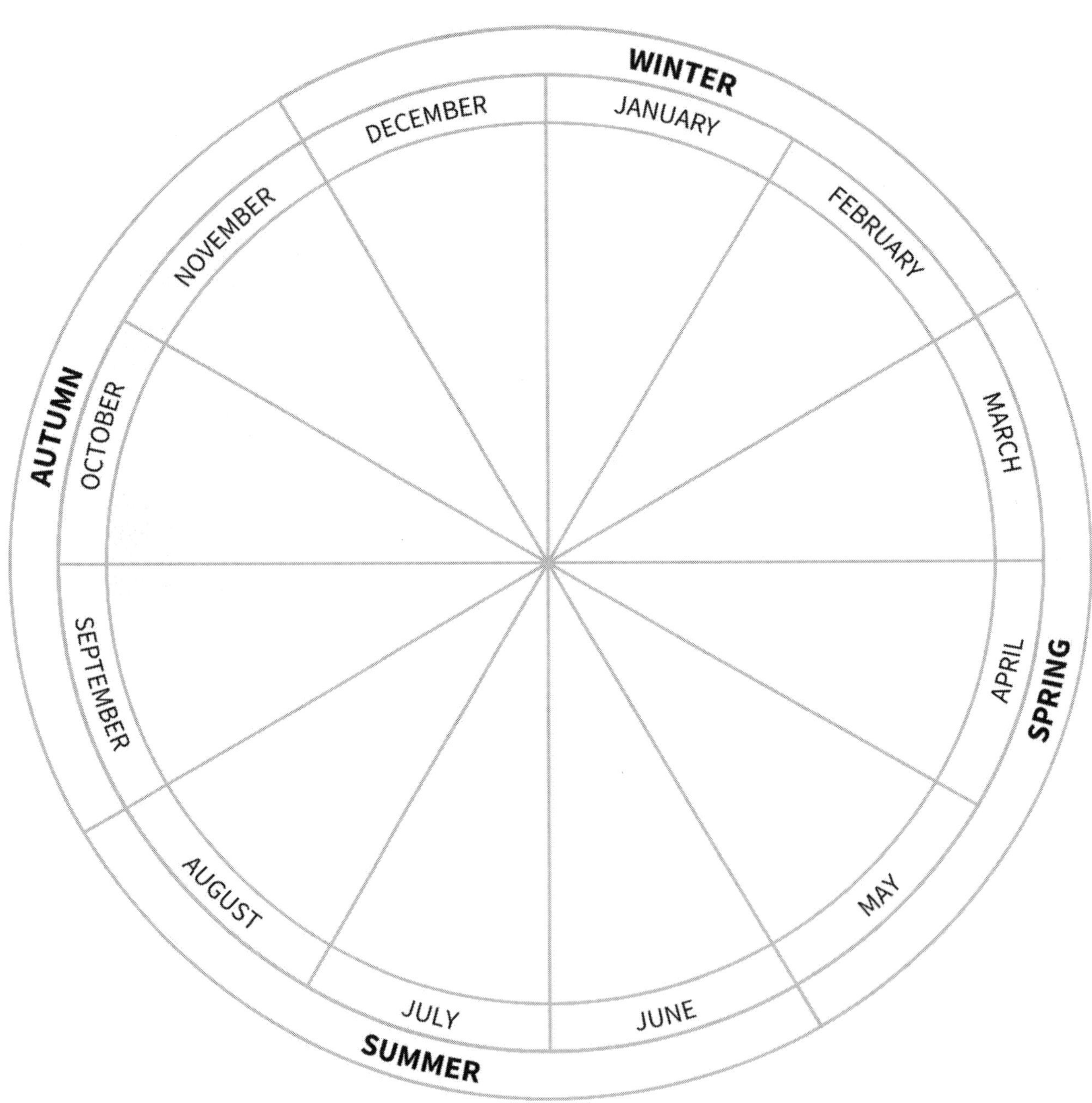

Day 263 - God has the Final Say and Judgement.

"Do not show partiality in judging; hear both small and great alike. Do not be afraid of anyone, for judgment belongs to God."
—Deuteronomy 1:17, NIV

BELOVED,
Don't be intimidated by anybody because it's 'really' God who is the judge. You are good enough, smart enough, sufficient enough, and strong enough for God. So stop proving yourself and people-pleasing. Always do your best for God. He is your only audience, core accountability, and final authority. Take your circumstances, problems, cases, and burdens to God. He has the final say, power, and influence, not man. He is the supreme judge over every complicated, complex, confusing, and chaotic case. *"May the LORD, therefore, judge which of us is right and punish the guilty one. He is my advocate, and he will rescue me from your power!"* (1 Samuel 24:15, NLT).
If you are maltreated, mistreated, wrongfully accused, outlooked, or misjudged by man for any cause, The Father says, take your case to Me, the Supreme Authority. I am aware of all I have seen and heard and will address it. I have the strategy and solution to every problem. Take the matter to Me. Wait to see how the case turns out for your good and My glory. *"Don't show any favoritism when you judge; whether a person is important or unimportant, hear him out. Don't be intimidated by anybody because God is the judge; you are His agents. If any case is too difficult for you, bring it to me, and I'll handle it."* (Deu 1:17, VOICE). Whatever you are facing today, be assured that as a child of God, surrender and invite God into the situation when you pray. He fights on your behalf, advocates, interceeds, defends, redeems, and rescues you. You're traveling from Genesis to Revelation, stopping at every instance of toxic dread in God's word. You should only fear God to trust, love, and obey Him. You camp at Deuteronomy 1:16-17 today. As the population grows, the people experience interpersonal troubles and take their concerns to Moses. Moses distributed cases to judges, advised them not to show partiality and favoritism, and encouraged the people not to be intimidated since God is the judge who has the final say, total control, sovereignty, and authority over your concerns. "*At the same time, I gave orders to your judges: "Listen carefully to complaints and accusations between your fellow Israelites. Judge fairly between each person and his fellow or foreigner. Don't play favorites; treat the little and the big alike; listen carefully to each. Don't be impressed by big names. This is God's judgment you're dealing with. Hard cases you can bring to me; I'll deal with them.'"* (Deu 1:16-17, MSG).

AFFIRMATIONS & DECLARATIONS
"But I say to you that everyone who is angry with his brother will be liable to judgment; whoever insults his brother will be liable to the council, and whoever says, 'You fool!' will be liable to the hell of fire." (Matthew 5:22, ESV)

- I have tremendous potential, capabilities, and capacity.
- I am capable of making wise decisions. I am capable of overcoming adversity.
- I am never alone as God is with me always, giving me wisdom and telling me what to say.

"For behold, the day is coming, burning like an oven, when all the arrogant and all evildoers will be stubble. The day that is coming shall set them ablaze, says the Lord of hosts, so that it will leave them neither root nor branch."
– Malachi 4:1, ESV

PRAYER
Father God, All-powerful God, Thanks because, right by my side, You have always been there for me through everything: every fight, every attack, and every storm. Whenever it poured, Lord, You reminded me that battle had won, and I would prevail if I persisted. There's nothing in the world like You. You are exalted, and I give praises and glory throughout the land. I proclaim that You, my Lord, never let me down and have received it. Thank You for everything and Who You have been to me.
Today the power of the Almighty God will reverse every evil plot and diabolical scheme and send their demonic curses back to them by the grace and power in the name of Jesus Christ. I pray that the Lord God Almighty will satisfy me with every good thing I desire in Jesus Christ's name. I will be a reference point for a life of significance to others; kings will be attracted to my light, gift, and vision. My God will plant and keep a permanent smile of satisfaction, peace, and joy on my face in Jesus' mighty name.

MY DOPE *faith journal*

Date S | M | T | W | T | F | S

Morning: I feel my emotion! My one-word check-in:

DECLARATION

Consider today's verse. I implore the Holy Spirit to reveal His wisdom and truth to me and I declare it over my life.

OBSERVATION

What does the message mean? Lord, help me see it.

PRAYER

What is my prayer request? Lord, I live fully in You.

EMPOWERMENT

How will Your word empower me? Lord, give me the insight to apply my faith to be more significant than my fears.

MY FEARLESS *journey*

Evening: Feel my emotion! My one-word check-up:

What is making me FEEL like this?

What lessons did I LEARNED?

What THOUGHTS did I had?

What prompted my GRATITUDE?

Who did I CONNECTED with?

What brought me JOY?

EVENING PRAYER

My treat for today is: ....

Nature Journal

Find a quiet spot in the outdoors to relax. Breathe more deeply and pay attention to your surroundings. What noises are present in your immediate surroundings? Develop a sense of smell. You smell how? What shades do you see? What shapes are you noticing? Post your ideas on this page. Note any epiphanies, thoughts, or memories that may have emerged throughout this practice.

Day 264 - When God says Go! Don't be afraid! Just do it!

"See, the Lord your God has given you the land. Go up and take possession of it as the Lord, the God of your ancestors, told you. Do not be afraid; do not be discouraged."
—Deuteronomy 1:21, NIV

BELOVED,

When God says, Go! Don't be afraid! Just do it! Let go of old endings and embrace new beginnings. Did God make you a promise? Are you standing on a promise of scripture for His performance? Are you waiting for answered prayers for a breakthrough or open doors? So how do you respond to the instruction when God says go? Often, the command or commission looks like a challenge, call, change, or character transformation, and you need God-courage and God-confidence to go. Is this what the season of waiting and wandering in the desert was about: preparing, positioning, and equipping you for God's divine purpose and the greenlight of your new beginning?

What does 'go' mean when commissioned and commanded by God?

When God says Go, it is a mandate from God. It is a movement, a motivation, a mission, a message, a messenger, a miracle, a ministry, and a marketplace mandate. Go! You are a history-maker, generational curse blocker, chain-breaker, game-changer, mover, and shaker. What does God's commissioning mean to you right now, based on where you are on your journey? What did God mean when He said to Moses, Esther, David, Joseph, Daniel, Ananias, Jonah, the Woman Caught in Adultery, and the Children of Israel, 'Go?' Also, Jesus said, 'Go therefore and make disciples,' as He gave you the Great Commission.

So, you're traveling from Genesis to Revelation, stopping at every instance of toxic fear in God's word and where He says be fearless. You should only fear God and trust and obey Him. Camp on Deuteronomy 1:21 today, read verses 5 through 21 to learn about Moses' servant leadership. Moses told the Israelites what the Lord had done. God is our Protector, Provider, Keeper, Guide, and Instructor. You must recall God's word, His character and behavior, His qualities and actions across generations, and how He displays His love and loyalty to you, your household, families, communities, and the nations. Knowing, experiencing, and confronting God's power should inspire fearless faith in His name, methods, words, and timing. Your bold confidence in God is strengthened as you recall how He has saved, redeemed, resurrected, restored, rejuvenated, and rebounded. He'll do it again. Same God back then, same God now.

'Now go up and take possession!'

AFFIRMATIONS & DECLARATIONS

Because I delight in the Lord, He directs my feet. He strengthens my efforts and guides my feet and steps. I'll hear His voice say, "This is the route to go; walk this way, whether I should turn left or right."
"Stalwart walks in step with God; his path blazed by God, he's happy. If he stumbles, he's not down for long; God has a grip on his hand." (Psalm 37:23-24, MSG).

- I am courageous and confident.
- I am ready to go forward.
- Lord, I will go where You send me.
- Lord, I will do what You ask of me.

"Therefore go and make disciples of all nations, baptizing them in the name of the Father and of the Son and of the Holy Spirit, and teaching them to obey everything I have commanded you. And surely I am with you always, to the very end of the age."
—Matthew 28:19-20, NIV

PRAYER

Almighty God, Abba Father, Faithful God, Lord, I worship You. You have been faithful in the past throughout generations. You have proven to be my Provider, Protector, Promoter, and Guide. You are the Promise-Keeping and Covenant-Fulfilment God. Lord, here I am today, having waited and wandered and wondered when I will ever go forward to claim the promise You have in store for me. Even the command to go seems scary, although I have prayed and trusted You. Lord, You promise to be with me. Lord, You promised never to leave me nor forsake me. Lord, strengthen my faith, equip my feeble knees, and give me the courage and confidence to go. Lord, You have prepared me to enter this new era and possess the promised land. Lord, You promised to go before me and lead me, and You are already there before I get there. Lord, You said You would go ahead of me and fight my battles. Lord, You said You would stay behind me and cover my back as my Rearguard. I am going forward. I am transitioning from wandering to possessing, by Your grace and all for Your glory. In Jesus' mighty and matchless name, I pray. Amen.

MY DOPE *faith journal*

Date S | M | T | W | T | F | S

Morning: I feel my emotion! My one-word check-in: ____________

DECLARATION

Consider today's verse. I implore the Holy Spirit to reveal His wisdom and truth to me and I declare it over my life.

OBSERVATION

What does the message mean? Lord, help me see it.

PRAYER

What is my prayer request? Lord, I live fully in You.

EMPOWERMENT

How will Your word empower me? Lord, give me the insight to apply my faith to be more significant than my fears.

MY FEARLESS *journey*

Evening: Feel my emotion! My one-word check-up:

What is making me FEEL like this?

What lessons did I LEARNED?

What THOUGHTS did I had?

What prompted my GRATITUDE?

Who did I CONNECTED with?

What brought me JOY?

EVENING PRAYER

My treat for today is: ....

Time Spent in Nature

THIS WEEK'S TASK

Try to spend time each day the outdoors this week. Write down your observations of what you hear, feel, see, and smell. Please record what you did and how it made you think.

	NATURE ACTIVITY	HOW IT MADE YOU THINK
MONDAY		
TUESDAY		
WEDNESDAY		
THURSDAY		
FRIDAY		
SATURDAY		
SUNDAY		

Day 265 - Don't be frightened; Don't be terrified by them.

"Then I said to you, Don't be frightened; don't be afraid of those people."
—Deuteronomy 1:29, NVC

BELOVED,

You must inform your current situation, yourself, and the current generation about the Lord's previous and ongoing favor on His people. This knowledge helps you place your confidence in God, who has already shown Himself as your Protector, Provider, Shepherd, Lover, Father, Guide, and Redeemer. Revelation 12:11 says you defeat the devil, his evil workers, toxic fear, and demonic tactics by the Blood of the Lamb and the word of your testimony.

You must lift the veil and see God's blessings in your life, journey, children, household, family, and land, which are undoubtedly inspiring and empowering against today's challenges. Recalling how God has supplied, protected, promoted, prepared, defended, and guided you in your life and past storms strengthens your trust, hope, and fearless faith in Him.

Now God has a message of encouragement for you amidst your storms.

God says, "Don't be fearful; don't be continuously frightened of these people. Like in prior struggles, I will go ahead and fight for you. You saw and heard me do that. I'll take care of you, even in your valley experience. I'll guide you to the prayer you requested and the relief I promised you."

"Then I said to you, 'Do not be shocked, nor fear them. The Lord your God who goes before you will fight for you Himself, just as He did for you in Egypt before your [very] eyes, and in the wilderness where you saw how the Lord your God carried and protected you, just as a man carries his son, all along the way which you traveled until you arrived at this place." (Deuteronomy 1:29-31, AMP).

In Deuteronomy 1:29-45, Moses instructed the new generation to support, serve, and steer the recent transition, change management plan, spiritual rebirth, and new organizational structure. Moses stressed recognizing duties, obligations, and connections to respect, trust, and be faithful to God, challenge and care for oneself, and interact with others. He assures them that they will confront many foes despite significant changes. It would help if you didn't let your opponents' poisonous dread cause you to worry or doubt God. He said God led them out of Egypt, through the desert, delaying, defeating, wounding every opponent, and eventually to the promised land. Moses said that despite all the wonders God performed for His people, He still travels with them, seeks refuge for them, and protects them day and night, yet they don't trust Him. When people question His loyalty, they grieve God's heart and fail to perceive His goodness. When you disobey God, your adversaries destroy you. Caleb and Joshua are the only ones who have seen the promised land and returned with a rejuvenated attitude, defined vision, and desire to progress. Your faithlessness and pessimism break God's heart. Don't doubt God; doubt your fears!

AFFIRMATIONS & DECLARATIONS

As a result, I say, "The Lord is with me; I will not be frightened." What are mere folks capable of doing to me? The Lord is my Helper; He is with me. I gaze triumphantly at my opponents. I prefer to seek shelter in the Lord than to put my confidence in human beings or be a people-pleaser.

- I am God's child. Whom should I be afraid of? There's no need to feel terrified, for God is with me.
- I have faith that my God will rescue me. I am guided, protected, and provided for by My God. He is my Shepherd, and I have no lack, fear, failure, or limitation.

"The Eternal is with me, so I will not be afraid of anything. If God is on my side, how can anyone hurt me? The Eternal is on my side, a champion for my cause; so when I look at those who hate me, victory will be in sight. It is better to put your faith in the Eternal for your security than to trust in people."
—Psalm 118:6-8, VOICE

PRAYER

Heavenly Father, I come before You. I cast all cares and concerns upon You. I put every decision, choice, and storm before You - spiritually, mentally, emotionally, physically, financially, and socially. I release my toxic fear, worry, anger, sadness, lack, sickness, hurtful ego, harmful stress, and anxiety at Your feet. I ask for Your help to overcome my doubts and fears when I feel that I am being crushed, persecuted, rejected, delayed, denied, abused, and wrongly accused by others. I choose instead to be inspired and influenced by fearless faith, a revitalized mentality, defined vision, unstoppable commitment, unwavering love, and hope for every goodness of my new beginning, promised deliverance and answered prayers with confidence in You and belief in myself. Please give me the unwavering trust in You that all things work out for my benefit and Your glory. In Jesus' name, I pray, Amen.

MY DOPE *faith journal*

Date S | M | T | W | T | F | S

Morning: I feel my emotion! My one-word check-in: ______

DECLARATION

Consider today's verse. I implore the Holy Spirit to reveal His wisdom and truth to me and I declare it over my life.

OBSERVATION

What does the message mean? Lord, help me see it.

PRAYER

What is my prayer request? Lord, I live fully in You.

EMPOWERMENT

How will Your word empower me? Lord, give me the insight to apply my faith to be more significant than my fears.

MY FEARLESS *journey*

Evening: Feel my emotion! My one-word check-up:

What is making me FEEL like this?

What lessons did I LEARNED?

What THOUGHTS did I had?

What prompted my GRATITUDE?

Who did I CONNECTED with?

What brought me JOY?

EVENING PRAYER

My treat for today is: ....

365 Journal

What I think about fearlessness in my life now...

DAY 266 - 273

Review and Reflect

Day 266 - The Lord, Your God, will fight for you.

[2] "The Lord said to me, Don't be afraid of Og, because I will hand him, his whole army, and his land over to you. Do to him what you did to Sihon king of the Amorites, who ruled in Heshbon." [22] "Don't be afraid of them, because the Lord your God will fight for you."
—Deuteronomy 3:2, 22, NCV

BELOVED,
Which 'Og' is trying to take you down today? What situation, burden, dilemma, financial crisis, illness, or sin has you in its grip?
The Father says, My triumph against every enemy, its entire army, and my promise of their land will end your fear. Treat these enemies like you would any other enemy you've faced, and I fought and defeated in the past. Grab on tight to My hand. Don't stick your head in the sand and push blindly through everything that comes your way. Despite it, turn to Me, your Great Savior, give Me the struggles, and let Me hold you with My righteous and victorious right hand. I will lead you, equip you, empower you, and enable you to overcome any obstacles. Despite all your concerns, I enjoy using the dire condition of your suffering to show you the truth of My strength, light, grace, glory, and love, which drowns out all fears, defeats your enemies, and rescues you. I am the Lord, your Defender, and your Deliverer. I will save you from harm and lift you beyond danger because you cling to Me in love. You will call on Me because you know My name, and I will respond. I'll be with you through thick and thin; I'll save you and give you dignity. I'll give you many beautiful years on this earth and let you see My salvation. (Psalm 91:14-16).
As you continue your journey from Genesis to Revelation, Deuteronomy 3:2, 22 is your emphasis today. *"Do not fear him, for I have handed him over to you, him and all his people and his land… Do not fear them, for it is the Lord your God who is fighting for you."* (Deu 3:2, 22, AMP). Read Deuteronomy 3 for context. The Israelites defeated Og as God promised and conquered all his 60 cities.
Moses continued to encourage the current generation by recalling God's love, generosity, and faithfulness to the preceding generation. Also, he revealed the God of Paradox of both mercy and justice! Moses was God's servant-leader. He received mercy and miracles while facing God's righteousness and judgment. Moses detailed his circumstances and massive failure, how he screwed up with God due to his disobedience, and the punishments he endured as proof of the justice of a Just God, who has the final say, final judgment, ultimate power, and the last word.

AFFIRMATIONS & DECLARATIONS
I'll stop fighting in my carnal flesh and being fearful of the wrong enemy. I will not be afraid of those who want to kill my body; they cannot touch my soul. I will have a healthy fear of God, who can destroy both soul and body in hell. (Matthew 10:28).

- I am still standing steadfast.
- I am standing firmly and boldly.
- I am pressing ahead courageously and confidently.
- I am unstoppable by foe, fear, or failure.

"Don't fear those who aim to kill just the body but are unable to touch the soul. The One to worry is He who can destroy you, soul and body, in the fires of hell."
—Matthew 10:28, VOICE

PRAYER
Heavenly Father, Thank You for making me righteous through the Blood of Jesus. I repent and confess all my sins in Jesus' name. Please show me Your grace, mercy, and forgiveness, and cleanse me from all unrighteousness. Change my mindset, thoughts, deeds, actions, and sins of commission in Jesus' name. Lord, I accept Your forgiveness, mercy, compassion, and love. I believe in Your promises, Your timeless and limitless character of faithfulness; I choose to trust that You are working behind the scenes on my behalf. Thank You for saving my life. Help me to maintain my gaze on You, even when I am rejected and dejected. May I remember that You can utilize everything for my good and Your glory! Give me a trusting heart and remove my urge to rely on my comprehension. Thank You for Your care, provision, protection, power, and presence! In the name of Jesus, I pray, Amen.

MY DOPE *faith journal*

Date S | M | T | W | T | F | S

Morning: I feel my emotion! My one-word check-in: ______

DECLARATION

Consider today's verse. I implore the Holy Spirit to reveal His wisdom and truth to me and I declare it over my life.

OBSERVATION

What does the message mean? Lord, help me see it.

PRAYER

What is my prayer request? Lord, I live fully in You.

EMPOWERMENT

How will Your word empower me? Lord, give me the insight to apply my faith to be more significant than my fears.

MY FEARLESS *journey*

Evening: Feel my emotion! My one-word check-up:

What is making me FEEL like this?

What lessons did I LEARNED?

What THOUGHTS did I had?

What prompted my GRATITUDE?

Who did I CONNECTED with?

What brought me JOY?

EVENING PRAYER

WATER:

FRUIT & VEG:

MY MOOD:

My treat for today is: ....

The Happiness Test

Give each assertion a score between 1 and 3, with 1 representing seldom true, 2 representing occasionally true, and 3 representing frequently true. When completed, put your points together to get your happiness score.	Rarely	Sometimes	Often
I am aware of my strengths.	1	2	3
My life has significance to me.	1	2	3
I am enthusiastic about the future.	1	2	3
I can concentrate on the now.	1	2	3
I take daily breaks from social media.	1	2	3
Every day, I engage in regular physical activity.	1	2	3
I frequently perform acts of kindness for others.	1	2	3
Using my abilities gives me a strong feeling of fulfillment in my life.	1	2	3
I express my emotions to family or friends.	1	2	3
I am grateful to individuals and events.	1	2	3
I'm a member of a spiritual community or group.	1	2	3
I participate in things that I find interesting and difficult.	1	2	3

Scores: 12 - 19

Not Happy

You are employing only a few abilities that add to your satisfaction. You may acquire pleasure by mastering these talents. Get expert assistance if you are experiencing a difficult time.

Scores: 20 - 28

Moderately Happy

You already have some happiness-enhancing abilities, but it would be beneficial to learn and practice a few other happiness-enhancing behaviors to find enjoyment in all aspects of your life.

Scores: 29 - 36

Extremely Happy

Since you employ many abilities that lead to happiness, you are joyful in all aspects of your life. Maintain using these abilitie and take pleasure in your joy.

YOUR HAPPINESS SCORE:	

Day 267 - Remember What God Did & Promised!

"But don't be afraid of them. Remember what the Lord your God did to all of Egypt and its king."
—Deuteronomy 7:18, NCV

BELOVED,
You may think, "These adversaries are stronger than I am. How can I overcome them?" But be fearless and remember what the Lord, your God, has done in the past and promised for your future. You must choose the Lord as your God to break every generational curse and pass on the legacy of faith, glory, and victory to your children and the generations. In Deuteronomy 7:6-24, Moses reminds the next generation of the Lord's goodness and the promises of generational benefits for obedience, loyalty, and trust, as well as generational curses for disobedience, worshipping other gods, and neglecting to obey the Lord's commands. You must be confident and committed to Jesus Christ as your Lord and Savior. Pray for your children, household, family, and the land. Declare Jesus' Blood, Name, and the Fire of the Holy Spirit over your children and generation. Your children are marked, saturated, submerged, and covered, and they are profitable in God's kingdom. Pray for your children's spouses so they don't intermarry and be unequally yoked to lose their faith in Christ. Declare: In the name of Jesus, this sickness, poverty, divorce, single-parenthood, curse, captivity, corruption, and ungodliness may have run in my family, generation, history, nationality, and culture, but it stops here for *"as for me and my house, we will serve the Lord."* (Joshua 24:15).
Family impacts your religion, values, virtues, financial literacy, God-accountability, and beliefs as a legacy to your children, home, and generations. A family demonstrating God's importance is crucial to creating a lifetime of faith. You must be confident in Jesus Christ as your Lord and Savior. Joshua 24:15 is a family rule. If serving the Lord Jesus looks undesirable, choose whom you will do today, but we shall serve the Lord. They should know you are a servant of God by your spiritual fruit, your connection with Christ by your character, and your conduct by the Fruit of the Spirit. You must produce memoirs, publish books, and recall God's magnificence to inspire future generations to be courageous and fearless. Remember what the Lord, your God, has done! Resolve to leave a faith-filled legacy that manifests God's promises.

AFFIRMATIONS & DECLARATIONS
I declare generational blessings in Jesus' name.
I sing praises, pray, and constantly remember my Limitless God, who has strength, power, wisdom, love, majesty, and peace beyond comprehension and measure.

- I am a courageous warrior.
- I will never forget what God has done for me.
- I am strong, brave, joyful, and self-assured.

"Now to the God who can do so many awe-inspiring things, immeasurable things, things greater than we ever could ask or imagine through the power at work in us, to Him be all glory in the church and in Jesus the Anointed from this generation to the next, forever and ever. Amen."
—Ephesians 3:20-21, VOICE

PRAYER
Heavenly Father, Thank You for making today a new day for me. This day is all about You. Thank You for Your message, which fills me with joy and inner strength as I recall Your goodness, faithfulness, and loving-kindness across generations, as well as personally in my own life and the lives of my children, household, and family. On this day, I chose to carry on my faith as a testimony, a tradition, a generational blessing, family salvation, and a way of life. Please help me understand and practice the concept that generosity begins at home. Make me busy doing good for others, but make me spend quality time alone with You as my Solace. Today, help me develop my love, dedication, obedience to You, self-love, and love for others. Make me healthy, wealthy, and wise through good works for You to be glorified globally and generationally. In Jesus' Name, I pray, Amen.

MY DOPE *faith journal*

Date S | M | T | W | T | F | S

Morning: I feel my emotion! My one-word check-in: ....

DECLARATION

Consider today's verse. I implore the Holy Spirit to reveal His wisdom and truth to me and I declare it over my life.

OBSERVATION

What does the message mean? Lord, help me see it.

PRAYER

What is my prayer request? Lord, I live fully in You.

EMPOWERMENT

How will Your word empower me? Lord, give me the insight to apply my faith to be more significant than my fears.

MY FEARLESS *journey*

Evening: Feel my emotion! My one-word check-up:

What is making me FEEL like this?

What lessons did I LEARNED?

What THOUGHTS did I had?

What prompted my GRATITUDE?

Who did I CONNECTED with?

What brought me JOY?

EVENING PRAYER

WATER:

FRUIT & VEG:

MY MOOD:

My treat for today is: ....

Happiness Test

Use this scale, where 1 is very happy (extremely sad), and 10 is very happy (extremely pleased, to gauge your overall happiness during the past month in each of the categories provided. To calculate your total level of happiness, add your scores.

	Very unhappy									Very happy
General happiness	1	2	3	4	5	6	7	8	9	10
Health	1	2	3	4	5	6	7	8	9	10
Career	1	2	3	4	5	6	7	8	9	10
Sleep	1	2	3	4	5	6	7	8	9	10
Communication	1	2	3	4	5	6	7	8	9	10
Family	1	2	3	4	5	6	7	8	9	10
Relationships	1	2	3	4	5	6	7	8	9	10
Emotional life	1	2	3	4	5	6	7	8	9	10
Strengths & Talents	1	2	3	4	5	6	7	8	9	10
Fitness	1	2	3	4	5	6	7	8	9	10
Optimism	1	2	3	4	5	6	7	8	9	10
Spirituality	1	2	3	4	5	6	7	8	9	10
Sex life	1	2	3	4	5	6	7	8	9	10
Nutrition	1	2	3	4	5	6	7	8	9	10
Finances	1	2	3	4	5	6	7	8	9	10
Environment	1	2	3	4	5	6	7	8	9	10
Learning & education	1	2	3	4	5	6	7	8	9	10
Personal growth	1	2	3	4	5	6	7	8	9	10
Recreation	1	2	3	4	5	6	7	8	9	10
Friendships	1	2	3	4	5	6	7	8	9	10

YOUR HAPPINESS SCORE:	

Day 268 - Be Battle-ready, Don't Panic & Run Away!

"He shall say: "Hear, Israel: Today you are going into battle against your enemies. Do not be fainthearted or afraid; do not panic or be terrified by them."
— Deuteronomy 20:3, NIV

BELOVED,
As you approach Battle Day, this is how you fight your battles; don't be scared, concerned, terrified, or anxious! Don't run away from your struggle because you're afraid; face it, and God will fight for you. As you meet your battles today, the Lord sends you breaking news and orders the command, 'Destroy them!' You will be blessed by God and be victorious in the struggle you are engaged in today. *"The eternal God is your refuge, and underneath are the everlasting arms. He will drive out your enemies before you, saying, 'Destroy them!'"* (Deuteronomy 33:27, NIV). To be victorious in a real fight against your enemies, you must be spiritually, physically, emotionally, and mentally prepared and entirely focused on facing the battle fearlessly with God. Give thanks to God as you face the struggle; the Lord prepares you to be strong and courageous; He is your rock and refuge. He trains your hands for war and gives your fingers skill for battle. (Psalm 144:1).
When experiencing a spiritual battle, remember what God has done for you and your previous wins, and do not be afraid. Also, be battle-ready and focused, not distracted, and committed to obeying God's laws. God's wisdom in Deuteronomy 20 equips and strengthens you for spiritual conflicts:

1. Face it and faith it! It is not the size of the army that matters, but who is with you!
2. Be Fearless! It is the battle day! Be battle-ready every day. Be encouraged, be strong and bold, and not afraid. You are on the most powerful squad, which has never lost a war; Jesus, the LORD your God, fights for you and saves you from your adversaries.
3. Trim the fat! A loyal, courageous, effective, and productive army would assist. Not everyone who started training with you will stick around. Sometimes, God does His best work in small groups.
4. Decide Peace or Fight? Don't fight unnecessary fights. Seek the path of peace before the battle.
5. Frazzle and finish those enemies! Destroy them!
6. Food vs. Foes? Know what is fighting you vs. what is feeding you. Spare the trees for food!

AFFIRMATIONS & DECLARATIONS
As far as I can tell, Jesus said it is finished! Jesus said these things to me so that I may have peace with Him. I will encounter difficulties in this life. But don't worry, there's hope! Jesus, He has overcome the world. I face my battle and I will not panic and run. "**Jesus:** Listen, if your hand is on the plow, but your eyes are looking backward, then you're not fit for the kingdom of God." (Luke 9:62, VOICE).

- I am prepared to battle for my life! Because I know God is with me.
- I am already a winner as I am on the undefeated team of Jesus.
- I am motivated to fight for my objectives.
- I seek Godly wisdom, strategies, solutions, and plan to win every battle.

"I have told you these things so that you will be whole and at peace. In this world, you will be plagued with times of trouble, but you need not fear; I have triumphed over this corrupt world order."
—John 16:33, VOICE

PRAYER
Thank You, Father God, for being there for me no matter what. It was Your response to my prayer request for wisdom that You give me challenges to make me more intelligent and wiser with inner strength, grit, and resilience. Through consistent prayer requests for virtues, you taught me how to exercise trust in You during the wilderness, the barrenness, and the process of preparation: plowing, planting, and pruning seasons, where I had no other choice than to sit still. While the seed was still in the barn, I learned to wait on You. The wait was challenging and scary, at times, through the wilderness to the Promised Land. Following my prayer request for bravery, Lord, You responded by teaching me the difference between toxic and wholesome fears in You. With You, I embrace the fresh starts and new beginnings with a renewed mindset, confident joy, unconditional love, steadfast endurance, and fearless faith in what You have prepared me for and planned for me. I know my faith is in You, and that victory of my battles is already Yours. In Jesus' mighty name, I pray, Amen.

MY DOPE *faith journal*

Date S | M | T | W | T | F | S

Morning: I feel my emotion! My one-word check-in: ____________

DECLARATION

Consider today's verse. I implore the Holy Spirit to reveal His wisdom and truth to me and I declare it over my life.

OBSERVATION

What does the message mean? Lord, help me see it.

PRAYER

What is my prayer request? Lord, I live fully in You.

EMPOWERMENT

How will Your word empower me? Lord, give me the insight to apply my faith to be more significant than my fears.

MY FEARLESS *journey*

Evening: Feel my emotion! My one-word check-up:

What is making me FEEL like this?

What lessons did I LEARNED?

What THOUGHTS did I had?

What prompted my GRATITUDE?

Who did I CONNECTED with?

What brought me JOY?

EVENING PRAYER

WATER:

FRUIT & VEG:

MY MOOD:

My treat for today is: ....

Happiness Review

You took a test to determine your happiness level at the start of this workbook. Return to this exam and check how your test score has changed.

HAPPINESS SCORE AT START	HAPPINESS SCORE NOW
What I've learned...	
What I believe happiness to be in my life right now...	

Day 269 - God never forsakes nor forgets you.

"Be strong and brave. Don't be afraid of them and don't be frightened, because the Lord your God will go with you. He will not leave you or forget you." Then Moses called Joshua and said to him in front of the people, "Be strong and brave, because you will lead these people into the land the Lord promised to give their ancestors, and help them take it as their own. The Lord himself will go before you. He will be with you; he will not leave you or forget you. Don't be afraid and don't worry."
—Deuteronomy 31:6-8, NCV

BELOVED,
God never forsakes nor forgets you. It would be best if you embraced this challenge or change to cross over by being bold, strong, and fearless about it. God says, Do not be scared or concerned; the Lord your God will be with you. Is that something you can do? When it comes to trusting God, there are many guarantees in the Bible that He would never leave or forsake you. Today, as you continue the journey from Genesis to Revelation, you are witnessing one of the most empowering events, God's faith hero Moses' farewell speech in Deuteronomy 31. God commanded and promised Israelites and Joshua before they entered the Promised Land, "Be strong and courageous!" God will go before you and defeat your enemies, just as He has done before. Do not be afraid, doubt God, or forget what God has done for you or what He has promised you and that He is with you always from the promise throughout the journey to the fulfillment to the Promised Land.
"***Moses:*** *I'm now 120 years old. I'm not physically able to lead you anymore, and the Eternal has told me, "You're not going to cross the Jordan River." Instead, it will be the Eternal your God who leads you across the Jordan. He'll clear out the nations who live there, and you'll take their place. As my successor and the Eternal's representative, Joshua will lead you across, just as He has said...Be strong and brave, and don't tremble in fear of them because the Eternal your God is going with you. He'll never fail you or abandon you!"* (Deu 31:1-4,6 VOICE).
You must faithfully and fearlessly serve in each assignment until God says it is time for succession, at which point you will train your successor and prepare for your next assignment as part of God's divine plan. God is looking for a new breed of servant leaders to serve, influence, partner with Him, and lead in humility, obedience, fearlessness, faithfulness, and love; He is anointing, appointing, and preparing you in the wilderness for the new era to cross over. God promises to be with you and never forsake you. Be confident of this truth: God goes with you, He goes before you, He is with you. God's got this! He confirms His promise and commitment in Hebrews 13:5, *"I will never leave you nor forsake you."*

AFFIRMATIONS & DECLARATIONS
God says to me today, "Have bravery and strength of character, and put in the effort to lead, learn, influence, be impactful, and inspire others. Embrace change and character transformation. Please don't be scared or disheartened. I am with you. I have anointed you for the assignment and appointment. I will not abandon you until all the labor in service to the My assignment and promise of victory have been completed." My God has never abandoned me, My lifetime God! He'll be with me for the rest of my life and beyond.

- I am already loved, prayed up, prepared, and chosen. I am enough. I am healed, well, and whole. I am complete because my God is with me always, and He is enough.

1 Chronicles 28:20, VOICE: *(to Solomon) "Be strong, courageous, and effective. Do not fear or be dismayed. I know that the Eternal God, who is my God, is with you. He will not abandon you or forsake you until you have finished all the work for the temple of the Eternal."*

PRAYER
Almighty Father, Thank You, Lord, for never abandoning me in any of my situations. Thank You for Your faithful love for me, blessings, and all of my circumstances because these have made me strong and confident. Every day, I am thankful because I know You are always by my side. Lord, allow me to focus solely on You today rather than being distracted by my thoughts, feelings, fear, and facts. Father, If I have ever given up on You because I thought You had forgotten about me, please have mercy and help me rebuild my trust in You. Please remember me always, in Jesus' name, Amen.

MY DOPE *faith journal*

Date S | M | T | W | T | F | S

Morning: I feel my emotion! My one-word check-in: ____________

DECLARATION

Consider today's verse. I implore the Holy Spirit to reveal His wisdom and truth to me and I declare it over my life.

OBSERVATION

What does the message mean? Lord, help me see it.

PRAYER

What is my prayer request? Lord, I live fully in You.

EMPOWERMENT

How will Your word empower me? Lord, give me the insight to apply my faith to be more significant than my fears.

MY FEARLESS *journey*

Evening: Feel my emotion! My one-word check-up:

What is making me FEEL like this?

What lessons did I LEARNED?

What THOUGHTS did I had?

What prompted my GRATITUDE?

Who did I CONNECTED with?

What brought me JOY?

EVENING PRAYER

WATER:

FRUIT & VEG:

MY MOOD:

My treat for today is:..

365 Journal

What I have learnt...

Day 270 - Be Strong and Courageous. Do not be Afraid.

"This is My command: be strong and courageous. Never be afraid or discouraged because I am your God, the Eternal One, and I will remain with you wherever you go."
—Joshua 1:9, VOICE

BELOVED,

It is time for a change. Be bold and powerful. Be strong. Be courageous. You are taking part in something brand new. It is a rebirth. It is a strategic renewal. It is a fresh start. It is transformational and revolutionary. It is an entirely new adventure, with new challenges, opportunities, and excitingly scary new beginnings. It's time to say goodbye to resisting change finally. You have a strong sense of personal transformation, change resilience, and change readiness—preparedness for the new era and epoch. The past is dead—the old relationship. - dead The old life - is dead. The old way of living, working, playing, and being - are dead. The old era - is dead. The old mentality- is dead. Dead! Yesterday is long gone; the way it used to be, the familiar and the comfort zone - are dead. The decades-old stuff - are now dead. The worldly ways of life - are dead. The carnal, fleshly view - is dead!

The Father is saying to you, Joshua, get ready. I anointed you in the wilderness, transformed your character, restored your attitude, refined your vision of the promised land, and gave you the faith to believe when others questioned Me. Moses' death did not surprise Me; I knew a new modern era was evolving and prepared you to emerge as a leader, singled you out for such a time as this. Are you fully ready? Are you brave and strong? Now go! Joshua 1:1-4 VOICE says, *"Moses served the Eternal One faithfully until the end of his days. After his death, the Eternal singled out Joshua, the son of Nun, who had walked at the right hand of Moses during the wilderness wanderings.* ***Eternal One*** *(to Joshua): Since My servant Moses is now dead, you and the Israelites must prepare to cross over the Jordan River to enter the land I have given you. I will give you every place you walk, wherever your feet touch, just as I promised Moses."*

The Father continues, "Never again will you be called "The Forsaken City" or "The Desolate Land." Your new name will be "The City of God's Delight" and "The Bride of God," for the LORD delights in you and will claim you as his bride.: (Isaiah 62:4, NLT). I will teach you why your disappointment in what you anticipated as different leads to a new adventure and anointing with Me in which you will be strong and fearless. Allow yourself to be freed from constraints, fear, and doubt. With Me, everything is made new. I will guide you personally, bring you to it, give it to you, tell you what to do, and even perform creative miracles. Don't fear, be brave! Get going; it is time to cross over. Victory is mine, and therefore joy is yours!

AFFIRMATIONS & DECLARATIONS

The Father tells me: Take command! Don't lose heart! Don't be concerned or disheartened. The Great I AM is with you in this; I will not walk away and abandon you. I will be at your side until every single element of God's worship and work is done. You have the anointing of a priest, prophet, and destiny helpers on your side, skilled craftsmen and artisans of all kinds ready to go to work. Both leaders and citizens are prepared. Utter the word! It has been completed successfully!"(1 Chronicles 28:20-21)

- God is my source of strength and provision and will provide for me.
- God is my source of courage and protection, and He will protect me and make me brave.
- My love and faith in Him are my antidotes against every lie, toxic fear, and demonic stronghold.

And he said, "O man greatly beloved, fear not, peace be with you; be strong and of good courage." And when he spoke to me, I was strengthened and said, "Let my lord speak, for you have strengthened me."
—Daniel 10:19 RSV

PRAYER

Dearest Father in Heaven, I am grateful that You have brought me nearer so I may face the new day with You at my side. Help me, Lord, use Your mighty Words to overcome my anxieties, quiet my fears, dry my tears, and solve my challenges. Would You please assist me in bringing my concerns to You at all times, trusting in Your ability to intervene and fulfill Your everlasting plans for me? Please give me a heart of gratitude that says, "Father, I am grateful for Your loving goodness to me. So, by Your grace, I trust You to carry out Your intentions for the benefit of others and Your greatness and my blessings." Would You please help me focus on the prize of eternal life that awaits those willing to run a good race to the finish to hear well done and follow Jesus? Would You please help me keep my eyes, heart, and mind focused on You? Please hear my humble prayer and meet my needs; my prayer is made in Jesus' mighty name, Amen.

MY DOPE *faith journal*

Date S | M | T | W | T | F | S

Morning: I feel my emotion! My one-word check-in: ....

DECLARATION

Consider today's verse. I implore the Holy Spirit to reveal His wisdom and truth to me and I declare it over my life.

OBSERVATION

What does the message mean? Lord, help me see it.

PRAYER

What is my prayer request? Lord, I live fully in You.

EMPOWERMENT

How will Your word empower me? Lord, give me the insight to apply my faith to be more significant than my fears.

MY FEARLESS *journey*

Evening: Feel my emotion! My one-word check-up:

What is making me FEEL like this?

What lessons did I LEARNED?

What THOUGHTS did I had?

What prompted my GRATITUDE?

Who did I CONNECTED with?

What brought me JOY?

EVENING PRAYER

WATER:

FRUIT & VEG:

MY MOOD:

My treat for today is: ....

365 Journal

What I think about fearlessness in my life now...

Day 271 - I Have Delivered Them Into Your Hands.

God said to Joshua, "Don't be timid and don't so much as hesitate. Take all your soldiers with you and go back to Ai. I have turned the king of Ai over to you—his people, his city, and his land."
—Joshua 8:1, MSG

BELOVED,

Yet again, God reminds you and His people like a broken record: Avoid trepidation; Do not be timid, anxious, worried, hesitant, intimidated, afraid, disheartened, angry, or scared.
"For God did not give us a spirit of timidity or cowardice or fear, but [He has given us a spirit] of power and of love and of sound judgment and personal discipline [abilities that result in a calm, well-balanced mind and self-control]." (2 Timothy 1:7, AMP).
The Father says, My word clearly stated in 2 Timothy 1:7 that fear is a spirit and not of Me. I have given you each a measure of faith (Romans 12:3). Your confidence in Me must be more significant than your fear. Be fearless and faithful! Depend on Me entirely for your strategy, strength, source, solution, and the shield to defeat, destroy, deliver, and defend you against every foe, falsehood, fear, fact, frustration, and failure. Never listen to the lies of the devil's prediction of the negative outcome of your battle. The battle is mine, and you belong to Me. I will deliver your enemies over to you, and you will destroy them by the Fire of the Holy Spirit. Trust Me; you do not need to fight or fear. Beloved, It's not over. I am the Author of your story. It's not over until it is well and you win! I lay forth the plan of attack for the current battle you are facing, how you will conquer the enemy, the rules of the war, and what to do and not to do. Stay prayed up to believe, listen, obey, and trust Me!
It is natural to be fearful or uncertain about a new beginning or facing our adversities and adversaries. Still, when you have a Father and a Friend who knows the way, His performance reviews are perfect and top-notch. The track record is undefeated, all-powerful, all-knowing, loyal, loving, kind, outstanding, sovereign, and trustworthy. The fear fades. Read Joshua 8 as you continue your journey from Genesis to Revelation. Here are three wisdom keys to apply and assess your life and situation.

1. **Lies vs. loyalty to the Lord:** Decide to doubt the Father of lies and believe the Father of Truth. Reject the lies of the enemy that comes to break your loyalty to God.
2. **Listen carefully and obey the laws of warfare.** What is God's strategy and plan of attack?
3. Learn from your past mistakes when you disobeyed and celebrate God's victories when you trusted God's plan, purpose, and promise.

AFFIRMATIONS & DECLARATIONS

"I will establish your borders from the Red Sea to the Mediterranean Sea and from the desert to the Euphrates River. I will give into your hands the people who live in the land, and you will drive them out before you." (Exodus 23:31 NIV). Lord, You have gone before me to drive out my enemies.

- I can overcome any barrier in my life because He who is in me is more prominent than He in the world. I have no fear of men, but I trust the Lord, who protects me.
- I am delivered and never defeated. I never lose; I with learn or win.
- I am a lifelong learner and a winner.
- I am not frightened of what anyone can do to me because I have faith in my faithful Father.

"Also they said unto Joshua, Surely the Lord hath delivered into our hands all the land: for even all the inhabitants of the country faint because of us."
—Joshua 2:24 GNV

PRAYER

Father God, I offer You everything I am: my spirit, mind, heart, body, life, family, relationship, career, hopes, concerns, dreams, and destiny. To You, I entrust everything I own and everything that I am. Thank You for being a good steward of my resources. In Your capable hands, I entrust my soul. Even if I feel like I am suffering or struggling right now, I am reminded that my life is a gift from God. You saved me, an intimate personal connection with You, and being part of the gospel of the Kingdom. Thanks for my deliverance! I give myself up to You, trust in Your faithfulness to help me stay fearless and steadfast in this situation to claim the success by Your power. In Jesus' name, I pray, AMEN.

MY DOPE *faith journal*

Date S | M | T | W | T | F | S

Morning: I feel my emotion! My one-word check-in: ....

DECLARATION

Consider today's verse. I implore the Holy Spirit to reveal His wisdom and truth to me and I declare it over my life.

OBSERVATION

What does the message mean? Lord, help me see it.

PRAYER

What is my prayer request? Lord, I live fully in You.

EMPOWERMENT

How will Your word empower me? Lord, give me the insight to apply my faith to be more significant than my fears.

MY FEARLESS *journey*

Evening: Feel my emotion! My one-word check-up:

What is making me FEEL like this?

What lessons did I LEARNED?

What THOUGHTS did I had?

What prompted my GRATITUDE?

Who did I CONNECTED with?

What brought me JOY?

EVENING PRAYER

WATER:

FRUIT & VEG:

MY MOOD:

My treat for today is: ....

365 Journal

What I think about fearlessness in my life now...

Day 272 - God will do it for you even if it takes a miracle!

And the Lord said to Joshua, "Do not fear them, for I have delivered them into your hand; not a man of them shall stand before you."
—Joshua 10:8, NKJV

BELOVED,
Facing a battle, amidst the fight and enduring a battle, God reminds you every step along the way not to fear and fight from a position of victory. Sometimes it seems as if the enemy has the upper hand, but God says, Do not be afraid or terrified of this current adversary, as I am putting these assailants into your hands. None of them will be strong enough to compete with you. *"Don't give them a second thought. I've put them under your thumb—not one of them will stand up to you."* (Joshua 10:8, MSG).
Pray and ask God for the impossible and the complicated. The Lord is the God of miracles, marvels, majesty, and might. Joshua prayed that the sun and moon would stand still until he defeated His enemy. God did it for Joshua; He will do it for you. *"So the sun stood still, And the moon stopped, Till the people had revenge Upon their enemies."* (Joshua 10:13, NKJV).
God is in the struggle and the storm with you. The impossible can become feasible when God is in it. Be calm, do not fear sudden disaster; God's got you! *"Stay calm; there is no need to be afraid of a sudden disaster or to worry when calamity strikes the wicked, For the Eternal is always there to protect you. He will safeguard your each and every step."* (Proverbs 3:25-27, VOICE). On your quest, today, visit Joshua 10 with Joshua on the battlefield. Joshua petitioned God to maintain the stillness of the daylight until he defeated his enemies. God granted the miracle. Pray for your God-sized dream. Are you fearless enough to command and claim the Lord's promises and power for you and your family? You are standing on Psalm 46:10-11 (TPT), which says, *"Surrender your anxiety. Be still and realize that I am God. I am God above all the nations, and I am exalted throughout the whole earth. The God of Jacob fights for us!"*

AFFIRMATIONS & DECLARATIONS
"Now God worked unusual miracles by the hands of Paul so that even handkerchiefs or aprons were brought from his body to the sick, and the diseases left them, and the evil spirits went out of them. (Acts 19:11-12, NKJV). Lord, as You did mighty and extraordinary miracles and impossible things through Paul, do it for me, heal me and make me whole. Right now, in the mighty and matchless name of Jesus, I am calling a miraculous breakthrough of magnificence, excellence, affluence, wellness, wholeness, wealth, wisdom, influence, and significance into existence in my life, living, and livelihood. The manifestation of divine plans and Covenant promises for my life today, this week, this season, this year, and in my future, destiny, and legacy! In the name of Jesus, I am positioned and put my name in the atmosphere to claim my mind-blowing miracle, no-eyes-have-seen, no-ears-have-heard, no-mind-can-conceive the manifestation of these dream-like blessings. Do it, God, even if it takes a gift!

- I have access to God's Shalom and Salvation. I don't have to settle with uncertainty.
- God has provided me with all I require to overcome trials, troubles, and temptations.

"To him who by means of his power working in us is able to do so much more than we can ever ask for, or even think of: to God be the glory in the church and in Christ Jesus for all time, forever and ever! Amen."
– Ephesians 3:20-21, GNT

PRAYER
Father in Heaven, Hallowed be Your name, Your Kingdom comes, and Your WILL be done on earth as it is in heaven. Lord, I come before You today to confess and repent my sins of omission and commission. O Lord, God of countless opportunities! Lord, I pray for Your mercy, grace, forgiveness, faithfulness, favor, and unwavering love for me. I announce today that I am a new creation and that it is a new season. I am a brilliant exhibition of the magnificence of God's glory. By God's grace, I claim the rewards of obedience outlined in Your word in my life, the lives of my children, my household, my family, in the Chayah Club community, in our finances, health, healing, wellness, in our careers/businesses, in our callings/ministries, in our academic/intellectual excellence, in the work of our hands, and life projects, vision, goals, and action plans. In our God-given destiny, divine purpose, and mission in Jesus' mighty name.
Lord, grant us the greatest gift of eternal life, for our visible problems, are only temporary and can not compare to the greater glory. I pray that I may hear the LORD and Master say, 'Well done, good and faithful servant, you've been faithful a little; now, I'll set you over a lot, enter into your Master's delight.' I pray, and proclaim these prophetic words, do it, Lord, even if it takes a miracle. I pray in Jesus' name. AMEN!

MY DOPE *faith journal*

Date S | M | T | W | T | F | S

Morning: I feel my emotion! My one-word check-in: ....

DECLARATION

Consider today's verse. I implore the Holy Spirit to reveal His wisdom and truth to me and I declare it over my life.

OBSERVATION

What does the message mean? Lord, help me see it.

PRAYER

What is my prayer request? Lord, I live fully in You.

EMPOWERMENT

How will Your word empower me? Lord, give me the insight to apply my faith to be more significant than my fears.

MY FEARLESS *journey*

Evening: Feel my emotion! My one-word check-up:

What is making me FEEL like this?

What lessons did I LEARNED?

What THOUGHTS did I had?

What prompted my GRATITUDE?

Who did I CONNECTED with?

What brought me JOY?

EVENING PRAYER

WATER:

FRUIT & VEG:

MY MOOD:

My treat for today is:..

365 Journal

What I think about fearlessness in my life now...

Day 273 - God has a plan!

"Then the LORD said to Joshua, Do not be afraid because of them, for tomorrow by this time I am going to hand over all of them slain [by the sword] to Israel; you shall hamstring (disable) their horses and set fire to their chariots."
—Joshua 11:6 , AMP

BELOVED,

When the adversary says it's too late, screwed up, you're too old, lost, broken, sick, jobless, cashless, helpless, thoughtless, lame, messed up, weak, hopeless, and even dead; God responds, "I still have a plan. You are Mine with Me have already won." God sent His Son, Jesus, who was born as a man and died on the cross for all past, present, and future sins. The sins of the world and people who put their faith in Him are washed away by the torrent of righteousness in Jesus' Blood. The Lord told Joshua, and He is speaking to you as well, do not be afraid of them, for I will turn over all your enemies to you by tomorrow by this time, and you must cripple their horses and set fire to their chariots. In Isaiah 59:19, God says, *"When the adversary comes in like a flood, I will establish a new order against them and send them to flight."* When the enemy attacks, God increases His power to defend you and destroy the Devil, demons, his diabolical plots, and weapons. "*So shall they fear The name of the Lord from the west, And His glory from the rising of the sun; When the enemy comes in like a flood, The Spirit of the Lord will lift up a standard against him.*" (Isaiah 59:19, NKJV). A torrent of Holy Spirit will rise against the adversary as they enter to affect, assault, or attack your life as *"the breath of the Almighty God"* that gives insight, knowledge, intelligence, and understanding (Job 32:80) will send hi, to flight, no matter what he tried, whenever and whatever he does.

Today is the concluding day of the 365 Live Fearlessly (Quarter 3) venture. You started on Day 182, on Day 250, when you began an adventure from Genesis to Revelation, pausing at every scripture or story where God instructs His children to be fearless. You've seen God's incredible work, His superabundant provision, and supernatural protection: along the journey from the covenant promise to the fulfillment, barren wombs giving birth to nations, the power of Blood to protect God's children, the separating of the Red Sea into a Highway, performing numerous creative miracles, defending and delivering His people, and a new generation and leader leaving the wilderness to occupy the Promised Land. God always defeats your enemies when you believe, obey, and follow His orders, standards, and strategies. As Quarter 3 ends, read Joshua 11, which describes Israel's conquest of the North Kingdom. They gathered together and came out to fight—so many warriors you couldn't count them like sand on a beach—led by horses and chariots. These kings pooled their troops and camped at Merom, ready to attack Israel. The Lord told Joshua, 'They're harmless. Tomorrow, I'll deliver you all their lifeless bodies. You'll burn their horses and chariots.' Joshua's troops assaulted them where they camped by the Merom River, and the Eternal handed them to Israel. (Joshua 11:4-8). Beloved, despite the plot, be fearless and faithful! God has a plan!

AFFIRMATIONS & DECLARATIONS

Jesus says, *"But the time is coming—indeed it's here now—when you will be scattered, each one going his own way, leaving me alone. Yet I am not alone because the Father is with me. I have told you all this so that you may have peace in me. Here on earth, you will have many trials and sorrows. But take heart because I have overcome the world."* (John 16:32-33 NLT)

- God has provided me with all I need to live my life as He created me, designed, and desires for me.
- God directs my steps because I choose to trust, obey, and honor Him in all I do, say, think, or ask.
- I surrender all my concerns and fears to my Lifetime God, who loves, cares, and protects me.
- I am an overcomer; I am never alone as God is with me always; I am at peace and filled with joy!

Matthew 6:33-34, NKJV: *"But seek first the kingdom of God and His righteousness, and all these things shall be added to you. Therefore do not worry about tomorrow, for tomorrow will worry about its own things. Sufficient for the day is its own trouble."*

PRAYER

Heavenly Father, Thank You for Your grand plans for my life, even if what I fear, think, see, or hear in front of me or chase me does not feel or look good or even sound stronger than me. I genuinely thank You, Lord, for providing me with the hope of an undefeatable victory. Would You please allow me to put my fearless trust in You and Your master plan that You will turn my mess into a masterpiece and make me a miracle of Your marvel and might? Would You please give me the divine assurance that You have nothing but a good and favorable outcome for me? Please remind me that even though I don't know and will never comprehend the entire plan, You do, and You are in total control and more powerful than everything that tries to overpower me to give up on Your schedule, strategy, and solution. Today, I lean into You with fearless faith. Please help me trust, wait, worship and exalt You in all things, and at all times, You are my God, my Peace, my Joy, my Hope, my Victory, my Eternal, and everything. Please help me persist, praise, and pray, not panic; Your thoughts and ways are higher than mine, and Your plans are bigger and better than mine, and nothing is impossible nor too tricky nor too powerful for You. Lead me every step of the way to a stunning victory, for You have already won, and I, too, am a winner. In Jesus' name, I pray, Amen.

MY DOPE *faith journal*

Date S | M | T | W | T | F | S

Morning: I feel my emotion! My one-word check-in: ____________

DECLARATION

Consider today's verse. I implore the Holy Spirit to reveal His wisdom and truth to me and I declare it over my life.

OBSERVATION

What does the message mean? Lord, help me see it.

PRAYER

What is my prayer request? Lord, I live fully in You.

EMPOWERMENT

How will Your word empower me? Lord, give me the insight to apply my faith to be more significant than my fears.

MY FEARLESS *journey*

Evening: Feel my emotion! My one-word check-up:

What is making me FEEL like this?

What lessons did I LEARNED?

What THOUGHTS did I had?

What prompted my GRATITUDE?

Who did I CONNECTED with?

What brought me JOY?

EVENING PRAYER

WATER:

FRUIT & VEG:

MY MOOD:

My treat for today is: ....

365 Self-care Plan

Be intention to plan self-care in your life.

This month, I've decided to be fearless, so I'll...

This Month's Affirmation

I am self-aware, reflective and innovative.
This Month's Question:

Answer:

3 Goals that will inspire and motivate me.
Monthly Inspiration:

Self-love: 5 things I will admire and adore.

1
2
3
4
5

Desires: Wouldn't it be great when God...

My Monthly Joy & Gratitude Planner

1
2
3
4
5
6
7
8
9
10

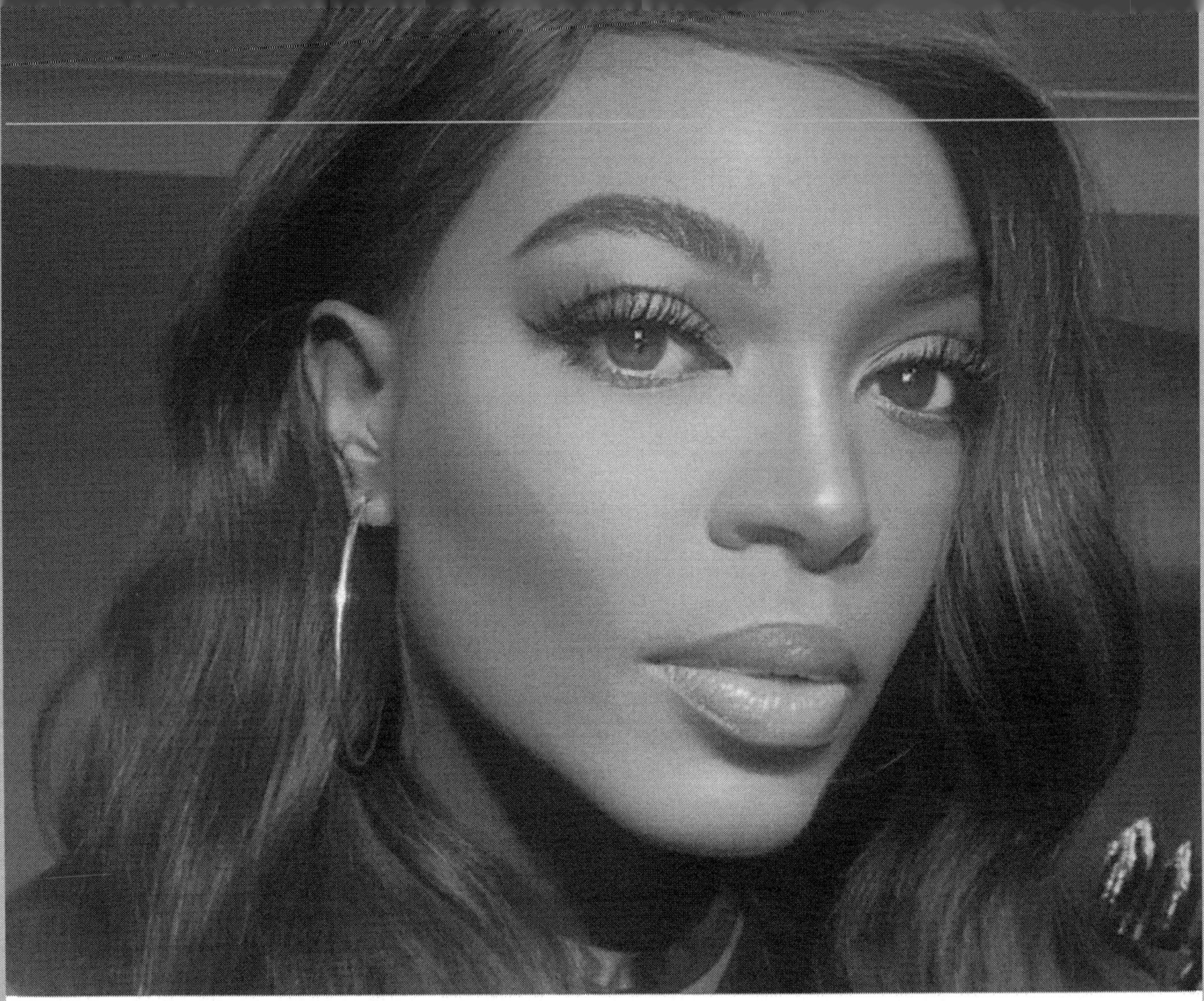

Congratulations

You have completed the 365 Live Fearlessly (Quarter 3) devotional and journal, your daily prayers, affirmations, declarations, and assignments. You are now well on your road to a happier, healthier, more faithful, fearless, and fulfilling lifestyle.

You conducted several happiness tests at the start of your 365 Live Fearless Quarter 3 journey. Return to these tests and observe how the results have changed. I hope you'll be pleased with the outcome!

I hope that now that you have concentrated on prioritizing God and self-coaching to address several aspects of your life, your life seems more balanced, fearless, limitless, faithful, and in sync with whom God created you to be and whom you are becoming. There has to be more to life than this, and there is, and you have it. God got you covered. You are cherished. Let's move to 365 Live Fearlessly (Quarter 4), get this book, finish strong and start the new season empowered.

REFERENCES

McFadden, N. (2022). 365 Live Fearlessly: A Fearless Faith Devotional & Journal for Life's Journey (Quarter 1 of 4). Nikimac Solutions Inc.

McFadden, N. (2022). 365 Live Fearlessly: A Fearless Faith Devotional & Journal for Life's Journey (Quarter 2 of 4). Nikimac Solutions Inc.

McFadden, N. (2020). *The Daniel Fast: Closing the GAP!: A 21-Day Prayer Journey to Wellness.* Nikimac Solutions Inc.

McFadden, N. (2018). R*ebound Faith: CHAYAH! (Full Volume): The Grit to Survive, Revive and Thrive from Devastation and Depression to Deliverance.* Nikimac Solutions Inc.

Images

Canva. (n.d.). Canva. https://www.canva.com/.

Life Coaching Templates

Home | Miri Campbell. (2021, November 12). Miri Campbell. http://miricampbell.com/.

Made in the USA
Columbia, SC
24 July 2022

63913166R00222